Norman K. Denzin

On Understanding Emotion

 Jossey-Bass Publishers
San Francisco • Washington • London • 1984

ON UNDERSTANDING EMOTION
by Norman K. Denzin

Copyright © 1984 by: Jossey-Bass Inc., Publishers
433 California Street
San Francisco, California 94104
&
Jossey-Bass Limited
28 Banner Street
London EC1Y 8QE

Library of Congress Cataloging in Publication Data

Denzin, Norman K.
On understanding emotion.

(The Jossey-Bass social and behavioral science series)
Bibliography: p. 285
Includes index.
1. Emotions I. Title. II. Series
BF531.D39   1984   152.4   83-23853
ISBN 0-87589-588-3

Manufactured in the United States of America

The paper in this book meets the guidelines for
permanence and durability of the Committee on
Production Guidelines for Book Longevity of the
Council on Library Resources.

JACKET DESIGN BY WILLI BAUM

FIRST EDITION

Code 8402

The Jossey-Bass
Social and Behavioral Science Series

Preface

The voluminous literature on the emotions does not contain any serious phenomenological account of the essential features of emotionality as lived experience. This book represents one attempt to fill this void. The centrality of the emotions at all levels of social life—micro, macro, personal, organizational, political, economic, cultural, and religious—is indisputable. While earlier discussions of the topic have examined the cognitive, interactional, psychoanalytic, structural, and cultural dimensions of emotion, a full phenomenological treatment has not been attempted. *On Understanding Emotion* offers a social phenomenological and interpretive perspective on the inner and outer worlds of emotional experience. This volume's thesis, which is developed in detail, is that self-feelings lie at the core of the emotional experience.

In part, this work grows out of a dissatisfaction with the cognitive and structural bias or heavily psychoanalytic orientation that characterize most current approaches to the study of emotion. With the major exception of the phenomenological

philosophers, including Scheler, Heidegger, and Sartre, the phenomenological point of view has not been developed and applied to the study of emotionality. My work is intended to
extend and build upon the writings of these investigators.

No sociologist or psychologist, to my knowledge, has analyzed in detail emotionality as a facet of lived consciousness, involving self-feelings, inner moral meanings, and intersubjectivity.
Nor has the general value or validity of the social phenomenological point of view for theoretical and research purposes been
well demonstrated in the social sciences. By taking on the difficult topic of emotion I hope to demonstrate how phenomenology, when combined with elements of symbolic interactionism
and interpretive theory, may generate an understanding of this
important pivotal issue in the human disciplines. I intend a theoretical and methodological contribution in attempting to combine phenomenology with elements of symbolic interactionist,
pragmatic, structuralist, Freudian, psychological, and existen-
tialist thought. I intend a substantive contribution as well, by
offering the analysis of domestic family violence and the study
of the emotionally divided self as demonstrations of the utility
of my approach. I also offer a theory of interpretation and understanding that draws upon the work of the Scottish moralists.

This book is directed to interpretive, critical, and structuralist theorists; to philosophers, anthropologists, psychologists, and sociologists who study emotion. While it is appropriate for advanced courses in theory, social psychology, and
emotion, it will also be of interest to clinical psychologists and
psychiatrists who must, in the course of their work, deal with
the selves of violent, emotionally divided individuals. It will be
useful to students of child and adolescent development because
it specifies an approach that examines the emotions of self and
significant others in interaction. It should also hold interest for
those who study the family from a historical, comparative point
of view because it conceptualizes emotionality as a relational
and historical phenomenon that is uniquely experienced within
each historical period. A glossary of terms is included to eluci-
date the somewhat specialized vocabulary that is used throughout the text.

Contents and Organization

The Introduction specifies the problem and situates this investigation in the literature on emotion. I specify in detail the social phenomenological and interpretive study of emotion and set out a number of points that are basic to my method. Chapter One critically reviews classical and current theories and views of emotion. I begin with the theory of William James, consider recent psychological and sociological formulations, and then move to the Freudian model of the emotions, reviewing some of the work of Jacques Lacan. I spend some time on the phenomenological theory of the emotions offered by Jean-Paul Sartre, for his views underlie many of my own. I offer a brief discussion of Thomas Scheff's theory of emotional catharsis and conclude with a comparison of James, Freud, Sartre, and Lacan. Chapter Two offers a brief presentation of the theoretical model that is developed in the remaining chapters. I define emotion as self-feeling, treat emotionality as symbolic interaction, and analyze the temporality of emotion in the circuit of selfness.

Chapter Three examines the essence of emotional experience while giving a detailed discussion of consciousness, temporality, the situation, the person, emotional associates, emotional reality, the world of emotion, and the double structure of emotional experience. Chapter Four focuses on the structures of lived emotion and involves a treatment of the lived body, intentional value feelings, sensible feelings, and feelings of the self and the moral person. Chapter Five builds on this analysis by moving to the examination of emotional intersubjectivity and the forms of fellow-feeling. The elements of a theory of emotional understanding are presented in this chapter.

Chapter Six is a phenomenological study of family violence. Various forms of violent conduct are identified, including those that are playful, spurious, inflicted, real, paradoxical, and enacted. Chapter Seven builds on the thesis of this work that self-feelings underlie emotionality by studying the emotionally divided self. I draw upon the work of William James, Jacques Lacan, Max Scheler, and R. D. Laing in this chapter. I develop a view of *ressentiment* that is applied to the emotionally divided self.

The Conclusion, "Reflections on Emotion," offers a theory of hermeneutics. It situates the study of emotionality in the lives of ordinary people. The work ends by returning full circle to the question that begins my first chapter: How is emotionality as a form of consciousness lived, experienced, articulated, and felt by people? The inquiry, which is unfinished, to be taken up again, concludes with the suggestion that without emotionality everyday life would be an endless empty exchange of repetitive, lifeless meanings, dull and devoid of inner, moral significance. Emotionality lies at the intersection of the person and society, for all persons are joined to their societies through the self-feelings and emotions they feel and experience on a daily basis. This is the reason the study of emotionality must occupy a central place in all the human disciplines, for to be human is to be emotional. How that is so is the topic of this book.

Champaign, Illinois   Norman K. Denzin
January 1984

Contents

The Author

Norman K. Denzin is professor of sociology and humanities at the University of Illinois at Urbana-Champaign. He received the B.A. degree (1963) and the Ph.D. degree (1966) in sociology from the University of Iowa.

Denzin's main research activities and interests have been in childhood socialization, the study of language, the self, interaction, interpretive theory, and phenomenology. He has been vice-president of the Society for the Study of Symbolic Interaction (1976-1977), and secretary of the Social Psychology Section of the American Sociological Association (1978-1980). Denzin is the author and editor of several books, including *Social Psychology* (1978, with A. Lindesmith and A. Strauss, 5th ed.), *Sociological Methods* (1978), *The Research Act* (1978, 2nd ed.), *Childhood Socialization* (1977), *Children and Their Caretakers* (1973), *The Values of Social Science* (1973), and *The Mental Patient* (1968, with S. P. Spitzer). He is the editor of *Studies in Symbolic Interaction: A Research Annual* and the author of over fifty articles, which have appeared in such journals as *American Journal of Sociology, American Sociological Review, British Journal of Sociology, Semiotica, Social Forces, Social Problems,* and *Sociological Quarterly.*

On Understanding
Emotion

These passions and thoughts and feelings are the general passions and thoughts and feelings of men. And with what are they connected? Undoubtedly with our moral sentiments and animal sensations, and with the causes which excite these; with the visible universe; with storms and sunshine, with the revolutions of the season, with heat and cold, with loss of friends and kindred, with injuries and resentments, gratitude and hope, with fear and sorrow. These, and the like, are the sensations and objects the Poet describes, as they are sensations of other men, and the objects which interest them.

——Wordsworth, Preface to the *Lyrical Ballads*

In connection with emotion, eidetic reflection will ask: after all, what is to be moved; what is the meaning of emotion? Can one conceive of a consciousness which is incapable of emotion, and if not, why not? One will understand emotion as a total act of consciousness, as a mode of our relation to the entire world, and one will seek to determine its sense.

——Merleau-Ponty, *The Primacy of Perception*

Introduction:
Studying Emotion

This volume constitutes an interpretive, social phenomenological, and interactionist examination of a basic question: How is emotion, as a form of consciousness, lived, experienced, articulated, and felt? The study of emotion lies at the heart of those social, anthropological, psychological, and humanistic disciplines that intend a deeper understanding of the phenomenon called person. Persons are moved by emotion. Emotional consciousness, to paraphrase Heidegger, dwells within emotion—within its own dwelling, which is emotion. In this study I attempt to examine the dwelling places of emotionality.

　　People are their emotions. To understand who a person is, it is necessary to understand emotion. Conversely, in order to understand emotion, an understanding of the phenomenon called person is required. The person is that temporal being already present in the world, ahead of itself, aware of itself, capable of expressing and acting on that being, awareness, and presence (Heidegger, 1927/1962). A person exists on two levels, the surface and the deep. These two levels will be examined in detail.

1

Emotions cut to the core of people. Within and through emotion people come to define the surface and essential, or core, meanings of who they are. Emotions and moods are ways of disclosing the world for the person. How this is so is both a topic and a resource of inquiry in the pages that follow.

Consider the following account of Stephen Dedalus about to take confession: "He bowed his head upon his hands, bidding his heart to be meek and humble that he might be like those who knelt beside him and his prayers acceptable as theirs. . . . His blood began to murmur in his veins, murmuring like a sinful city summoned from its sleep to hear its doom. . . . He could still leave the chapel. . . . He could still escape from the shame. . . . The slide was shot to suddenly. The penitent came out. He was next. He stood up in terror and walked blindly into the box. . . . The slide clicked back and his heart bounded in his breast. The face of the old priest was at the grating averted from him, leaning upon a hand" (Joyce, 1976, pp. 400-402).

In this passage James Joyce places Stephen in a highly charged emotional experience. He is lodged in the emotionality that draws him to the priest and to the confessional situation. The emotions that he feels—shame, guilt, fear, terror—are both in him and in the situation. They are part of the self and the selfness that he feels as he draws near to the moment of confession. In these feelings Stephen reveals himself to himself as a moral person. His emotionality, as a lived experience, points to and illustrates some of the emotional experiences that are the subject matter of this book.

After a considerable period of neglect, philosophical, sociological, anthropological, psychological, and social psychological conceptions of emotion are taking root in the human disciplines (see Candland, 1977, for a review).* These approaches

---

*Many theories have been set forth: situational (Lazarus, Averill, and Opton, 1970), cognitive (Arnold, 1960a, 1960b, 1970; Schachter and Singer, 1962), cognitive-affective (Singer, 1973, 1974; Tomkins, 1962, 1963), psychoanalytic (Keen, 1977), interactionist and psychoanalytic (Hochschild, 1979, 1983; Scheff, 1979, 1983), sociological-structural (Collins, 1981), structural-exchange and reinforcement (Kemper, 1978, 1981), symbolic interactionist (Shott, 1979; Gordon, 1981), structural-psychological (Plutchik, 1962, 1977), cross-cultural and nonverbal (Ekman, 1973, 1980; Averill, 1980), and emotional-motivational (Izard, 1972, 1977).

are in agreement, at least partly, on the following three fundamental components of all emotions: (1) each emotion has a determined neural substrate, (2) each emotion has a characteristic
neuromuscular-expressive pattern, and (3) each emotion has a
"distinct subjective or phenomenological quality" (Izard, 1972,
p. 2). The phenomenological and interpretive perspective I develop assumes each of these points.

     My thesis may be succinctly stated: *Emotions* are self-
feelings. *Emotionality,* the process of being emotional, locates
the person in the world of social interaction. *Self-feelings* are sequences of lived emotionality, often involving the feeling and
experiencing of more than one specific, named emotion. Such
experiences always have self-referents; that is, they refer back to
the self of the person who feels them. *Moods* are emotional
states of mind that transcend specific situational experiences.
Feelings are sensations of the lived body. All emotions refer
back to the person who feels, defines, and experiences them.
Yet emotionality draws the person to others, for emotions are
felt in relation to other interactants, or *emotional associates.*
There is a world of social emotion that can be entered at any
moment by the person. All experiences of being emotional are
situational, reflective, and relational. A person cannot experience an emotion without the implicit or imagined presence of
others. There is a temporal structure to emotional experience
that is at once forward- and backward-looking (see Heidegger,
1927/1962, pp. 395-401). Emotionality radiates through the
lived body of the person. The study of emotionality requires a
conception of the human body as a structure of ongoing lived
experience (see Merleau-Ponty, 1963; Plessner, 1970). The self
of the person stands in the center of the emotions that are experienced. Self-feelings constitute the inner essence, or core, of
emotionality.

     Various attempts to catalogue the full range of human
emotions have been developed. Darwin (1872/1955) examined
the emotions of anxiety, grief, despair, joy, hatred, anger, disgust, guilt, pride, surprise, fear, horror, shame, and shyness.
James (1890/1950, vol. 2, pp. 449-468), following Darwin
somewhat, classified the emotions into two categories, the
coarser (grief, fear, rage, and love) and the *subtler* (moral, intel-

lectual, and esthetic feelings). Sartre (1939/1962) used a pas-
sive/active dimension to analyze fear, sadness, and joy; in subsequent works (1943/1978, 1976, 1981) he examined love,
masochism, indifference, desire, hate, sadism, terror, and ressentiment. Freud (1954) emphasized aggression, hostility, anger,
fear, and the ambivalence of love and affect in his investigations. Plutchik (1962) considers as primary the following emotions: fear, anger, joy, grief, acceptance, disgust, surprise, and
expectation. Izard (1972, 1977) suggests that patterns of emotion interact and that interest, joy, surprise, distress, anger, disgust, contempt, fear, shame, and guilt are fundamental emotions. Arnold's (1960a, pp. 193-196) extremely useful scheme
classifies the conditions under which any given object can affect
us. Three dichotomies are utilized: whether the object is good
or bad for us, whether it is absent or present, and whether it is
easy or difficult to attain. Basic emotions occur as a reaction to
these basic conditions (Arnold, 1960a, p. 193). This model re-
lates emotions to social objects in the person's field of experience. Arnold distinguishes positive, negative, impulse, and con-
tending emotions. This permits an analysis of love, wanting, joy,
hate, aversion, sorrow, hope, hopelessness, daring, fear, anger,
and dejection. Kemper (1978b, pp. 47-49) classifies emotions
in terms of their duration (long- or short-term); their real, imagined, and anticipated outcomes in social relationships; whether
they are structural, anticipatory, or consequent; and whether
they are negative or positive. The specific emotions he analyzes
include guilt, anxiety, security, fear, shame, happiness, depression, anger, frustration, gratitude, liking, trust, love, sadness, joy
at the misfortune of others, and desire. Scheff (1979) analyzes
the distress emotions grief, fear, anger, and boredom. Hochschild
(1979, 1983) examines the rules that appear to suppress the
open display of true (negative) feelings. Shott (1979) investi-
gates guilt, shame, embarrassment, pride, vanity, and empathy.

The emotions that have received the greatest attention
appear to be negative ones, including anger, fear, guilt, and anxiety. These are partly situational, partly relational. There is some
suggestion that the more extreme forms of these emotions refer
to lasting relational bonds between persons, as do love and the
positive emotions or sentiments of friendship and intimacy.

It would be pointless to propose yet another classification system for the emotions. The present inquiry assumes that all experiences of emotionality involve positive and negative situational experiences that may or may not endure in the relational worlds of the person. It is also assumed that all emotional experiences involve reflection, feeling, cognition, and interpretation. Many emotional experiences are purely private; others are public or collective in nature. Many emotions are ritually inspired by groups or larger social structures; others (for example, love) are dyadic, involving the close primary relationship. Whatever form emotional experience takes, it locates the person in a world of emotionality. It is the experiencing of emotion within that world that concerns me the most. Because no emotional experience is ever experienced exactly the same way a second time, as James (1890/1950) and Arnold (1960a) have observed, the labels applied to emotional experience are always shifting and are subject to new or different interpretation. The meaning of a given emotion lies in the interpretations a person brings to it. One person's joy may be another's sorrow, and so on. Because the meaning of the experience lies in the experience, and only partly in the word or term brought to it, it is the structure of emotional consciousness that must be analyzed.

The two case studies of lived emotionality included in this work (Chapters Six and Seven) focus mainly on what H. S. Sullivan (1953a, p. 72) termed the *uncanny emotions* of awe, dread, loathing, and horror. These negative emotions are examined for what they reveal about the underlying thesis of this work: that self-feelings lie at the core of all emotional experiences. Examining the negative emotions enables us to disclose the various negative features of self that become intertwined in emotionality.

The emphasis on the negative forms of emotional experience seems consistent with the present historical moment, which is one of reflection, analysis, hesitation, ressentiment, and what Laing (1965) terms ontological insecurity. Northrop Frye (1982, p. 232) writes of "man's fear of freedom and his resentment of the discipline and responsibility that freedom brings." Nietzsche, Marx, Freud, Weber, Heidegger, James, Sartre, Merleau-Ponty, Foucault, and Mills have commented on the crisis of meaning, self, and understanding that confronts the twentieth-century individual. If the human's assignment is to find meaning in the world and if that world and the person's relationship to it are continually shifting and changing, then the negative, ambiguous, doubting, halting, indecisive, and potentially inauthentic and insincere elements of everyday life are ever present. The emotions and emotional experiences that have preoccupied the human disciplines reflect the stance of the twentieth-century scholar toward the human experience. Recent attempts to displace the human subject and to give primacy to language, power, the state, or unconscious desire merely shift the ground of discussion. It is the feeling, thinking, interpreting subject who stands at the core of all discourse, no matter how disguised that discourse may be. The subject who is located in a world of *intersubjective* experience emotionally, cognitively, and interactionally provides the point of departure for the analysis that follows. That subject is historically self-aware and embodies in his or her lifetime the experiences, feelings, and moods of the historical moment.

The inquiry that follows is interpretive, social phenomenological, and interactionist. Emotion is interpreted from within as a lived experience. The works of Heidegger (1927/1962, 1977, 1975/1982), Sartre (1939/1962, 1943/1978, 1976, 1981), Merleau-Ponty (1962, 1963, 1964a, 1964b, 1964c, 1969, 1973a, 1973b, 1973c, 1974), Scheler (1913/1970, 1916/1973, 1912/1961), Husserl (1913/1962), and James (1890/1950) are basic to the argument I will develop. It is these phenomenological investigators who have brought the emotions and human feelings most clearly into focus.

It is necessary to speak to the social phenomenological and interpretive perspective that will be used in this investigation. The social phenomenological study of emotion involves the following assumptions and steps. First, as a method of inquiry, social phenomenology directs the investigator to study lived human emotion from within (Husserl, 1913/1962, p. 108; Sartre, 1939/1962, p. 21; Heidegger, 1977, p. 74; Merleau-Ponty, 1962; Denzin, 1980). The individual feeling and experiencing emotion is located in the world interactively, reflectively, and unreflectively. People act in the world so as to make that world a part of themselves and a part of their emotionality. There is no division between people, their emotion, and the world. The phenomenological and interactional streams of emotional experience of the person are connected and joined to the world in and through the circuit of selfness and self-feeling (see Sartre, 1943/1978, pp. 155–158, on the circuit of selfness).

Second, emotional human interaction must be situated in the natural world. That is, interaction must be confronted and examined in its natural fullness in the world of lived experience. Multiple instances of emotionality must be secured. The use of multiple, triangulated methods is required. Any instance of emotion, whether derived from experiments, case studies, open-ended interviews, field conversations, free fancy, imagination, history, art, poetry, literature, myth, film, music, or fiction, is suitable for phenomenological purposes (Husserl, 1913/1962; Sartre, 1940/1972). The emotional phenomena that are secured must be situated by time and place and recorded within the language and meanings of the world being investigated. The "prose" of lived emotion must be captured (Merleau-Ponty, 1973c).

Third, once we have obtained multiple instances of emotion naturalistically, it must be bracketed and cut loose from the natural world. This procedure leads the investigator to suspend the findings, facts, and propositions of previous investigators who have studied the phenomenon of emotion from the standpoint of their "natural science theories" (Husserl, 1913/ 1962, p. 86). The meanings of emotion are often covered up, hidden, distorted, or buried within the everyday world or clouded by prior "scientific" understandings. The phenomenal structures of emotion must be uncovered, laid bare, and explicated phenomenologically. "Everything that belongs to this manner of indication and explication constitutes the conceptual tools of this research [and] is called phenomenological" (Heidegger, 1977, p. 85).

This alteration of what Husserl terms the "natural thesis" is based on the assumption that "every individual event has its essence which can be grasped in its eidetic purity" (Husserl, 1913/1962, p. 104). The search for the essence, the recurring facticity, and the descriptive core of the phenomenon of emotion-as-a-process is a basic goal of descriptive phenomenology (see Merleau-Ponty, 1962, pp. xiv–xvii). The phenomenon of emotion that is engaged is a reflection both of its location in the world and of the meanings brought to it by the investigator (see Blumer, 1969; Merleau-Ponty, 1962; Heidegger, 1927/1962). The essence, or changing inner reflective meaning, of an emotional phenomenon lies in this double transaction with the world. This assumption joins Husserl's and Merleau-Ponty's phenomenology with the pragmatism of James, Peirce, Mead, Dewey, and Blumer (see Denzin, in press-a).

Fourth, once the essential properties of the phenomenon have been disclosed, factual information and phenomenal structures may be classified, compared, ordered, and synthesized. Factual inquiry alone will not provide adequate foundations for an understanding and interpretation of emotion. The core of the phenomenon of emotion must first be discovered, interrogated, and described. Phenomenological inquiry is first descriptive and then interpretive.

Fifth, "the methodological meaning of phenomenological description is *interpretation* . . . or *hermeneutics* which is the work of interpretation" (Heidegger, 1977, p. 86). Interpretation reveals and engulfs all that is known about the phenomenon at the everyday and bracketed levels of meaning. This knowledge and understanding are then fitted into an "interpreted totality." This interpreted totality discloses the phenomenon in its fullness, revealing its structures and their interrelations.

Sixth, the interpretive study of emotion seeks understanding entirely from within emotion as a phenomenon-in-the-world. Inquiry is confined solely to the phenomenon in question, whether this is the emotions (Sartre, 1939/1962), the ways of the music-making hand (Sudnow, 1978, 1979), the Balinese cockfight (Geertz, 1973), or the procedures of scientific discovery used by astronomers (Garfinkel, Lynch, and Livingston, 1981). Interpretations from outside the lived experience of emotion, or the phenomenon in question, are not sought. They are actively rejected. A social phenomenological interpretation always stays within the phenomenon, seeking understanding from within the lived experience. Understanding, explanation, or prediction is not sought in terms of forces or factors external to the phenomenon, nor are properties or disturbances internal to the emotional world of the person, yet outside the person's field of consciousness, sought and examined.

Seventh, the following questions constitute steps toward an interpretation of emotion. They are also criteria for judging a phenomenological interpretation.

1. Does the interpretation of emotion illuminate, disclose, and reveal lived emotion?
2. Does the interpretation rest on thickly contextualized, thickly described materials and on concepts near to experience?
3. Is the interpretation historically embedded and temporally grounded?
4. Does the interpretation reflect the emotion as a process that is relational and interactive?
5. Does the interpretation engulf what is known about the phenomenon?
6. Does the interpretation incorporate prior understandings and interpretations (the investigator's and others', including emergent ones) as part of the final interpreted, understood structural totality?
7. Does the interpretation cohere?
8. Does the interpretation of emotion produce understanding; that is, do the elements that are interpreted coalesce into a meaningful whole?
9. Is the interpretation unfinished? All interpretation is necessarily provisional and incomplete, to begin anew when the investigator returns to the phenomenon.

These criteria should be applied to the work that follows. It can be seen that interpretation involves a grasping of what is and was understood about a phenomenon as one begins inquiry. Prior understandings are brought to bear on emotion even before the investigation begins. Every reader and every investigator approaches the task of interpretation from the hermeneutical situation (Heidegger, 1927/1962, p. 275). My purpose, in this investigation, is to let go of prior conceptions of emotion so as to more clearly see it from within as a lived, interactional experience.

Interpretation is necessarily a temporal process. What has been interpreted provides the horizon for what is interpreted now. What is interpreted now is shaped by what will be interpreted. The hermeneutical circle of interpretation moves forward and backward, always starting from the present. Hence it is never closed or final, nor can we ever get outside it.

Eighth, the social phenomenological method can now be seen as having five components, or phases: deconstruction, capture, reduction, construction, and contextualization (see Heidegger, 1975/1982, p. 23). In deconstruction traditional concepts, understandings, and theories that surround the phenomenon of emotion are deconstructed—taken apart and traced back to their original sources and meanings. This permits a laying bare of prior understandings and misunderstandings (and their sources) of emotion.

In phenomenological capture, as indicated earlier, multiple instances of the phenomenon are obtained. Phenomenological reduction brackets the natural attitudes surrounding emotion. This permits a move to the essential features of the phenomenon. This movement is progressive and regressive, forward- and backward-looking at the same time (see Sartre, 1939/1962, pp. 93-94; 1963, pp. 85-166). Reduction moves forward, progressively, to a free projection, or construction, of the phenomenon in its fullest, interpreted forms. In the case of emotion this requires locating emotion in the lives of interacting individuals.

Interwoven with construction is contextualization. This requires a situating of the phenomenon of emotion back in the world. By contextualizing, the investigator places and studies emotion in the world of lived experience. Emotion is located in the personal biographies of interacting individuals. Contextualizing isolates its meaning for them, presenting it in terms of their languages, meanings, and understandings (point 2 above). In contextualizing, the social phenomenologist returns emotion (or any phenomenon), which was previously bracketed, to the world of interaction. Emotion's meanings, nuances, subtleties, innuendoes, distortions, and significations are brought to life and thickly described within the lived experiences of ordinary people. This investigation is a study of emotion as it is lived by ordinary people.

Summarizing and applying these structures and assumptions to the study of emotion suggests the following conclusions:

1. Emotion must be studied as a lived experience in the phenomenological and interactional streams of interacting individuals.
2. Emotion must not be studied as a social fact that is episodic, accidental, or incidental to social experience.
3. The natural scientific attitudes regarding emotions must be suspended. This includes whether they are naive, real, coarse, subtle, spurious, rational, irrational, conscious, unconscious, subconscious, physiological in origin, or the products of social and cultural forces.
4. Emotion must be grasped in its entirety, as fully and as clearly as possible, although the grasping will involve successive glimpses, interrogations, and judgments.
5. The essence, core, or kernel of emotion-as-a-process must be captured and carefully described. The universal, or generic, features of emotion must then be interpreted.
6. Emotion must be understood from within, as a process that has its own trajectory, or stream of experience. As a phenomenon it dwells within its own dwelling.
7. Emotion is a process that turns on itself, elaborates itself, gets out of hand. It requires what came before it in time for what follows in its development.
8. The phenomenological understanding and interpretation of emotion will not be causal. It will be descriptive, interpretive, and processual. Variables, factors, and causal agents will not be sought.
9. Phenomenological interpretation proceeds neither from strict induction (the gathering up of facts for theory) nor from deduction (theory to facts to hypotheses), but

moves forward, carefully, through rigorous intuition, abductive interrogation, and understanding. The phenomenon itself is uncovered and interpreted in consciousness and in the world of lived experience.

10. Theory testing is not the goal. The intention is descriptive interpretation; the goal is seeing, inspecting, and studying the interiority of emotion as lived experience. Social phenomenology is a descriptive, interpretive discipline. As such it seems particularly well suited to the study of emotion and emotionality.

This study is intended as a beginning for a phenomenological sociology and psychology of emotion and emotionality. A clarification and interpretation of emotion is intended. Accordingly, I will argue that although existing theories of emotion call attention to the centrality of the phenomenon for an understanding of human conduct, they must be temporarily suspended in favor of a social phenomenological and interactionist exploration and interpretation of emotion.

PART ONE

Differing Views
of Emotion

Chapters One and Two of this investigation locate the study of
emotion and emotionality within a point of view that is interpretive, phenomenological, and interactionist. These three terms
require brief elaboration. *Interpretation* is the clarification of
meaning. It occurs through the process of translating, describ-
ing, dissecting, recording, and piecing together the meanings of
another's actions and placing those actions within a meaningful
sequence or totality. To interpret is to give meaning to an act,
event, or object. A point of view is *phenomenological* when it
attempts to secure the interpretation and understanding of a
phenomenon from within. That is, phenomenological inquiry is
a return to the thing itself, as Husserl argued so many times.
The thing, the phenomenon, is studied as a process in its own
right. Inquiry endeavors to reveal and unravel the structures,
logic, and interrelationships that obtain in the phenomenon under inspection. The variant and invariant features of the phenomenon are thereby disclosed through successive glimpses, re-

flections, and analyses. *Interactionist* study locates the phenomenon of human experience in the world of social interaction. It directs attention to the emergent, conflictual, dialectical, problematic features of ongoing interaction.

To surround the study of emotionality with these three terms is to increase the likelihood that analysis will be grounded in the lived experiences of interacting individuals. Chapter One deconstructs previous theories of emotion, turning principally on the formulations of William James and Sigmund Freud, the two theorists who have dominated the study of emotion in the twentieth-century. By inserting the phenomenological perspective between James and Freud, and by drawing on the symbolic interactionist thought of Mead and Blumer, I offer a conception of emotionality that seems more consistent with the view of human nature that I develop in Part Two.

Critical to this point of view are lessons I take from the classical sociological theorists: The human subject's emotional experiences are grounded in practical activities taken up in the face of an obdurate social world. The material world is constituted through the ensembles of social relationships that bind subjects to one another. The fields of emotional experience that subjects produce are separate social realities that are layered over or exist alongside the everyday world they take for granted. The subject is connected to and in the world intersubjectively, in a circuit of selfness. The natural emotional attitude is one that takes the experiencing of emotionality for granted. The phenomenological perspective I adopt makes that natural attitude problematic so that these taken-for-granted features of emotionality may be better illuminated.

In Chapter One bits and pieces from a number of theorists are adopted as I lay the foundations for Chapter Two, wherein the topics of emotionality, self, and interaction are brought together in a somewhat formal fashion. I try to steer a course between structuralist, Freudian, psychological, behavioral, evolutionary, and cognitive perspectives while remaining true to Merleau-Ponty's charge to uncover the essential meaning of emotionality.

Chapter One

Classical
and Contemporary
Theories

The philosophical, psychological, psychiatric, sociological, and anthropological traditions that surround and embed contemporary understandings of the emotions run so deep and are still so influential that their effects on any understanding of emotion cannot be overestimated. This chapter is devoted to a discussion of these traditional concepts, understandings, formulations, and theories. It follows Heidegger's (1975/1982, p. 12) suggestion that the progressive phenomenological understanding of a phenomenon proceeds through a *deconstruction* of prior theories and formulations. Such an unraveling or unveiling of prior formulations of emotion is necessary if its social phenomenological interpretation is to have solid footing.

The following theories and views of emotion will be reviewed: (1) the James-Lange theory of emotion, (2) the recent psychological formulations of Lazarus, Averill and Opton, Ar-

nold, Singer, Plutchik, Ekman, and Izard, (3) the recent sociological formulations of Kemper, Hochschild, Shott, Scheff, and
Collins and the more classic sociological formulations of Marx,
Weber, Durkheim, and Simmel, (4) Freud's model of the emotions, (5) Lacan's psychoanalytic theory of the Other, speech,
desire, and history, (6) Scheff's theory of emotional catharsis,
(7) Sartre's theory of emotion.

The etymology of the word *emotion* suggests the following meanings: (1) an agitation of the passions or sensibilities,
often involving physiological changes, (2) any strong feeling
arising subjectively rather than through conscious mental effort,
(3) to excite, to move out, to stir up, to move. The prevailing
meaning of *emotion* in the theories to be reviewed stresses the
physiological and nonconscious mental features of emotion. It
is necessary to begin with the James-Lange theory of the emotions, for here the physiological position is most forcefully and
most clearly stated.

The James-Lange Theory of Emotion

The James-Lange theory of emotion has been the subject
of considerable scientific debate since its (1890) publication by
William James in *Principles of Psychology* (see Wundt, 1891;
Worcester, 1893; Dewey, 1894, 1895; Irons, 1894; Stratton,
1895; Baldwin, 1894; Mead, 1895, 1982a; Cannon, 1929; Sartre,
1939/1962; Schachter and Singer, 1962; Kemper, 1978b;
Scheff, 1979, 1983). Portions of James's theory were formulated by the Danish psychologist Carl Georg Lange in 1885, and
James combined his views with those of Lange. The James-Lange
theory offers a physiological accounting of the constitution, organization, and conditioning of the "coarser" emotions such as
grief, fear, rage, and love, in which "everyone recognizes strong
organic reverberations," and the subtler "emotions, or those
whose organic reverberations [are] less obvious and strong,"
such as moral, intellectual, and esthetic feelings (James, 1890/
1950, vol. 2, p. 449).

The general causes of the emotions are assumed to be internal, physiological, nervous processes, not mental or psycho-

logical processes. Moods, affections, and emotions are "constituted and made up of those bodily changes which we ordinarily
call their expression or consequence" (James, 1890/1950, vol.
2, p. 452). A purely disembodied emotion—for example, the
emotion of fear without a quickened heartbeat, sharp breathing,
or weakened limbs—would be a nonentity for this theory. The
emotions are the result of bodily changes that occur as a reflex
effect of an exciting object or fact confronted by the person.

An emotional experience follows this sequence: (1) the
perception of an exciting fact or object by the person, (2) a
bodily expression such as weeping, striking out, or fleeing the
situation, (3) a mental affection or emotion, such as feeling
afraid or angry. Many theories of emotion, as well as common
sense, place the bodily expression of weeping or striking out or
fleeing *after* the emotion of feeling anger or fear. The James-
Lange theory alters this sequence, placing bodily expressions *between* the perception of the exciting fact and the emotion. In
everyday terms, we "cry and then feel sad"—not "we feel sad
and then cry." *"The bodily changes follow directly the perception of the exciting fact . . . our feeling [*them*] as they occur is
the emotion"* (James, 1890/1950, vol. 2, p. 449). This is a
physiological-cognitive theory of emotion. Physiological processes, however, take precedence over cognitive states. In the
theory, the word *emotion* refers to "the rank feeling of excitement" that comes from the physiological sensations felt by the
person (James, 1894, p. 525).

The debate and criticism that have surrounded the theory
involve the following points. Considerable controversy and
words have been wasted over whether the James-Lange theory is
a centralist, a peripheral, a specificity, or an antispecificity
theory of emotion. Rather than placing the critics of the theory
(or the theory itself) into these categories, I shall avoid labels
and treat each critic in turn, regardless of classification. First,
Wundt (1891) argued that James gave insufficient attention to
the fact that emotions intensify and develop as they are experienced. Second, Irons (1894, 1895) argued that the theory did
not deal with the place of the self and subjective feelings in the
experiencing of emotion. He stated: "Not the mere object as

such is what determines the physical effects, but the subjective feeling toward the object" (1894, p. 78). Irons further stated that the theory did not belong to psychology because it ignored the self and its unity. Third, Worcester (1893) suggested that the theory did not have a place for self-feelings and emotional reactions of the self. He proposed the term *feeling-attitude* for these feelings. Fourth, Baldwin (1894, pp. 610–623), who termed the James-Lange theory a peripheral theory of the emotions, suggested that the "coarser" emotions the theory dealt with were phenomena of *instinct*. Many of the emotions the theory's critics focused on were learned emotions that emerge during a child's moral, social, and intellectual development. It is true that the original theory drew heavily on Darwin's works (1859, 1872/1955) and did not satisfactorily treat the "subtle" emotions. Anger, fear, and rage were primary emotions discussed by James. Baldwin's point was well taken.

James's responses to these criticisms were to sharpen his conception of the physiological meanings of the term *emotion* and admit into his formulations a broader interpretive stance on the part of the person experiencing an emotion. He stated: *"Such organic sensations being also presumably due to incoming currents, the result is that the whole of my consciousness* (whatever its inner contrasts be) *seems to me to be outwardly mediated by these* [physiological sensations] " (1894, pp. 523–524). He did not develop Dewey's position, discussed next, that emotion is an inhibition to acting habitually.

Fifth, John Dewey (1894, 1895), elaborating Baldwin's Darwinian observation, proposed the following conception of emotion: "Certain movements, formerly useful in themselves, become reduced to tendencies to action, to attitudes. As such they serve, when instinctively aroused into actions, as means for realizing ends. But so far as there is difficulty in adjusting the organic activity represented by the attitude with that which stands for the idea or end, there is a temporary struggle and partial inhibition. This is reported as *affect,* or emotional seizure. Let the coordination be effected in one act, instead of in a successive series of mutually exclusive stimuli, and we have interest. Let such coordinations become thoroughly habitual and hereditary, and we have *Gefuhlston* [emotional disturbance or affect] " (1895, p. 32).

Sixth, G. H. Mead, whose fuller reactions to the James-Lange theory have only just become available, developed Dewey's modification of the theory as follows: "The point of view of Dewey assumes that the emotion as such arises through the inhibition of a tendency to act. There is of course an affective side of all consciousness, but this does not appear as an emotion unless there is an inhibition of a tendency to act. . . . If the emotion is to be regarded as a function of inhibition, we cannot accept Wundt's theory or the James-Lange theory. The clenching of the fist does not cause the emotion, but the inhibition of the act of striking does produce the emotion" (Mead, 1982a, p. 40). In his brief comment on James's theory in 1895, Mead (1895, pp. 162–164) basically supported James's formulations but drew attention to the inhibition to response that occurs on perception of the exciting fact. Thus, and most important, Dewey and Mead insert an inhibitory phase between stimulus and reaction.

Seventh, Cannon (1929) argued that the thalamic neurons are the cause of the emotions. The thalamic theory of the emotions modifies the James-Lange theory by asserting:

> An external situation stimulates receptors and the consequent excitation starts impulses toward the cortex. Arrival of the impulses towards the cortex is associated with conditioned processes which determine the direction of the response. Either because the response is initiated in a certain mode or figure and the cortical neurons therefore stimulate the thalamic processes, or because on their inward course the impulses from the receptors excite thalamic processes, they are roused and ready for discharge. That the thalamic neurons act in a special combination in a given emotional expression is proved by the reaction patterns typical of the several affective states. These neurons do not require detailed innervation from above in order to be driven into action. Being *released* for action is a primary condition for their service to the

body—they then discharge precipitately and intensely. . . . The theory which naturally presents
itself is that *the peculiar quality of the emotion is
added to simple sensation when the thalamic processes are roused* [Cannon, 1929, p. 200].

Eighth, in a study now regarded as near classic, in which
some subjects were injected with epinephrine and others with
an inert substance, Schachter and Singer (1962) argued that "an
emotional state may be considered a state of physiological
arousal and of a cognition appropriate to this state of arousal.
. . . It is the cognition that determines whether the state of
physiological arousal will be labeled as 'anger,' 'joy,' or whatever" (p. 380). This formulation significantly modified James's
theory. The experiment designed to test this hypothesis has
been subjected to considerable interpretation and criticism. The
findings appear to be inconclusive (Kemper, 1978b, pp. 166–
187; Scheff, 1979, pp. 92–100).

Ninth, Jean-Paul Sartre (1939/1962) critically evaluated
the James-Lange theory from a phenomenological perspective
and rejected it on the following grounds. First, behavior, physiological or expressive, is not emotion, nor is the awareness of
that behavior emotion. Second, the body does not call out its
own interpretations, which are given in the field of consciousness of the person. Third, the bodily disturbances present in
emotion are disorders of the most ordinary kind but are not the
causes of emotion. They ratify the existence of emotion for the
person; they give emotion its believability. Fourth, to consider
only the biological body, as the James-Lange theory does, independent of the lived body, and the person's consciousness of his
or her body as the source of his or her emotion, is to treat the
body as a thing and to locate emotion in disorders of the body
(Plessner, 1970; Meinong, 1972). Emotion as a part of the person's lived experiences in the lifeworld has not yet been given
adequate attention by either the critics or the followers of the
James-Lange theory (see Scheler, 1916/1973).

The factors isolated in the theory are not disputed. The
perception of the sequence of the factors and the emphasis on
strictly physiological as opposed to social, psychological, and in-

teractional processes are the sources of current controversy (see Kemper, 1981). Furthermore, the production of a crucial, incontrovertible experiment that would clarify once and for all the centralist/peripheralist debate is still sought (Scheff, 1983).

Sartre's critique, which is accepted in this text, would, if adopted, put an end to sociologists' preoccupation with physiological definitions and formulations of the emotions. Sartre's work, however, has been largely ignored in the recent literature, as the following discussion will reveal. His criticisms of James apply, as well, to recent theorists who have used James's definition of emotion.

Recent Psychological Formulations

A number of recent psychological theorists have significantly advanced beyond James's physiologically grounded theory by emphasizing the cognitive, affective, phenomenological, situational, motivational, and interactional dimensions of emotion and emotionality. Candland (1977, pp. 1–85) provides an extremely useful review and statement of these theories, as do Izard (1977), Arnold (1970), and Plutchik (1962, 1977). Arnold's theory, which is cognitive, interpretive, and phenomenological, stresses the individual's active appraisal of a social situation as an emotional line of action is built up toward a social object. Her theory has certain similarities to Meinong's (1972) theory of emotional presentation. Arnold suggests that a sequence of emotional experience begins with appraisal and interpretation. Meinong proposes that an emotional field of experience presents itself to the person as a situation to be lived through and given meaning. In this sense emotions exist ahead of the person, as fields of experience that must be constructed. Plessner (1970), Strasser (1963, 1970), Binswanger (1963), Giorgi (1970), and Schmalenbach (1977), in more fully developed phenomenological statements, have made similar arguments, as have Allport (1955), Kelly (1955), May (1958), Rogers (1961), Smith (1974), Harré and Secord (1973), Icheiser (1970), and Riezler (1950).

Averill, Opton, and Lazarus (1969), Lazarus and Averill

(1972), and Averill (1980) have developed a model of emotion that is quite close to Arnold's appraisal theory. They assume a threefold emotional response system that elaborates Dewey's (1895) suggestion that an inhibition of action occurs between stimulus and response and that inhibition may redefine the stimulus. First, emotional responses may serve as stimuli that contribute to an emotional experience. The emotional response system they develop suggests, second, that emotions are social constructions (Averill, 1980, p. 38) that are shaped by primary and secondary appraisal processes, which operate within the human brain and the individual's sociocultural system. The third element of the emotional response system consists of cognitive, expressive, and instrumental responses to the emotional stimulus situation.

Izard (1977) develops an interactional-motivational theory of emotionality that incorporates physiological processes into the personality system. Termed the "differential emotions theory," Izard's formulation suggests that emotions interact, so that one emotion may "activate, amplify, or attenuate another" (Izard, 1977, p. 43). This model suggests comparisons with Plutchik's, which combines an evolutionary model of human development with a differentiation of what Plutchik terms the primary emotions (as discussed earlier) into primary, secondary, and tertiary dyadic complexes, or structures. Such a mixed, or interactive, model of the emotions assumes that there are only a small "number of pure or primary emotions" (Plutchik, 1962, p. 41). Ekman's (1973, 1980) investigations indicate that certain emotions, those termed primary or fundamental by Izard (1977), have the same expressions and experiential qualities in "widely different cultures from virtually every continent on the globe, including preliterate cultures having had virtually no contact with Western civilization" (Izard, 1977, p. 6). The expressions, or languages, of emotion as given in the human face and in nonverbal communication appear to be universal (Darwin, 1872/1955; Ekman, 1973, p. 259). A further elaboration of the cognitive and affective approach to emotions is given in Singer's (1973, 1974) and Tomkins's (1962, 1963) works, which stress the importance of fantasy processes, dreams, and imagery in the person's emotional and motivational system. These theorists, with Izard (1977) and Mowrer (1960), assume that emotions constitute the primary motivational system for human beings (Izard, 1977, p. 38).

These psychological formulations have importance for the perspective developed in this book. They bring emotions out of the unconscious into the conscious world of the person. They situate emotions in the social and cultural world. They speak to the universal modes and forms of emotional experience. They suggest that interpretation, thought, cognition, and feeling are all involved in emotionality. They assume, also, that the physiological and neurological substrate of emotions must be taken into account before psychological accounts or theories can be built. However, they suggest that psychological and phenomenological theorizing can and must occur at a level that is above the physiological level of analysis (Boyle, 1984). The repeated attempts to isolate the primary, universal, or fundamental emotions and the marked similarity in all such schemes indicate that the phenomena of emotion have at least been consensually captured. Accordingly, when the social phenomenologist speaks of emotionality, of the emotions, or of emotional experience, a common universe of meaning (Mead, 1938) is understood.

This recent work by the psychologists of emotion contains few if any referents to the self, to interaction, to interaction ritual, to social structure, to ideology, history, feeling rules, or emotional marketplaces. The concern for human motivation and the place of emotions in motivational theory run counter to the phenomenological and interactionist view that the constancy of human activity requires no theory of motivation (Stone and Farberman, 1981, p. 317). John Dewey (1922, p. 119) observed that the person is "an active being and that is all there is to be said on that score." Consequently, it can be assumed that emotions and emotionality are a constant presence in the stream of activity that is the person. What require analysis are the motives and meanings that people bring to bear on the organization of their own behavior. These emotional vocabularies of motive are discussed in the next chapter.

Finally, this body of recent psychological work understandably does not locate the emotions and emotional experience in the social, cultural, and historical milieu of the person; nor does it treat the place of the emotions in human nature. The emotions of love, hate, envy, pride, rage, humility, anger, desire, and hope are more than specific cognitive and affective responses or interpretations to social situations and social objects: They are the basic elements of sociological human nature. They lie at the core of the human being and are experienced in the presence of other humans.

The present work assumes that the way people act is very much determined by the moods, feelings, and emotions they experience and bring into their situations of social interaction (Denzin, 1980, p. 251). These emotional features of the human condition lie at the center of the intersection of mind, culture, and society. A society and its laws enter directly into the organization and experiencing of everyday phenomenological life through the structuring and sanctioning of the moods, emotions, and emotional experiences felt by its members. In everyday life the moods that people experience and establish can be as basic to the organization of their joint actions as are their claims to power, influence, or status. As society reaches out and enters into the person, as seen in emotionality and social interaction, alterations occur in the person's inner phenomenological stream of consciousness (Goffman, 1983). Individuals are connected to society through the emotions they experience. Herein lies the importance of mood and emotion for the study of society and social organization. A social psychology and social phenomenology that desires to study the subjective and intersubjective sides of social life must bring the emotions squarely into focus. This the literature cited above attempts to do. It remains to situate emotionality more centrally in the social world. Recent and classical sociological theory has attempted to do this.

Recent and Classical Sociological Developments

After decades of speaking to and about the emotions, sociologists are now taking them seriously and attempting to construct theories that give human emotionality a central place in the sociological view of individuals and their societies (Gordon, 1981; Parsons, 1978; Scheff, 1979). Recent efforts to contribute to a sociology and social psychology of the emotions (Scheff, 1979, 1983; Shott, 1979; Hochschild, 1979, 1983; Kemper, 1978b, 1981; Collins, 1975, 1981) are to be applauded. Shott's application of principles from symbolic interactionism, Scheff's catharsis theory, Hochschild's conceptions of emotion rules and emotion management strategies, Kemper's social relational theory of emotion, and Collins's emotion marketplace theory constitute significant advances over previous formulations. Together, this body of work has several distinct merits: It treats emotions sociologically, relationally, and interactionally. It synthesizes wide-ranging literatures in experimental psychology, physiology, social psychology, anthropology, and sociology. It offers innumerable propositions that could be examined empirically and comparatively in different societies, cultures, and social classes. It speaks to the emotions as sociological processes, not strictly physiological or psychological ones.

These advantages notwithstanding, this current body of work suffers from two basic problems that need correcting. The first is definitional and involves how the phenomena of emotion are to be formulated sociologically. The second is one of domain priorities and involves the place of somatic processes in a sociological view of emotion. The two problems tend to blur together.

Scheff, Collins, Hochschild, Shott, and Kemper, following James, treat emotions as states of physiological arousal, which are defined by the person, using emotional labels. Emotions, they suggest, are responses to certain forms of stimuli—physiological, cultural, structural, interactional, and relational. Shott (1979, p. 1318) states: "I shall use Schachter's (1971, pp. 23-24) conception of emotion as a state of physiological arousal defined by the actor as emotionally induced." Hochschild (1979, p. 551) defines emotion as "bodily cooperation with an image, a thought, a memory—a cooperation of which the individual is aware." Kemper (1981, p. 339) states that "different outcomes in power and status relations instigate different physiological processes which are in turn related to different emotions." Elsewhere (1978b, pp. 47–48) he defines emotion as a "relatively short-term evaluative response essentially positive or negative in nature involving distinct somatic (and often cognitive) components." Scheff (1979, p. 91) postulates a "discrete set of physiological changes for each emotion." He states that "my approach is close to James's except that I take his definition, with its physiological emphasis, a step further: emotions are specific patterns of bodily changes, whether or not there is conscious awareness. This step is necessary if one is to speak of unconscious emotions." Collins's emotions are automatically aroused emotional responses (Collins, 1975, p. 153).

Following James, these authors posit a direct causal relation between the perception of an exciting social fact or social situation, internal bodily reactions, and overt behaviors, which are then labeled, inhibited, or disguised in terms of social, relational, ritual, and structural factors, as well as by emotional rules and cultural-sexual ideologies. What unites these theorists is a search for an explanation of emotion that is not in the lived reality or experience of the person who experiences emotion but, rather, in factors that lie outside emotion itself. Emotion is seen as either the cause or the consequence of factors external to emotional consciousness (Sartre, 1939/1962). Whether the emphasis is on cultural factors (feeling rules, emotion, work, ideology), on structural, ritual, and relational factors, or on the socialization process, the explanation and interpretation of emotion are located in the development and appearance of the emotion as that development is conditioned and shaped by factors external to the person. Emotions are treated like stones or ponds or static objects that are given labels. They are not treated as processes lived by self-reflective individuals in interactional experience.

These theorists appear to await a crucial experiment that will resolve once and for all the controversy over whether the "cause" of emotions is physiological, cognitive, or structural. Lacking this experiment, Scheff (1979) and Kemper (1978a, 1978b, 1981) have offered labored interpretations of the inconclusive findings from the classic Schachter and Singer study mentioned earlier. Both authors seek support for their respective theoretical positions. After a long reanalysis of Schachter and Singer's study, Scheff (1979, pp. 99, 98) states: "My conclusion is that the subject's state of information, a peripheral variable, had a very weak effect on emotional state in both the anger and happiness condition, but that no effect was found for the second peripheral variable, the social environment. . . . What I am saying is that the laboratory conditions of the experiment, which lead to very low levels of intensity and small effects, are the very conditions most likely to support the peripheral hypothesis. A much more rigorous test would be under conditions of high intensity and strong changes."

Kemper similarly concludes that Schachter and Singer's study yielded inconclusive results. He states: "Unfortunately, the experiment contains a flaw that invalidates any interpretation at all . . . the flaw is that the experimental paradigm allowed the supposedly high-fear subjects to experience fear arousal and its symptoms *before* learning that they would also be ingesting a (placebo) drug" (1981, p. 340). Faced with this conclusion, Kemper (1978b; 1981, p. 342) interprets Funkenstein's (1955) hypothesis that "anger directed outward is associated with the secretion of norepinephrine while depression and anxiety are associated with the secretion of epinephrine" to support his position of specificity that "different emotions are associated with different physiological response configurations" (Kemper, 1978b, pp. 151, 153). The suggestion by both Scheff and Kemper that a discrete physiological and neurological substrate is associated with each emotion is in line with the arguments of Izard (1972), Plutchik (1962), and Arnold (1960a, 1960b, 1970).

Collins's Theory of the Emotional Marketplace. Of the recent sociological theories of emotion, Randall Collins's is the most explicitly structural and the most directly connected to the sociological theories of Marx, Weber, Durkheim, and Goffman. He develops a model of ritual interaction chains in which everyday encounters become marketplaces for the exchange of cultural and emotional resources (Collins, 1981). Building from a Darwinian organismic theory of emotion, Collins assumes that emotions are aroused by basic social ties that are ritualistically

controlled and exchanged through the chains of ritual interaction that society's participants routinely and regularly produce.
His emotions cluster around the social processes of conflict,
domination, subordination, and ritual solidarity. The theory
examines the exchange and expenditure of emotional energies
and resources in a society at any given moment. Collins's model
assumes that social structures and social change rest on fluctua-
tions in the emotional and cultural resources of interacting individuals.

This is a quasi-exchange, quasi-equilibrium, structural
model of emotional interaction that assumes certain reinforcement principles at the psychological level. It moves quickly
from the stage of emotional arousal to the level of ritual interaction, while treating emotions as objects, or commodities, not
as processes. The theory has the strength of connecting emotions to the level of large-scale social structures and hence extends Weber, Durkheim, and Garfinkel in important new directions. However, Collins gives little if any systematic attention to
the self-feelings of the interactant who experiences emotional
arousal, the feeling rules analyzed by Hochschild (1979), the interactional, intersubjective meaning of ritual, the situational
world of emotionality, and the place of the lived body in emotional experience. The forms of emotional ritual—spatial, temporal, linguistic, and interactional—recently identified by Power
(1984) in the contexts of early childhood socialization suggest
that Collins's formulations of ritual interaction require additional development.

A major strength of his formulations is the location of
emotionality in every interaction that occurs within a society
and the attempt to build a structural theory of emotionality out
of face-to-face interaction processes. Still, it is difficult to accept Collins's basic assumption that the emotional energies in a
social collectivity are transmitted "by contagion among members of a group, in flows that operate very much like the set of
negotiations which produce prices within a market" (1981, p.
272). Such a view ignores the multiple forms of fellow-feeling
and emotional intersubjectivity that exist in everyday interaction. It assumes too, as just noted, that emotions are commodi-

ties. Missing in Collins's theory is a well-worked-out conception of emotional intersubjectivity and emotional understanding.

Hochschild's Theory of the Managed Heart. In a major interactionist investigation that extends her earlier (1979) analysis of emotional feeling rules, Arlie Hochschild (1983) offers an interactive model of emotions fitted to the special case of female participation in the labor force. Drawing on a large body of theory, including Marx, Lionel Trilling, and a critique of the work of Erving Goffman, Hochschild examines the pressures and ideologies that work against women's expression of deep, sincere, authentic, inner feelings in the emotional and work marketplace. The feeling rules, cultural ideologies, sexual stereotypes, and economic factors that shape emotional display while demeaning the female's dignity to herself and to others are dramatically highlighted in Hochschild's interviews with female airline flight attendants. Central to her theory is the premise that the management of emotion has become an added qualification for female participation in the labor force. The managed heart is twisted to fit the culturally and economically dominant male conception of femininity in public places. It suggests that virtually one half of the workers in postcapitalist societies are working under conditions that suppress and distort their inner emotional experiences. This insight extends Freud's (1933) observations on women and the internalization of the feminine sex role. It elevates to even greater importance Freud's charge to women to interrogate their own experience. Women must seize the means and the language to conceptualize their experience within their own terms. Hochschild's work is an important step in this direction.

Her work complements Scheler's, Nietzsche's, and Weber's on the place of ressentiment in the lives of modern men and women (see Chapter Seven). Women repeatedly experience emotional situations that subordinate them to men sexually, politically, economically, and intellectually. These negative emotional experiences produce suppressed wrath, hatred, and other hostile emotions. They are interiorized in the body, often producing a hatred of the body or a splitting of the real self from the public body that is gazed on and evaluated by others. The body of the person of ressentiment becomes a source of pain, guilt, and self-torment. Joyce Carol Oates (1982) has suggested that the modern woman is invisible in public places. That is, her inner self is invisible; she is judged publicly only in terms of her body and its attractiveness. This is precisely the situation of the women studied by Hochschild. The essence of public femininity produces a distortion of self and emotionality that cuts to the woman's inner core, thereby debasing the essence of being human for women.

Hochschild's investigation suggests a required thickening of phenomenological analysis so that the lived experiences of repressed and suppressed female emotionality can be more fully revealed. Her work also suggests the need for a deeper radical feminist critique of Freud (Irigaray, 1980). Extensions in Lacan's reformulations of Freud as well as in a feminist semiology are also called for (Clough, 1982).

Although the content of emotion feeling rules remains somewhat unclear in Hochschild's work, a comparative study of emotion management by males seems warranted. Whether the phenomenological structures Hochschild uncovers are universal or unique to the experiences of women at this particular moment in postcapitalist societies is also uncertain. Her investigation adds another dimension to Collins's conception of the emotional marketplace, for it suggests that there are at least two emotional marketplaces at work in American society—one for men and one for women. Her subtle analysis of the microactions of emotion management fills in the rather large gap that exists in Collins's move from the micro- to the macrolevels of social structure.

Interpretation. Emotions are embodied experiences. The place of the body as an instrument in the expression of the emotion cannot be denied. However, the body does not call out interpretations. Interpretations of bodily states are given in the individual's field of experience. Pure behavior, as noted earlier, is not emotion. The simple awareness or defining of that behavior as emotion is also not emotion (Sartre, 1939/1962, p. 74). The body adjusts itself to emotional consciousness. The bodily disturbance present during emotion is most typically "a disorder of the most ordinary description" (Sartre, 1939/1962, p.

78). At bottom, these disorders, Sartre argues, "resemble those of fever, of artificial overexcitation, etc. . . . They merely represent a complete and commonplace upset of the body . . . the bodily disturbance is nothing more than the belief [in the emotion] lived by the consciousness as it is seen from the outside" (Sartre, 1939/1962, pp. 78-79). The search for the unifying physiological states or structural conditions that would account for the emotions will not speak to the basic question that guides this investigation: How is emotion as a form of consciousness lived, experienced, and articulated in the everyday lifeworld? Although scientific analysis "may be able to distinguish, in the biological body, in the body as a thing, the local disorder of this or that organ" (Sartre, 1939/1962, p. 79), such discoveries have reference to the physiological, not the phenomenological, understanding of emotion.

Perhaps, as Sartre (1940/1972) argued, following Husserl in his attempts to lay the foundations of a phenomenological psychology, great strides will be made in the sociological understanding of the emotions when sociologists (and psychologists) "cease to burden themselves with ambiguous and contradictory experiments and start bringing to light the essential structures constituting the subject of [their] investigations. . . . In a word psychology [and sociology] is an empirical discipline that is still looking for its eidetic principles. Eidetic description is the required starting point. The way is open for a phenomenological psychology [sociology]" (pp. 129-130, 143). This is not to deny the importance of experimentation and careful gathering of facts in the study of emotion. But before experimenting, observing, or gathering facts, it is essential that one "know as exactly as possible *what* one is going to experiment *upon*" (Sartre, 1940/1972, p. 129).

The second problem with the current literature on the emotions is one of domain priorities and involves the place of somatic processes in a sociological theory of emotion. It must be granted that emotion is a social, interactional, linguistic, and physiological process that draws its resources from the human body, from human consciousness, and from the world that surrounds the person. The sociological and phenomenological

analysis of emotion cannot begin, however, with the physiological and neurological structures of the human body and the
brain. Nor can such a study begin by examining factors outside
the field of interaction wherein emotion is felt and experienced.
Physiological, neurological, social, cultural, ritual, structural,
and relational interpretations of emotion must be temporarily
suspended while emotion is defined and studied from within, as
a lived, interactional process that has the self of the person centrally in its organization.

*Emotion in the Works of Marx, Weber, Durkheim, and
Simmel.* The recent sociological works just discussed extend the
insights of a number of classical sociologists on emotion and social structure. Contrary to the observations of Scheff (1979, pp.
3-5) and Hochschild (1975, pp. 284-285), the emotions and
emotionality do occupy a significant position in the works of
Marx, Weber, Durkheim, and Simmel.

Marx saw human emotionality and consciousness as shaped
by social situations and social structures. He saw too that a dialectical relation exists between the person's sensuous relations
with the material world and the meanings brought to and developed in relation to that world (Marx, 1888/1983d, p. 156). He
understood that the essence of the individual lies in the *ensemble* of social relations that bind him or her to the social and material world (Marx, 1888/1983d, p. 157). There is no such thing
as an isolated individual, only the person in relations with others. Emotionality, including alienation (Marx, 1845-1846/
1983b, p, 178), estrangement, and disenchantment with the
world, translates into the material economic practices that reduce individuals to being defined in monetary, labor-value
terms. If all social life is essentially practical, involving human
practices in the world, then emotions are grounded in the practical activities that locate individuals in the world. The emotional fields of experience that confront the person in the capitalist and postcapitalist society are alienating and self-destructive.
The values of men and women are defined in monetary, not human, terms, as seen in the fetishism of commodities. Commodity values are even placed on emotional experiences.

Marx demonstrates how ideas, ideals, and emotions can

support a repressive, alienating social structure (1852/1983c, pp. 287-323). Emotionality is located in history and in the person's relation to that history. The *Economico-Philosophical Manuscripts of 1844* (1844/1983a) make clear Marx's position that emotionality may be externalized in material commodities, thereby driving a wedge between inner feelings and economic-material practical activities. Central to Marx's position is the intersubjective, relational component of social conduct. If people are cut off from one another, and if class consciousness does not develop, private, isolated worlds of emotionality are built up. These worlds perpetuate the dominating emotional attitudes of ressentiment and alienation. Such conditions promote the emotional and political subordination of social collectivities to an executive authority. This increases the likelihood that exploitation, political terror, and violence will occur (Marx, 1852/1983c, p. 312).

Marx's emotions are social, interactional, and historical productions grounded in the person's and the group's material and interactional relationship to the world. The modern individual, Marx proposes, lacking the ability to make his own history, to structure the circumstances and conditions that he confronts in the world, experiences the emotions of previous generations. These emotions and emotional experiences, like the traditions, languages, and rhetorics of all dead generations, weigh on the consciousness and the lives of each succeeding generation (Marx, 1852/1983c, p. 287).

I turn now to Max Weber, who builds his entire analysis of capitalism on the fact that it is anchored in deeply held religious and emotional attitudes. The irony that infuses his work turns on the observation that once capitalism is "in the saddle," it no longer requires emotional attitudes "or needs religious motives" (Gerth and Mills, 1946, p. 68). The formal rationality of capitalism has no or little place for human feelings and sentiments. Capitalism requires that emotionality be managed and controlled and, if experienced, kept in the private spheres of the individual's life. The disenchantment that characterizes the modern world stems from the growing rationality that infuses organizational, bureaucratic, and everyday life. The structures of the modern lifeworld are based on an autonomous, rational logic that has no place for emotionality and self-feeling. The more deeply capitalism infuses itself in bureaucratic structures, the more dehumanizing it becomes. And the more "completely it succeeds in eliminating from official business love, hatred, and all purely personal, irrational, and emotional elements which escape calculation" (Weber, 1946, p. 216).

Weber understood the importance of status sentiments and self-feelings in the maintenance of bureaucratic structures and bureaucratic social relations. He also understood how important the manipulation of emotional attitudes is for the organization of the modern military (Weber, 1946, p. 254). His theory of the charismatic leader assumed that emotionality constitutes a basic mode of meaningful social action. His analysis of eroticism and sexual intimacy (Weber, 1946, pp. 343-350) rivals Simmel's (1950) treatment of these modes of emotional interaction.

Perhaps Weber's greatest insight (shared partly with Durkheim) into emotionality and the rational attitude of the modern world was to see that the distinction between the content of an emotional belief or action cannot be clearly differentiated from cognitions and thoughts about that belief or action. With Marx and Durkheim he saw that even religion and emotionality are subjected to the pressures of rationality and science (Weber, 1946, pp. 286-297). More important, he saw that all modes of emotional-affective conduct are infused with cognitions and the "rational" attitude. This position, of course, echoes the recent arguments of Arnold (1960a, 1960b), Izard (1977), and other cognitive psychologists on the emotions. It also suggests compatibilities with William James, whose work on the varieties of religious experience influenced Weber (Weber, 1946, p. 308). It is not possible, given the above points, to allow Scheff's (1979, p. 5) and Hochschild's (1975, pp. 284-285) conclusion that Weber misunderstood the importance of the emotions for the inner workings of social structure. It can, in fact, be argued that Weber anticipated many of Hochschild's observations.

A similar conclusion must be reached in regard to Durkheim, who, contrary to Scheff (1979, p. 3), did not see emotions as antisocial and irrational. Emotions and emotional experience, for Durkheim (1912/1973), are social facts and social currents. Their location is in society, which is a reality that comes before the person (Durkheim, 1912/1973, p. 191). The feelings, sentiments, and emotional attitudes of the person are "ways of acting, thinking, and feeling that present the noteworthy property of existing outside the individual consciousness" (Durkheim, 1895/1964, p. 2). These social facts exist as pressures against the person. "Let an individual attempt to oppose one of these collective manifestations and the emotions that he denies will turn against him" (1895/1964, p. 5). The feelings and emotions the person feels, Durkheim suggested, are not private or the sole construction of the person. Rather, "we are then the victims of the illusion of having ourselves created that which is actually forced itself from without" (1895/1964, p. 5). Individuals contribute spontaneously to the common emotions that coerce them and make them act and feel in emotionally obligatory ways. The emotions that the person feels often appear strange and not of the person's own making. This is because they have been forced on the person "to a much greater extent than they were created" (1895/1964, p. 5).

The emotions that a person feels are often solidified into rituals, both profane and sacred, which define individuals in moral terms. All societies uphold at regular intervals the collective sentiments and ideals that give them unity (Durkheim, 1912/1973, p. 201). This moral remaking of society occurs through the ceremonial occasions of social interaction wherein the common moral sentiments of the group are reaffirmed. These structures of experience have been well analyzed by Goffman (1983) and provide the foundations for Collins's theory of the emotional marketplace.

Like Weber, Durkheim found the impulse for society and science in religion. He also analyzed the tensions between emotional beliefs and rational, cognitive thought. Although he too drew on William James, Durkheim, more than Weber, located the content of emotionality in society, not in individual consciousness (Durkheim, 1912/1973, pp. 190, 208, 216). Durkheim's work, as Michael Hammond (1983, pp. 90–119) notes, offers the foundations of a sociological theory of the emotions. His theory, however, is structural, not phenomenological. It does suggest that the emotions a person feels in relation to others are social in origin and not entirely of the person's own making. This point is critically important, for social phenomenology must be able to work its way back to the structures of experience that move through the person's phenomenological relationship to the world.

Georg Simmel's (1924, 1950) work opens important avenues for a social phenomenology of emotion and emotional experience. His analyses of intimacy, the emotional instability of dyads, the isolation of the modern individual, the expressive nature of visual interaction, and the place of the face and feelings in social interaction suggest basic themes for inquiry.

Simmel builds his observations on the fact that it is through the medium of the senses and sense impressions that people perceive one another. The sense impressions of any person produce emotional and cognitive interpretations that provide bridges to the self of the other (Simmel, 1924, p. 357). Emotional and cognitive impressions merge and intertwine and may be directed to a person's emotional value or focused on the deliberate attempt to understand the other person. The tone of another's voice, as well as the content of her utterances, merges with her appearance and the meaning of her individuality into a single field of experience that joins two parties. Emotionality, for Simmel, is grounded in face-to-face interaction. The emotional union of two parties may be given in the mutual exchange of glances or in other forms of visual interaction. Through the glance the person expresses an experiential orientation to the situation and to the person who is glanced at. Openness, closedness, friendliness, coquetry, hostility, anger, disdain, pleasure, and sorrow are all emotional definitions of the situation that are communicated nonverbally through visual interaction.

The human face is, for Simmel, a structure of experience (see also Ekman, 1973; Izard, 1977). It is an embodiment of the inner essence or meaning of the person at a particular moment. The face makes a claim to emotional and moral character, or presence. As it gives off impressions of calmness, beauty, individuality, and sincerity, the face presents the emotional self of the person to others. The face as a moving structure of experience is seen as a repository of the person's past. It is a moving yet fixed testimony to the inner emotional self of the individual. The face and its looks, whether dour, sarcastic, grim, or cheerful, assume multiple forms. Its halves move in unison as it expresses the eyes and the self it extends. The face announces the person's moods, just as it lags behind his spoken emotionality, when a quick shift in mood or emotional self-feeling occurs. The face accompanies the person wherever he goes, always moving, never fixed, always expressive of moving internal mood and of emotional and cognitive intentions.

The meanings of the face are given through the eyes. Because of the norm of civil inattention (Goffman, 1963), people cannot stare at one another, so they work from first impressions, gleaned through glances. The initial impressions of the other remain a keynote to the other's appearance, his mood, his situational intentions, his past, and the degree that he is in emotional control of himself. The face hidden with the hands, the covered eyes, the head that is turned away or down—these faces and others like them convey a distance between the person and the situation. The face is unlike a statue or a photograph that expresses a fixed ideal. The face is always somewhat flawed in its expressions. It is always changing. Its very being changes its meaning. That meaning, in turn, reflects on the emotional meaning of the person who lays claim to the face that is presented.

In the modern social world, one typically sees the other before one hears her. Visual impressions and visual interaction affect and structure our modern mentality. The normative structure of everyday life shapes and is geared to the organization and control of visual interaction (Simmel, 1924).

Individuals present "normal appearances" (Goffman, 1971) to others, controlling their emotional definitions of self while in public places. Selves are presented as serious, unproblematic participants in the public order. People come and go from one another's visual presence, affirming their mutual respect with their eyes, their glances, their smiles, and their reciprocal courtesies. All that is asked is a nod of mutual recognition.

The self gives itself to the other visually. Respect for the public order is given through appearance, clothing, gestures, comportment, gait, and the eyes and the face. This public order, which is emotional throughout, is based on visual interaction. It may be the person's primary contact with society at large.

Simmel's emotionality is based on self-feelings that are communicated interactionally, through talk, gestures, and the eyes. The self of the person, always private, lies behind the public self that is given in the arena of visual interaction. That private self, too, is tied to other selves in the shifting emotional alignments that characterize dyadic and triadic social structures. One's emotional life, for Simmel (1950), is always changing, always lodged in the interaction process, and always somewhat at a distance from one's true, inner feelings.

To summarize: Marx, Weber, Durkheim, and Simmel offer views of emotion and emotionality that are structural, historical, economic, and interactional. Each theorist places emotionality at a distance from the person, either in rational rules, in economic practices, in power relations, in social interaction, or in the collective representations of society, including rituals. Each speaks to a political economy of emotions in which feelings, moods, and selves are structurally produced and distributed throughout a society. Each also suggests that emotionality, in its main forms, is a fundamental link between the person and society. In these respects the classical social theorists do make emotional experience a primary component of their theories. These points of view suggest necessary ingredients that must be included in a fully developed social psychological and social phenomenological study of emotionality.

The Freudian Model of the Emotions

William James's conception of emotion has been a dominant force in contemporary theories of emotion, as we have seen in the foregoing discussion. The second major force in theories of emotion has been Sigmund Freud. Freud's conception of the unconscious, of the physiological basis of emotion, and of the signification of emotional behaviors provides a second backdrop against which this study of emotion must be situated.

The underlying physiological foundations of Freud's theories of consciousness and affect are evident in the following statements:

> The essence of consciousness, for us the state of becoming conscious, is a special psychic act, different from and independent of the process of becoming fixed or represented, and consciousness appears to us as a sensory organ which perceives a content proceeding from another source [Freud, 1938, p. 224].

> The nature and development of affect . . . is regarded as a motor or secretory function, the key to the innervation of which is to be found in the ideas of the [unconscious]. Through the domination of the [preconscious] these ideas are as it were strangled, that is, inhibited from sending out the impulse that would develop the affect. The danger which arises if cathexis by the [preconscious] ceases thus consists in the fact that the unconscious excitations would liberate an affect that —in consequence of the repression that has previously occurred—could only be felt as pain or anxiety [Freud, 1938, p. 521; see also Freud, 1900/ 1965, p. 621].

> The source of affect is somatic, or experiences or thoughts of the day [1938, p. 455].

The Freudian model of the emotions, long familiar to the social scientist, posits a causal relation between unconscious sexual desires, overt behaviors (for example, fear of a laurel bush), and a state of consciousness (for example, fear). The primordial triadic family complex of mother, father, and child is the seat of adult emotionality and emotional disorders (Freud, 1900/1965). A state of consciousness, for Freud, signifies something other than itself. What is signified and significant must be discovered by the analyst. That discovery is made by unlocking the doors to the unconscious.

The meaning of an emotion, mood, or feeling lies not in the state of consciousness where the feeling is felt but, rather, outside consciousness, in the unconscious. Through dream work, hypnosis, catharsis, free association, and psychoanalysis more generally, the symbolic meanings of the emotion can be uncovered. The development of affect lies in the unconscious. When ideas in the unconscious are "strangled," or inhibited through repression, then pain or anxiety, as physiological reactions, are felt.

Emotions, or feelings, for Freud, are suffered, they surprise, they paralyze, they develop according to their own momentum and laws. Conscious efforts cannot modify their course. Freud separates the organized character of emotion (its structure, functions, goals, and aims) from its overt expression in the person's behavior and states of consciousness. He relegates emotion's organized features to the unconscious and its distorted, painful feelings to consciousness (Sartre, 1939/1962, pp. 48–55).

Psychoanalytic explanations view the conscious phenomenon as "the symbolic realization of a desire repressed by the censor." The significance of emotional consciousness lies entirely outside consciousness, in the unconscious. "What is *signified* is entirely cut off from the *signifying*" (Sartre, 1939/1962, p. 51). Emotions, for Freud, receive their meaning and significance from outside consciousness.

From a social phenomenological point of view there are five basic flaws in Freud's model of the emotions. First, Freud attempts to establish bare causal relationships regarding emotion which are outside of consciousness. He makes no explicit reference to the field of consciousness in which emotion is experienced. To look for explanations of emotion outside consciousness, in the unconscious, is, like the physiological and structural theorists, to conceive of consciousness passively (Sartre, 1939/1962). Such a view runs counter to current and classical theories of mind, thought, consciousness, being, and self (see Mead, 1934, 1982a; James, 1890/1950; Brentano, 1924/1973; Husserl, 1913/1962; Peirce, 1931; Heidegger, 1927/1962, 1975/1982; Sartre, 1939/1962, 1943/1978; Luria, 1978; Vygotsky, 1978; Wittgenstein, 1981).

Second, consciousness must be conceptualized processually, not passively. Emotionality and emotion must be confronted on their own terms within the lived experience of the person. It is not necessary to look outside consciousness to locate the signification of emotion.

Third, Freud's causal interpretations are backward-looking, into the subject's past. Time is in the past. The meaning of emotion does not lie in the present or the future for Freud, although events encountered in the present do symbolically evoke the past. Fourth, and closely related to the third point, the existential temporality of mood, emotion, and states of mind is not well treated in Freud's work. Fifth, the world of interaction and directly lived experience is not directly examined by Freud, although it is illuminated in his studies of dreams.

Freud's model of the unconscious as the source of meaning of emotion, coupled with his physiological/somatic view of the body, consciousness, and affect, must be set aside in favor of a social phenomenological conception of emotion, consciousness, interaction, and the person. Jacques Lacan addresses many of the problems noted above in his revisions and readings of Freud's work. It is to his perspective that I turn next.

Jacques Lacan: The Other, Speech, and History

In a path-breaking series of lectures and other works, the brilliant French psychoanalyst Jacques Lacan has significantly reworked and restructured Freud's basic theory of personality and psychoanalysis (Lacan, 1966, 1968, 1977, 1978). Central to Lacan's theories are the following points: (1) The human subject is located as language's referent in language. (2) Language is central to the uncovering of the processes that operate in the unconscious of the subject. (3) In language, conceived in part in Saussurian terms, the subject conducts transactions with the world and with the psychoanalyst. The structure of these speech acts constitutes a central topic of concern for the psychoanalyst. (4) The Other is basic to the emergence of the personality in the "mirror stage" of development, in which the infant first develops a unified sense of self and "I." In this stage a counterpart of the self and body of the infant is grasped (Merleau-Ponty, 1964a, pp. 96-155). The Other emerges as an objectifying link in the linguistic chain of concept and sound. In the Other, first perceived as the counterpart of the infant's self, the self as a unified object appears. The Other reappears in the castration complex as a missing Other. (5) Lacan states: "What we teach the subject, is to recognize as his unconscious is his history—that is to say, we help him to perfect the contemporary historization of the facts which have already determined a certain number of the historical turning points in his existence. But if they have played this role, it is already as facts of history, that is to say, insofar as they have been recognized in one particular sense or censored in a certain order" (Lacan, 1968, p. 23). Lacan's subject is a historicizing, temporalizing subject, located in the structures of language, yet lodged in the triadic structure of interactions in the human family.

Desire animates and propels the subject in the world. Lacan's subject is located in a world where desire cannot be fulfilled. Desire, or the demand for love, for the presence of the Other, for the fulfillment of biological needs, for control over one's world, is experienced, Lacan (1966) argues, as absence and loss. "Desire outlines itself in the border where demand tears itself away from need, this border being that which demand . . . opens under the form of possible failing that demand can bring to bear on it as not providing universal satisfaction" (p. 814). This failure to find and control the object(s) of one's desires has been developed by Marx, Hegel, Freud, and more recently Deleuze and Guattari (1977) and Coward and Ellis (1977).

Lacan advances Freud's theory significantly, most particularly in his emphasis on the linguistic foundations of the subject and the unconscious. Furthermore, his insightful introduction of the Other and desire into the Freudian personality complex opens the way for a more meaningful analysis of the personal biographical history of each individual. The reduction of emotion and affect to desire, however, precludes an examination of the phenomenology of emotion as lived experience. (Lacan, of course, rejects a phenomenological treatment of consciousness and a Sartrean theory of self.)

Still, the historicality of Lacan's subject, captured in its own past, attempting through remembering to find its own past, is like Heidegger's being who "thus has been" (Lacan, 1968, p. 17). The subject is a victim of its own historicizing abilities.

In "The Empty Word and the Full Word" Lacan (1968, p. 12) reminds the reader that "the unconscious is that chapter of my history which is marked by a blank or occupied by a falsehood: it is the censored chapter. But Truth can be found again; it is most often already written down elsewhere." That blank, empty past of the person is written down, Lacan (1968, p. 21) suggests, in (1) my body, which is a monument, or repository of my past, (2) my childhood memories and archival documents from my childhood (see Denzin, 1982d, pp. 29-46), (3) my traditions, rituals, and legends of myself and my family, and (4) buried memories from my past and the traces that connect one segment, or chapter, of my past with another. In short, the archeology of my past is accessible to me, but only with assistance. Further, there are breaks in my past that have "epistemic" features, permitting them to be viewed as ruptures (Althusser, 1969; Foucault, 1977).

Without accepting Lacan's conception of the unconscious, it is possible to move forward phenomenologically with his insights (but see Giddens, 1979, pp. 120-123). My body and my stream of consciousness are moving emotional sites. They are filled with emotional memories, childhood experiences, semirecognizable images of my parents (missing and absent fathers and mothers), and interiorized images (imago) of myself as a distinct object and subject. My dreams, fantasies, and conversations are played out in the dramas of my primordial family situation. I relive my past, emotionally, in the present. I do so in terms of the repertoires of feeling, expression, repression, distortion, and signification that were acquired in my original family situation. These repertoires of feeling and thinking are today reworked through my present situation as it comes toward me from the past.

I and my emotionality are linguistic constructions lodged in the interiority of my consciousness and in the circuit of selfness that connects me to the present and to my past. I am a victim, emotionally, of my own temporality. My knowledge of

temporality comes to me through my language, as a set of struc-
tured experiences, relationships, presences, differences, absences,
and contradictions (Derrida, 1973). The Other is the mirror to
my emotionality, and I see and feel my emotions in the expressions of others toward me (Cooley, 1902/1956).

Thomas Scheff: Catharsis

A modified Freudian view of emotion is found in the recent work of Thomas Scheff on catharsis, healing, and ritual. As
noted earlier in this chapter, Scheff (1979, p. 49) views emotions as states of bodily tension produced by stress. In the absence of interference (socialization and interaction) these tension states will be spontaneously discharged. Scheff distinguishes
two emotional states: emotional distress (grief, fear, anger,
boredom) and emotional discharge. Emotions are discharged
through catharsis, a distancing of the distressful emotion, which
may be overdistanced, underdistanced, or esthetically balanced.

Scheff's emotions, like Freud's, are physical tension
states. Unlike Freud, Scheff stresses four basic distress emotions:
grief, fear, anger, and boredom. With no interference, these tension states will be spontaneously discharged through weeping
(for grief), shivering and cold perspiration (for fear), spontaneous laughter (for embarrassment and anger), and "storming"
(Scheff, 1979, p. 49). Emotions are discharged either spontaneously or through catharsis.

If Freud locates the meaning and origin of emotions outside consciousness, in the unconscious, Scheff locates them in
the body but also out of the range of the person's consciousness. Scheff's explanations are causal, not interpretive. He nar-
rows the phenomenon of emotion to felt states of physical tension and their discharge. Still, it must be remembered that
Scheff's is a theory of catharsis based on the cathartic theory of
reevaluation counseling. Although his work deals with only a
small portion of Freud's more general theory, it attests to the
vitality of the physiological/unconscious view of emotions.
Scheff's theory carries, too, a form of behaviorism that, in Lacan's words (1968, p. 6), is "entirely unfaithful . . . to the psychoanalysis inspired by Freud."

Jean-Paul Sartre's Theory of Emotion

In *Sketch for a theory of the Emotions* Jean-Paul Sartre
(1939/1962) outlines a phenomenological theory of emotion
that critically departs from the theories of William James and
Sigmund Freud. Unlike Freud and James, Sartre studies emotion *in* lived consciousness, not in the body or in the unconscious. Emotion, for Sartre, is a form of lived consciousness that
transforms, by means of incantation and magic, the individual's
relationship to the self and to the objects in the individual's environment. Sartre, like James, isolates three closely interrelated
factors in the sequence of an emotional experience: (1) a perceiving subject who *intentionally* (in Husserl's sense) perceives
or encounters an emotional object or fact hatefully, with desire,
fearfully, joyfully, with terror, or otherwise, (2) an unsuccessful
attempt by the person to realize her definitions of the emotional object, whether to bestow wrath on it, escape from it, or
grasp it, (3) a nondeterministic transformation of the world and
of consciousness, by means of magic and incantation, so that
the person-in-consciousness *symbolically* confers on the object
and herself the qualities that cannot be given deterministically
in the real world. To this third phase, or factor, may be added a
fourth, the bodily feeling by the person of a sense of rage, terror, joy, or fear.

An emotion, for Sartre, is a transformation of the world
that occurs through consciousness. When the paths in the world
are blocked, yet action must go forward, either through neces-
sity or because of desire, the person attempts to change the
world by changing his consciousness. "To put it simply, since
the seizure of one object is impossible, or sets up unbearable
tension, the consciousness seizes or tries to seize it otherwise;
that is, it transforms itself in order to transform the object"
(Sartre, 1939/1962, p. 63). This transformation in consciousness *is not self-reflective*. It occurs within consciousness, however. The particular emotional label given to such experiences
(by an observer or the person), whether "anger," "fear," "ter-

*I am grateful to William Schroeder for his comments on my dis-
cussion of Sartre's theory of emotion.

ror," "joy," or "depression," arises *during* the conscious experience itself. It is not given after the feeling of sensations or after
the experience, as it is for James and Freud.

Sartre discusses a variety of emotions, including those he
terms weak, strong, spurious, playful, real, serious, and pretended (1939/1962, pp. 63-91). In each case the emotional
transformation of consciousness arises either out of confronta-
tions the person has with the world or out of the world's forcing itself on the person. "Thus there are two forms of emotion,
according to whether it is we who constitute the magic of the
world to replace a deterministic activity which cannot be realized, or whether the world itself is unrealizable and reveals itself
suddenly as a magical environment. In the state of horror (for
example), we are suddenly made aware that the deterministic
barriers have given way" (1939/1962, p. 86).

Emotional consciousness, for Sartre, is caught in its own
snare, yet it is a mode of consciousness that is not self-reflective. It is magical, uncanny, and nonreflective. Emotional consciousness has an animism and spontaneity that allow it to perpetuate itself (see Sartre, 1943/1978, p. 441). The consciousness
is "moved by its emotion" (Sartre, 1939/1962, p. 81). In emotionality a *debasement* of consciousness occurs. In the face of a
frightening situation, the person faints, thereby avoiding what is
frightening.

Sartre offers several examples to support his formulations. In passive fear a person faints when confronted by a fero-
cious beast. Flight, fainting away in action, occurs when a person wants to put the greatest distance between himself and
some danger. Passive sadness occurs as a mode of retreat and
refuge from a hostile world. A patient throws a fit rather than
make a confession to a psychiatrist. A joyful person cannot
keep still while she waits for the arrival of a friend. In fainting,
flight, passive sadness, and fits of temper, individuals symbolically confer new meanings on themselves and their emotional
objects. They receive release from a difficult world but do so
nondeterministically.

Sartre's theory, though attractive in most respects, raises
certain conceptual problems. First, how is *magical* to be conceptualized? Second, how does consciousness perform its own mag-

ical transformations and debasements? Third, how is debasement felt, if not reflectively—retrospectively, or not at all? Fourth, there is a questionable acceptance in Sartre's scheme of the frustration-aggression hypothesis of Dembo and others (Sartre, 1939/1962, pp. 41-48): Sartre assumes that blocked or frustrated acts provoke responses that reduce, however indirectly and symbolically, the frustration felt from the deflection of the act. He does not discuss the fact that individuals may walk away from frustrating, blocked acts. "Being unable, in a state of high emotion, to find the delicate and precise answer to the problem, we act upon ourselves, we abase and transform ourselves into a being for whom the grossest and least adapted solutions are good enough (for example, tearing up the paper on which a problem is stated). This anger now appears as an escape; the angry subject is like the man who is unable to untie the knots of the cords that bind him, and who writhes about in his bonds. And the 'angry' conduct, though less well adapted to the problem than the superior—and impossible—behavior that would solve it, is still precisely and perfectly adapted to his need to break the tension, to shake the leaden weight off his shoulders" (1939/1962, p. 45). Sartre's individual is locked into the emotionally frustrating situation and forced by the situation to act.

G. H. Mead's (1934, 1938, 1982b) conception of the blocked, suspended, inhibited, and redirected act would suggest that we can redefine our emotional situations, not in self-debasing but in self-adjusting ways. Such readjustments permit us to process conflict into our ongoing field of action. Thus the magical transformation of consciousness in the face of conflict and blocked, intentional acts may be only one of several adjustments (emotional or otherwise) that we make to a current problematic situation.

James, Freud, Sartre, Lacan

Freud locates emotion in the unconscious as a neurological disturbance, whereas James regards emotions as labels or ideas that individuals give to their physiological feelings and sensations. Sartre applies the term *emotion* to the entirety of an episode of consciousness. Bodily sensations confer the important element of believability on emotional consciousness, but they are not the source of the emotion. The source of the emotion lies in the person's relationship to the emotional object. The reality of emotion is to be found in the person's consciousness and in his relationship to the world, interactionally, symbolically, and immediately. Emotion is lodged in the circuit of selfness that attaches the person to the world. *It is in consciousness, in the world, and in the person* (Sartre, 1943/1978, pp. 156-158). *Emotional* is the term to be given to a particular mode of consciousness and of being-in-the-world. It is not a term to be applied to the sensations one attributes to interior bodily states and feelings. Emotion must be studied from within consciousness, not in terms of physiological processes or unconscious mechanisms. The study of emotion must be located in the interaction process, for all forms of emotionality arise from the interactions the person has with himself and others in the world.

Sartre's views of emotion are processual, not mechanistically causal. He does not seek universal symbolism in the meaning of emotional acts. His theory is not animated by a libido, by the "fundamental complex" of child, mother, and father, nor do the underlying drives of desire, life, and sexuality propel his human, as they do for Freud and Lacan. His theory has no unconscious. His human in emotionality is faced with choices in the immediate situation at hand. His existential psychoanalysis aims to understand the total person, not a slice of the person in terms of a complex, a disorder, a fixation, or a repressed drive (Binswanger, 1963; Sartre, 1943/1978, pp. 732-734, 1981). Sartre's views, as indicated earlier, set a fundamental foundation for the analysis that follows.

for early suggestions in this regard). Emotions are lodged in social acts and interactions with others. All emotion terms used in
everyday language refer to embodied feelings, mental states, and
interactional experiences with real and imagined others that the
person feels and directs inward, to herself, or outward, to others. Emotional terms carry a double referent: They reflect feelings felt by the self, and they reference feelings the person feels
or directs toward others, including social objects (see Plutchik,
1977, pp. 191-192). This appears to be the case for the following emotional terms: being angry, resentful, sad, joyful, depressed, hostile, enraged, ashamed, proud, affectionate, friend-
ly, embarrassed, rejected, guilty, shameful, in pain, or in love. At
one level emotions are, like the subject who feels them, linguistic phenomena.

     An emotional experience that does not in some way have
the self, the self-system, or the self or self-system of the other as
its referent seems inconceivable (see Sullivan, 1956, pp. 4-5, 92;
Laing, 1965, pp. 94-95; Lacan, 1968; Sartre, 1943/1978). It is
this self-referencing element of emotion that is absent in the
definitions of emotion offered by James, Freud, Lacan, Shott,
Schachter and Singer, Hochschild, Kemper, Scheff, Collins, and
others in the literature on emotions. Hochschild (1979, pp. 554-
555, 558) does call for a theory of the self and emotions. Her
notion of the self as emotion manager is suggestive. Emotions
are not things; they are processes. What is managed in an emotional experience is not an emotion but the self in the feeling
that is being felt.

     Use of the term *self-feeling* expands the traditional view
of self-feeling. James (1890/1950, vol. 1, pp. 305-306), Bain
(1859, pp. 125-126), and Cooley (1902/1956, pp. 183-185) included as self-feelings such emotions as pride, vanity, arrogance,
shame, mortification, and personal despair. These authors referred only a small class of the emotions to the self. Current literature on the emotions has followed this path (but see Arnold,
1960a; Izard, 1977; Plessner, 1970; Keen, 1977; Averill, 1980).

     My change in James's, Bain's, and Cooley's meaning sug-
gests that although emotions may not have their *origins* in the
self, as do self-pride and vanity, their *referent* is always back to

the self that feels (see Heidegger, 1975/1982, pp. 136-138). Many emotions arise in the field of social experience and then are directed back to the self, either by the person or by his emotional associates—for example, shame, guilt, and embarrassment (Hochschild, 1979; Goffman, 1956; Gross and Stone, 1964; Shott, 1979; Kemper, 1981).

Self-feeling refers to any emotion the person feels. Emotionality refers to the process of being emotional, or of feeling an emotion. Emotions are processes, not static things. What is felt in an emotion is a feeling of and for one's self, or a component of one's self. Self-feelings include bodily sensations, sensible feelings, intentional value feeling states, and feelings of self as a moral, sacred, or profane object (Scheler, 1916/1973, pp. 330-333; Durkheim, 1912/1973; Goffman, 1971, p. 63). The feelings that a person feels in emotionality have a threefold structure: (1) a sense of the feeling in terms of awareness and definition, (2) a sense of the self feeling the feeling (one brings the feeling into self-awareness and feels the feeling), and (3) a revealing of the moral, inner, deep feeling self through this experience (Heidegger, 1975/1982, p. 137). The feeling person, the person in emotional consciousness, feels his self in emotion. Feelings disclose the person to himself.

The self will be defined as (1) all that I call mine at a particular moment in time, including my feelings, my actions, my material possessions, my body, and my relations to others (James, 1890/1950, vol. 1, pp. 291-292), (2) the meaning of me to myself as a distinct object and subject at any given moment in my existence (Mead, 1982a; Heidegger, 1927/1962, p. 153) and (3) the meaning of my being to myself as I turn back on myself in reflection and self-apprehension (Heidegger, 1975/1982, p. 159). The self is not a thing or a substance. It is that structure of experience that I call mine. The self is not in consciousness, but in the world of social interaction. It haunts the person.

The self of the person may be authentically or inauthentically felt (Heidegger, 1927/1962). It may be divided against itself (James, 1904/1961). It may be a false-self system (Laing, 1965). It may be a self with no sense of objective existence

(Lacan, 1968, p. 44; Wilden, 1968, pp. 284-292). It may be a self that can neither feel its feelings nor recognize and define them. It may be a hypothetical self (Mead, 1982a, pp. 187-188). It may be a self that feels its feelings totally through others. However, the feelings that are felt and not felt in emotionality have their referents back to the self of the person, no matter how distorted, divided, false, troubled, or inauthentic that self and person may be.

The emotionality of emotion is temporally and relationally rooted in the social situation. Goffman (1971), Gross and Stone (1964), and Hochschild (1979) have shown how interactional rules of conduct shape and modify the situational organization, feeling, and display of emotionality. Rules and emotional management strategies concerning the extent, direction, and duration of feeling in situations are implicit, Hochschild (1979, pp. 564, 566) argues, in the framing rules of ideology. Temporally, emotionality moves forward and backward in the interactional situation, just as time itself moves forward and backward in the person's biography.

All emotions are relational phenomena. They are learned in social relationships, initially the primary group of the family (Cooley, 1902/1956). They are felt relationally (Freud, 1938; Lacan, 1968; Merleau-Ponty, 1963). They are interpreted in terms of social relationships (Lacan, 1977). The vocabularies of emotional meaning that people bring to bear on their emotional experiences are also relationally grounded (Mills, 1940; Freud, 1938; Lacan, 1968; Merleau-Ponty, 1963). These vocabularies include both the terms and the feelings for such emotions as fear, anger, desire, shame, disgust, pride, and love.

The historicity of emotionality is a relational, primary-group phenomenon. The emotionality of self-other feelings is lived and played out in the internal drama of the human family or its equivalent. The family provides the setting in which the person's emotionality is learned, felt, expressed, and interpreted. Hence, self-feelings must be seen as relationally specific feelings. These relational feelings are embedded, hidden, and lodged in the person's interactional biography. They are, in Lacan's terms, a part of one's relational history. The study of emotionality is necessarily historical (Sartre, 1981). That history will be part family, part sexual, part educational, part occupational, and part friendship, both adult and child.

The interpretation of emotionality, in addition to containing vocabularies of emotional meaning, rests on self-justification. All emotions carry or call for justification within the person's present world of involvement. Their meanings are negotiated within emotion contexts of interaction (Sugrue, 1982, pp. 280-281).

The self-justifying nature of self-feeling offers to the person and his or her associates an account, or reason, for the emotion that is currently felt and expressed (see Scott and Lyman, 1968). Such justifications may be termed "emotional accounts." Self-justifications may follow an emotional episode, may be expressed during emotionality, or may be offered beforehand, as preinterpretations. Such justifications, whether pre-, post-, or expressed during emotionality (as lived justifications), are basic to an understanding of self-feeling. Emotionality, at least in Western culture, appears to require justification. Accordingly, the justifications and disclaimers a person gives for his or her feelings require careful investigation (see Hewitt and Stokes, 1975, on disclaimers). It appears, as Hochschild (1979), Kemper (1981), and Scheff (1979) have argued, that the self-justifying features of emotionality vary by ideology, perhaps by social class, certainly by sex, perhaps also by race, age, education, occupation, and ethnicity. In short, many of the feelings people feel and the reasons they give for their feelings are social, structural, cultural, and relational in origin.

There is a stratification to the person's emotional life that moves outward from feelings of the lived body to the surrounding interactional world (Scheler, 1916/1973, p. 330). This stratification of emotional life corresponds to the structures of the person's lifeworld (Schutz and Luckmann, 1973). Such matters and processes as modes of fellow-feeling, mood joining, structures of relevancy, emotional intersubjectivity, stocks of knowledge, vocabularies of motive, typifications, and idealizations are intimately connected to the person's inner and outer emotional life. Basic to the stratification of emotional life are the grammars of emotional expression and the vocabularies of emotional understanding that accompany everyday emotional experience (Scheler, 1916/1973, pp. 333–335). In order to interpret and give meaning to lived emotion and to their self-feelings, people must possess a vocabulary of terms that confer understanding and meaning on their experiences (Lacan, 1977, 1978; Mead, 1934). People interpret their self-feelings by making reference to certain recurring value-meaning-emotional contexts, by reproducing certain emotional experiences, by sharing in emotional experiences with others, and by "knowing" on the basis of previous experiences what self-feelings they are currently experiencing (Scheler, 1913/1970, p. 11; Merleau-Ponty, 1973b; Lacan, 1968; Power, 1982). People also feel the feelings they are told to feel (Kemper, 1981).

Emotionality as Symbolic Interaction

Defining emotions as self-feelings felt in emotionality has the advantage of placing their study directly in the field of social interaction. Mead's (1934, 1938, 1982a), James's (1890/1950), Cooley's (1902/1956), Peirce's (1934), and Blumer's (1969) views of the self, the social act, symbolic interaction, nonsymbolic interaction, significant gestures, firstness, secondness, thirdness, the looking-glass self, the I and the me, self-interaction, the triadic structure of meaning, temporality, social objects, and joint acts can now be brought directly to bear on the study of emotion and emotionality.

If emotionality is conceptualized as a process of self-feeling, then it can be seen as arising out of the self-interactions that individuals direct toward themselves and out of the reflected appraisals of others, both imagined and real (Sullivan, 1956). Figure 1 describes the process of emotional self-interaction (see Denzin, 1980, 1983b). Imagine an argument between two persons, A and B. It starts with A saying something critical to B (number 1) in Figure 1. That statement is heard by B and enters her phenomenological stream of consciousness (numbers 2-6). She takes her own attitude towards herself (B-B), and toward A. She turns that attitude back from A to herself.

She calls out an angry response to A and directs that to him (6-7) in the interactional stream that connects the two of them. A receives that action, and it enters his side of the phenomenological stream (9-12). Here he calls out an angry reaction to B's angry reaction to his initial critical statement. This attitude is reflected back to B in his final action (13).

Stated more abstractly, the phenomenological stream (Numbers 2-6, 8-12 in Figure 1) describes the inner side of interaction that occurs when the person interacts with himself and with another in a social situation. In the phenomenological stream, the person takes his own attitude toward self (A-A) and toward the other (A-B) and turns the imagined attitude of the other toward himself (B-A). The interactional stream (Numbers 1, 7, 13 in Figure 1) points to the co-present, or imagined, situation. The actual utterances and actions of the other are available to both parties. Emotional self-interaction involves person A's initiating a line of action toward B (act 1), which calls out in B (act 2) a significant emotional gesture that is present in A's action and thought. A turns this emotional gesture inward (act 8), judging and interpreting B's actions in light of A's own incipient emotional attitude(s) (A-A, A-B, B-A). This interpretation becomes part of A's emotional self-feeling, which is then incorporated into A's next gesture or statement to B (acts 12-13). A's self-feeling becomes part of an emotional social act, which enters B's inner phenomenological stream and becomes part of B's emotional social act (both toward B and toward A). For both A and B, emotional self-feelings are lodged in the interactional stream that connects them and in their inner phenomenological streams of consciousness. They both feel inwardly what they may or may not express outwardly in the interactional stream.

The sequence of emotional self-interaction appears to have the following trajectory: (1) The person is interactively located in the world with others, engaged in an interpretive practice, however mundane or problematic. (2) An interaction occurs between the person and a social object (including another person), which brings the object into the person's phenomenological field. (3) As the object enters the person's field, it is defined in self-feeling terms such as anger, fear, or anticipation. (4) These anticipatory self-feelings are ratified through physical feelings and sensations felt in the lived body, such as tenseness and anxiousness. (5) The person imagines his appearance and actions in the eyes of his interactional fellow(s), real and imagined (Cooley, 1902/1956). (6) An interpretation of the judgment of the other follows, as well as some sort of inner self-feeling that accompanies that judgment (Cooley, 1902/1956, p. 184). (7) A feeling is built up toward the other regarding the feelings that have been imputed to her. (8) That feeling is incorporated into the feelings the person feels toward himself. (9) The person experiences a feeling of moral self-worth regarding himself and the other. (10) A summary or gloss emotional self-definition is produced, including an emotional definition of the other's self and the object around which the interaction was focused. These emotional terms are significant symbols (Mead, 1934). Emotionality dwells in these interactions, as indicated below.

The Dwelling Place of Emotion

This sequence may be termed the hermeneutic circle of emotionality. It is not a straight linear sequence of action, emotion, and feeling. Rather, as Weber (1946), Mead (1982a), and James (1890/1950) have noted, emotional thoughts are not strictly divided in the field of experience of the person. They merge and run together. Therefore, the potential for emotionality is always present in the self and the situation of the person. Furthermore, it is impossible, as Heidegger (1927/1962, p. 275) noted, to approach a situation free of preinterpretations, foreunderstandings, and foreconceptions. Emotionality arises out of the hermeneutic situation of preemotional understandings, preemotional interpretations, and preemotional dispositions to act emotionally. Emotionality is a form of action, self-conversation, and interaction that is born out of the interplay of cognitions and emotional thoughts in the person's field of experience. Emotionality is a dialogue with the world, carried on in and through emotional thoughts, acts, words, gestures, and meanings. Like all dialogue, it turns back on itself, redefines itself, reexpresses itself, and assumes new forms and dimensions as it moves forward. *Emotionality is a circular process that begins and ends with the transactions and actions of the self in the social situation interacting with self and others.* The emotions that the self feels are, in many significant respects, present in the actions others take toward the person. Others in the social situation, joined with the imagined emotional attitudes and judgments of generalized others (Mead, 1982a), are at the basis of the person's self-feelings and emotionality.

Social Acts. Emotions may be studied as social acts, with covert and overt, inner and outer dimensions. As social acts, emotions have phases, including beginnings, middles, and ends. Many emotional acts are retrospective, backward-looking, locked in the temporality of the past. Other emotional acts lie in anticipated futures, and some are realized in the immediate present (Heidegger, 1927/1962). Emotional acts may be inhibited, blunted, checked, or redefined. They may be reflectively and unreflectively organized (Athens, 1980; Mead, 1982b).

Temporality. The temporality of emotion is circular. The future, the past, and the present are vividly and reflectively interconnected in the person's lived emotional acts. The temporality of emotion as lived experience blurs the distinctions among past, present, and future. In emotion the person sits "perched" looking in two directions at the same time. In the "saddleback" element of emotional time, the person looks forward and backward at the same time, while being pulled into and through the present (James, 1890/1950, vol. 1, p. 609). Intense emotionality appears to stop time. The present is the process the person is currently alongside. The future is that which is drawing near, and the past provides the horizon of acts and experiences that have just occurred. Yet, to catch the meaning of emotion in the present, individuals must draw on the past and the future as they interpret and anticipate the actions of the other in the interactional stream.

Others. Emotions without the presence of others are unimaginable. Accordingly, others are central to the study of the social acts that produce and make up emotion. Emotional terms link selves together in joint activities, or social acts. Emotional associates are inside the emotions that people feel (see Figure

1). How others enter into the inner side of emotionality deserves detailed study, but clearly they enter through significant
symbols and "other-taking" emotions, including shame, guilt,
and embarrassment (Shott, 1979, pp. 1325-1330). To bring the
other into an emotional act is to call out in one's self an emotional attitude toward the other and then to build up a line of
emotional activity regarding that attitude.

The emotional "interiority" of the other rests on a lodging of the self in the imagined emotional life of the other. Such
a lodging of the self implicates, or entangles, one's emotions
and feelings around thoughts and feelings for the other. The
other comes to live in one's emotional life. And, borrowing a
phrase from James Joyce (1976, p. 122), individuals "emotion-
alize" their mental life around these imagined and "real" relations with the other. This emotionalized other becomes a recurring part of one's inner, emotional life. One entangles one's
thoughts with one's thoughts of the other. And one enters into
the other's thoughts as well. Their emotional lives merge and
run together.

Others may knowingly be brought into a person's emotional acts. Mixed contexts of emotional awareness (open,
closed, pretended, suspected) may obtain (Glaser and Strauss,
1967). Individuals may be joined through conflicting, as well as
cooperative and complementary, emotional lines of action
(Athens, 1980).

Emotional Reality. Emotional acts have a lived "realness"
that is not doubted. The emotional experience, in the form of
embodied self-feelings, radiates through the person's inner and
outer streams of experience. During its occurrence emotional
experience is lived as absolute reality (Sartre, 1939/1962). The
emotional act grips the person and, when out of control, can
carry the person into and through violent acts (Athens, 1980).
Emotional consciousness captures the person and moves him or
her into the world of emotion (Sartre, 1939/1962). In this
world the codes of everyday life are broken and suspended.
Temper tantrums, acts of physical violence, fainting spells,
weeping, tearful confessions, loud verbal outbursts, rapid movements of flight, extraordinary profanity, the destruction of val-

ued objects, and the taking of chances are common in the world
of emotion. The world and reality of emotion is neither wholly
rational nor fully deterministic, nor is it a world where things
are entirely as they appear to be. It is a world filled with nuance,
the uncanny, symbolism, and hidden, indirect meaning. It is a
world that arises through the processes of one person taking the
attitude of another in a concrete social situation.

The Circuit of Selfness. A circuit of selfness (Sartre,
1943/1978, pp. 155-158) attaches the person to the world. In
that circuit emotionality, meaning, and the other are joined. In
the circuit of selfness there is no separation between the person,
others, objective social structures, cultural systems, or subjective meaning systems. There is only the person in the world,
feeling, thinking, acting, and joining his or her actions with
those of others. In the circuit of selfness, the person and others
jointly produce a field of experience that each enters into. This
field of experience anchors the self in the other's phenomenological and interactional streams. It is in the merger of these two
streams of experience that emotional self-feelings are lodged.

The structure of self-feeling may be described in circular
terms as the circuit of self-feeling. In the sequence of emotional
self-feeling what is first felt is a feeling for oneself or for the self
of another. This feeling, in turn, becomes part of the inner
moral feeling that is the emotion that is experienced. However,
what is experienced in the self of the person is an emotional experience. Emotions cannot be studied independent of the selves
that feel and experience them.

This feeling experience has a double structure. In any
emotional self-feeling there is a core, or essential emotional experience that is named and felt—perhaps anger or fear or guilt.
Surrounding that core feeling is a horizon of interrelated feelings, thoughts, and memories that are passed through, as in
emotional memory, when the person moves into the core emotional experience (Stanislavski, 1936, p. 158). The spheres of
emotion that encircle the core emotional self-feeling may be
termed the horizon of the emotion. The self takes on different
feelings as it passes through the horizons of a core feeling to the
feeling itself.

Conclusions

Emotions are not mere cognitive responses to physiological, cultural, or structural factors. They are interactive processes best studied as social acts involving interactions with self and interactions with others. The sociological study and definition of emotion must begin with the study of selves and others, joined and separated in episodes of copresent interaction. Defining emotion as self-feeling returns the sociology of emotion to the world of lived, interactional experience.

Although emotions may not lie at the base of the genesis or foundations of self, as Mead (1934) argued, they certainly figure centrally in its elaboration, destruction, collapse, and reorganization (Sullivan, 1956, p. 145; Bateson, 1972, p. 326). Perhaps for this reason alone the place of the self must be firmly secured in the study of emotion. Sociologists must attempt to build theories of emotion that study emotion from the perspective of interacting individuals.

In Chapter Three the topics of the stream of emotional consciousness, the situation, temporality, the person, emotional associates, reality, world, and the essence of emotion will be taken up in greater detail and depth.

PART TWO

Emotionality, Self, and Interaction

In Part Two of this investigation multiple instances of lived emotionality are presented and subjected to bracketing, reflection, or phenomenological reduction. The intention is to lay bare the essential structures or interrelated features of emotionality. Chapter Three moves to the essence of emotionality, elaborating and developing the theoretical points made in Chapter Two. Chapters Four and Five examine the structures of lived emotion and emotional intersubjectivity.

The empirical materials presented in this and following chapters are taken from an ongoing naturalistic investigation of the display and meaning of emotionality in everyday life. In addition to instances of reported emotionality given by students in my classes in introductory social psychology, small groups, and social interaction over the past several years, I have regularly gathered instances of expressed emotionality from newspapers, literature, film, field conversations, and open-ended interviews. The Emotions Project is the title I give to this ongoing investigation. I have made it a point to draw out individuals who have made their emotionality public, following up their emotional actions with open-ended interviewing and conversation, in an attempt to secure their interpretations of their emotional conduct. Following Husserl (1913/1962) and Sartre (1940/1972), I have assumed that, as stated in my Introduction, any instance of expressed emotionality is suitable for phenomenological purposes.

The lived body of the human subject is an important point of departure for Chapters Three and Four. The phenomenological perspective suggests that the subject inhabits and interprets a lived structure of experience that is *in* the lived body. Emotion's body is the stable point against which all emotional experiences are grounded. Accordingly, a phenomenological account of the human body is required, and that is the topic of Chapter Four. However, the phenomenon of person must be brought to the study of the body, and this is the problem addressed by Chapter Three. A phenomenology of the person, coupled with the analysis of emotion's body, complements the physiological and cognitive views of emotionality. In this discussion I hope to move beyond those theories and views of emotion that remain attached to primarily neurological or physiological positions. A phenomenology of the lived body is sketched in these chapters.

Chapter Five moves deeply into the interiority of emotionality, noting and developing distinctions among several forms of emotional intersubjectivity, including feelings in common, fellow-feelings, emotional infection, emotional identification, shared emotionality, and spurious emotionality. The temporality of emotional understanding is analyzed, and a clarification of the essential features of emotional understanding is presented.

Together Chapters Three, Four, and Five present the full structure of my social phenomenological view of emotionality. They constitute the backdrop against which the remainder of my analysis should be understood.

Chapter Three

Essence of Emotional Experience

"Today I was the first to have emotion memory checked. 'Do you remember,' asked the director, 'that you once told me about the great impression Moskvin made on you when he came to your town on a tour? Can you recall his performance vividly enough so that the very thought of it now, six years later, brings back the flush of enthusiasm you felt at the time?' 'Perhaps the feelings are not as keen as they once were,' I replied, 'but I certainly am moved by them very much even now.' 'Are they strong enough to make you blush and feel your heart pound?' 'Perhaps, if I let myself go entirely, they would.' 'What do you feel, either spiritually or physically, when you recall the tragic death of an intimate friend you told me about?' 'I try to avoid that memory, because it depresses me so much.' 'That type of memory, which makes you relive the sensations you once felt when seeing Moskvin act, or when your friend died, is what we call *emotion memory*' " (Stanislavski, 1936, p. 158).

Stanislavski's analysis of emotion memory contains the basic elements of emotion. *Emotion is a lived, believed-in, situated, temporally embodied experience that radiates through a person's stream of consciousness, is felt in and runs through his body, and, in the process of being lived, plunges the person and his associates into a wholly new and transformed reality—the reality of a world that is being constituted by the emotional experience.* Emotion moves people. It alters their stream of consciousness. It changes the perceptions and feelings of their bodies. Emotion locates people in a particular time and place. It relives past memories and sensations and moves against a horizon of previous emotional experience. Emotion socially places the person in the real or imagined company of others. It is moved by other emotions. While felt, emotion constitutes a reality, or a world, unique and solely contained within itself. *Emotion is self-feeling.*

The Structures of Emotion

The analysis of the essence of emotion requires that the critical elements in the definition above be carefully dissected and made clear. The critical terms are (1) *stream of consciousness* and *experience*, (2) *situation*, (3) *time*, (4) *person*, (5) *associates*, (6) *reality*, (7) *world*. Each term will be treated in turn.

Streams of Experience. Emotions are located in the ongoing stream of consciousness of the person. Indeed, they constitute a distinct form, or mode, of consciousness (Sartre, 1939/1962, p. 56; Peirce, 1931, vol. 1, p. 152). Consciousness consists of the stream of thoughts, feelings, sensations, perceptions, and awareness that the person is in at any moment in time (James, 1890/1950, vol. 1, pp. 186, 224, 229). Consciousness is simultaneously directed to an inner world of thought and experience and to an outer world of events and experiences that surround the person (Husserl, 1913/1962, p. 103). These two worlds, the inner and the outer, are, respectively, the phenomenological stream of consciousness and the interactional stream of experience. The phenomenological stream of consciousness involves the person caught up in her own flow of inner experience. The interactional stream of experience is public and observable in the gestures, speech, communicative acts, interactions, encounters, and language games of the person and her associates (Searle, 1970; Stone, 1982; Mead, 1934, 1938; Goffman, 1961b; Blumer, 1969; Wittgenstein, 1981; Denzin, 1980, p. 255).

Emotional consciousness, or conscious experience, has a double structure: an inner phenomenological dimension (Peirce, 1931, vol. 1, p. 141) and an outer interactional dimension. These two dimensions are united in the stream of emotional experience, or the stream of emotional consciousness (Husserl, 1913/1962, p. 105; James, 1890/1950, vol. I, pp. 224-225).

Emotional consciousness is intentional; that is, it is directed toward an object or a set of objects. Consciousness is consciousness of something (Husserl, 1913/1962, p. 103; Mead, 1938, p. 7). Consciousness is that phenomenon which is conscious of its own consciousness and, as such, is "a concrete being *sui generis*" (Sartre, 1943/1978, p. 323). It is the starting point for a phenomenology of emotion. On this point William James (1890/1950, vol. 1, p. 224) asserts: "The only thing which psychology has a right to postulate at the outset is the fact of thinking itself . . . the universal conscious fact is . . . 'I think' and 'I feel.' " To this postulate, the interpretive interactionist can reply: "The only thing that social phenomenology has a right to postulate at the outset is the fact of interaction itself. And basic to interaction are the thoughts and feelings that individuals have of themselves while interacting. 'I interact, I think, and I feel.' " The starting point for the analysis of emotionality is the interaction process that joins the person's inner and outer streams of experience. Interaction is the point of reference for emotional consciousness.

Emotional consciousness is directed toward itself and the person as its own object of consciousness. Consciousness has no content; it is simply a spontaneity, a sheer activity, a "multiplicity of interpenetration," to use Bergson's phrase. Consciousness, in itself, contains no objects and no intentions. Intentionality is consciousness, and consciousness has only objects of intention. Consciousness is a process. The objects of emotional consciousness are not in consciousness but in a world made emotional and interiorized and lived within emotional consciousness through reflection and nonreflection.

Every object experienced in consciousness and reflected on can, through bracketing, or reflection, be discovered to have "its own *essence open to intuition,* "a content" which can be considered in its *singularity in and for itself*" (Husserl, 1913/ 1962, p. 105). The objects of emotional consciousness have an inner essence, or meaningful core, which can be discovered. It is this inner meaning of emotion that the person attempts to catch and give meaning to when he or she acts emotionally. The fact that the inner meaning of emotion continually eludes the person will be treated in detail below in the discussion of living an emotion.

The object of emotional consciousness is made problematic through reflection and interaction. Emotional consciousness assumes the dimensions of an "inner conversation" the person carries on in the field of symbols between herself and another object, event, situation, or person (see Mead, 1938, p. 709). The person reflecting on her emotional consciousness is "wide awake," aware of the tensions in her own consciousness and acting on the objects present in that field of experience (Schutz and Luckmann, 1973, p. 26). These objects become the topics and resources of her emotional consciousness.

Features of Emotional Consciousness. In addition to being intentional and having inner and outer dimensions, emotional consciousness is regarded by the person as being strictly unique and belonging solely to him. The stream of emotional experiences that make up inner consciousness is perceived as being sensibly continuous. The changes that occur within the stream are never absolutely abrupt (James, 1890/1950, vol. 1, p. 237). The stream of inner emotional thoughts that the person experiences occurs against a moving "horizon" of previously thought and felt thoughts. This continuity in experience is characterized by movement and rest, or, in James's words, "flights and perchings" (1890/1950, vol. 1, p. 243). The resting places of thoughts, the substantive parts, the objects of reflection and thought, are the places that emotional thought moves to as it is dislodged from one thought, feeling, or emotion and moves to another. The main use of the transitive, flightlike portions of emotional thought is to lead the thinker to another substantive emotional thought, or point of rest (James, 1890/1950, vol. 1, p. 243). Thought, feelings, and emotions, within the stream of thought, move to conclusions, or reach ending points. Once an emotional thought has been completed, what remains is its meaning to the person—the meaning being a condensation of the thought into a particular word, phrase, image, or answer to a problem that was troubling the thinker (for example, anger, love). The meaning of a thought or experience can be reconstructed through cognitive and emotional memory, in which case the thought, feeling, or emotion is thought and felt anew.

The inner stream of emotional consciousness consists of a continuous flow of feelings as well as thoughts, but no single term, other than *experience,* serves to designate the fluid inter-relationship between the thoughts people have of their feelings and the feelings they have for their thoughts.

The things that are thought, are reflected on, and appear in the inner stream of emotional experience are thought as uni-ties, or associative wholes in a "single pulse of subjectivity" (James, 1890/1950, vol. 1, p. 278; Saussure, 1959). When peo-ple think of an emotional experience—for example, being angry at another—they do not dissect the thought into its constituent elements. Rather, the word *anger* or the phrase *angry at* desig-nates the totality of the other who is the object of the emotion-al experience. If asked to dissect the emotion, the person could do so, polythetically, step by step, but the emotional thought is felt and remembered as a total experience, glossed under the meaning of a single word or a handful of words. As with James's example of the-pack-of-cards-is-on-the-table, the person who is-angry-at-his-mother thinks, feels, and sees that thought and feel-ing all at once.

The inner stream of consciousness is visceral, cinematic, and acoustical. Thoughts and experiences are felt, seen, and heard (Denzin, 1982c). They are given as instantaneous glimpses of experience, which are remembered and become part of the person's emotional and sensation memories (Stanislavski, 1936,

p. 159). As such, they can be drawn on for future thought and feeling, although the person will be selectively attentive and inattentive to what is remembered, recollected, and felt.

Firstness, Secondness, and Thirdness. Peirce's categories of firstness, secondness, and thirdness may be applied to the analysis of emotional consciousness (Peirce, 1931, vol. I, pp. 280-305). Consider the following:

> I tell ya, my mind just went blank when you mentioned relationships. I couldn't think of anything to say. I hadn't thought of those six brothers-in-law for years. You know, they ruined me. I came along. I was the last son. My father had no choice but to set up my sisters in business. There was no place for me. I was a failure for thirty years just to prove my father was right. There wasn't no place for me. How could there be? And here I am today. Those bastards are failures. The old man would turn over in his grave if he seen them today. If there's a heaven, I hope the folks can see me today, and I hope I can talk to them. I think dad would be proud today. You know, today I leave them alone, I have nothin' to do with 'em. I live my life, they lead theirs. I ain't got nothin' to say to 'em, even my sisters [Field conversation, fifty-seven-year-old male, Emotions Project, spring 1982].

In this statement three levels, or modes, of being aware of an object of emotional consciousness are evident. *Firstness* refers to the becoming aware of a new object or event in the stream of consciousness. The word *relationship* signaled this new awareness. *Secondness* is seen in the recognition of the word *relationship* as being-in-the-consciousness-of the person. *Thirdness* places that awareness (firstness) and recognition (secondness) into an interpreted context of emotional memory. With firstness, the sound of the word, consciousness "went blank." Secondness grasped that awareness and focused attention and intention on it. Thirdness interpreted the totality of that experience in relation to what had come into awareness and had been recognized. At each level—firstness, secondness, and thirdness—the emotional experience is transformed and the consciousness of it is altered and changed. There is, then, immediate experience in the emotional stream of consciousness; then an awareness and recognition of that experience; then a building of an emotional memory around that recognition, and an interpretation, in the here and now, of that experience, its immediacy, its awareness, and its recognition. A new emotional experience is generated, out of an old emotional memory, occurring over thirty years, and it is built up through the three levels of firstness, secondness, and thirdness.

It is important to note that a person cannot move to the interpretation of a slice of his consciousness without having first been confronted with the experience in a nascent form, as an idea, a sound, an image, a word, a feeling, or a memory. Then, second, the impulse for the thought must be recognized and, third, acted on and interpreted in experience. Emotional experience turns "on itself." It becomes ensnared within its own structure. It transforms itself.

A large amount of emotional experience, of course, occurs at the level of firstness only. There is no reason to assume, as Mead observed, that "experience as such involves in itself an awareness of the experience" (1938, p. 656). Hence, many people are not aware of the emotions they might feel or are feeling at the level of firstness.

Unreflective and Reflective Emotional Consciousness. Emotional consciousness that is not reflective is lived from within. The person is not explicitly aware of her feelings, thoughts, movements, actions, or statements, except as these are further elements of the emotion being experienced. There is no attempt to make an object out of the emotional consciousness and to stand outside that experience, as there is in reflective emotional consciousness. Nonreflective emotional consciousness is completely self-contained. The person is in the emotion and unable or unwilling to make her emotional experience an object of intentional reflection. The following excerpt represents a forty-three-year-old Latin mother sunk in nonreflective emotional consciousness.

I don't know what to do. My children don't call me. They know my phone number, my mother,

she's eighty-five years old, was here for a week and
they never called to ask how grandma was. I was
raised right. I respect my mother. I call her every
Friday and she calls me every Saturday. And then I
call her the next Saturday and she calls me on Friday. My daughter lives twenty blocks from me. She
knows my phone number. I call her and she says I
woke her up. I can't call. Everybody's gone, no-
body cares. I don't know what to do. Your children are supposed to care for you and call you. I
just don't know. My life is over. I'm in the condo
all by myself, the rooms are all empty. My young-
est son is gone. I raised him! Now what do I do?
I'm just so depressed. I don't want to go out. I
don't want my old job back. I'm just worthless
[Field conversation, Emotions Project, fall 1981].

The speaker is totally absorbed within her own emotional experience and is living that experience as a stream of events and objects that is acting on her. She is passive within her own consciousness and has generated a field of emotional experience
that turns in on her. She is being unreflectively engulfed and
crushed by her own emotional field.

In nonreflective emotional consciousness, consciousness
reflects on itself but does not stand out from itself and become
a distinct object of self-reflection. The experience of the emotion builds on itself internally, reflecting back on itself. The person in this mode of emotional consciousness may be said to be
experiencing a form of what Scheff (1979, p. 59) terms "underdistanced" emotion: "In dramatic criticism, a drama is considered to be underdistanced if it evokes raw emotion in audiences
to the point that its members become so drawn into the dramatic action that they forget where they are; they react as if
they were participants in, rather than observers of, the drama."
The Latin mother speaking earlier was experiencing her depression as underdistanced emotion, as pure emotional subjectivity.

In reflective emotional consciousness people attempt to
become objects in their own emotional stream of consciousness.
They stand out from consciousness. As observers, they situate
themselves within consciousness and reflect both on conscious-

ness and on themselves as objects in that stream. They turn attention to the thoughts and feelings they are thinking and feeling. Most important, they situate themselves biographically, in the lived present, in the emotion, and reflect the emotion onto themselves, asking, perhaps, "Is this how I want to feel and present myself as feeling now?" In this double reflection, the self of the person feels, reflects the emotion, and reflects on the emotion. In Heidegger's terms, "What is phenomenologically decisive in the phenomenon of feeling is that it directly uncovers and makes accessible what is felt. . . . Feeling is having a feeling-for, and so much so that in it the feeling ego at the same time feels its own self" (1975/1982, pp. 132, 135).

Consider the following:

> My husband became so angry yesterday, he screamed at me. I felt his anger in my body. I wanted to scream and run away. I thought about it all day—his screaming. It ruined my day, I couldn't get it off my mind. It made me angry. I had a headache. I was angry at work. I couldn't get it off my mind. I tried to put it out of my mind. Every time I thought about it, I got angry at him, and then I got angry at myself. I couldn't help it [Field conversation, twenty-eight-year-old graduate student in psychology].

In reflection, the woman continued to feel the emotion of her husband's anger. His anger became her anger. She felt the anger throughout her body, and it permeated the other dealings in her day. His anger became part of her world and a focal point of her "selfness" in the world. The emotion was not just a part of her consciousness, it was a part of *her*. Hence Heidegger's observation that what is decisive about the phenomenon of feeling is a feeling of the self or the ego in the feeling.

In reflective emotional consciousness the person attempts to guide and direct the feeling of the emotion and to shape the interpretations he gives to his emotion. A labeling of the emotion, a definition of the situation, and a definition of the person in the situation are involved in reflective consciousness. The following excerpt exemplifies these features.

I was stuck in a snowbank. My battery was
dead. I was shoveling out my car. This sonofabitch
pulled up behind me and honked. He wanted me to
move my car. I pointed to my car and the hood
and the snowbank and shrugged my shoulders. He
leaned on his horn and said, "Move it." As if he
had a right to my parking place! I looked at him. I
felt myself getting mad and out of control. I gave
him the finger. "Can you start it?" I said, and
pointed to my car. "Get the hell out of here if you
can't help!" I told him to "go _____ off" and got
back in my car and just sat there until he drove off.
I was seething. I didn't know what to do. I was losing control. I got out and walked across the street
and went into my apartment and tried to calm
down [Field conversation, thirty-five-year-old engi-
neer].

The engineer was in a problematic situation. Another person
challenged his definition of the situation. He became angry, felt
himself losing control, tried to check his feelings, got back in his
car, and then walked away from the situation, carrying his angry emotional consciousness with him. Unlike the Latin mother, who did not reflect on her emotional consciousness, the
engineer turned his consciousness and self-awareness inward, on
the emotional experience. The feeling of the self in the emotion
is central to reflective emotional consciousness. Of equal importance, however, is reflection on the consciousness of the experience. By reflecting on the experience and turning it into an object of reflection, not just living emotion as a phase in experience,
the person transforms experience. The engineer tried to check,
control, and alter his emotional consciousness. The levels of
firstness, secondness, and thirdness are present in reflective
emotional consciousness. The self of the person moves through
the experience, reinterpreting what has been recognized and
drawn into conscious awareness. In this mode of emotional consciousness the self is in the field of emotion, living within emotion as a part of the "who" of the "who I am at the moment."

Emotional consciousness is both reflective and unreflective. Individuals are differentially aware of their emotions and,

as indicated above, may have feelings they are unaware of, just as they may misidentify their feelings or pass over feelings they might act and reflect on. In addition, individuals may reinterpret their feeling states, returning at a later time to a neglected feeling, or they may dwell, as in ressentiment, on a long-held emotion. The fifty-seven-year-old male quoted earlier is reinterpreting a long-held ressentiment. The engineer, in contrast, may be seen to be interpreting an emotion-as-it-occurs. Reflection may be backward-looking in time or turned directly to the present. Reflection, backward looking, reconstructs, through emotional memory, a previously felt emotion. Reflection-in-the-present alters emotional consciousness as it is occurring. These two modes of reflection thus produce two entirely different forms of emotion, which may be termed "reconstructed emotion" and "altered emotion." Unreflected emotional consciousness produces a third emotional form: directly lived emotion. Reflection on past emotional states may produce a redefinition of the previously felt emotion. Redefined and reconstructed emotions flow from backward-looking reflection, which is always conducted from the standpoint of the present and the oncoming future. Individuals redefine themselves in terms of the emotions and the feelings they once felt toward themselves and others. This fourth form of emotional consciousness will be termed "redefined emotion."

Reconstructed emotional consciousness produces new emotion and new feelings, as well as redefined emotions. The new emotions produced may be "pretended," or dramaturgical approximations of an earlier emotional consciousness. Spurious, or pretended, emotion, a fifth emotional form, often follows elaborate attempts to reproduce socially an emotional happening or "feeling of togetherness" between persons who have long since cut emotional bonds with one another. The following statement, from a description of a family Christmas dinner, displays these points:

> Every year my great-aunt organizes Christmas dinner. And every year it's always the same. My uncle gets drunk after we toast from the bottle of

> Polish wine. My mother gets mad at her sister, and
> grandmother won't speak to grandfather. The kids
> all try to eat in the kitchen and stay away from the
> older relatives. But it never works. We all sit at the
> big dining room table. Everybody is uncomfort-
> able, and my great-aunt looks like she is in her glory.
> I think she lives for this day when the whole family
> is together once a year [Field interview, eighteen-
> year-old undergraduate female, January 1981].

The "spurious," pretended, dramaturgically induced emotion—
family togetherness—which produces the underlying reason for
the social occasion rests on top of deep, underlying emotional
feelings that contradict the surface feelings of the participants.
Both layers of feeling are dulled in the occasion of interaction.
Family ritual and ceremony distort the personal feeling structures of the family gathering.

To understand and interpret emotional consciousness reflectively, individuals must situate themselves within the world-
at-hand. Emotions arise out of and in situations and are situated
in the world. Although normative standards adhere to the situated display of emotion, and rules specific to emotion work in
situations have been identified, the phenomenology of situations remains an underdeveloped area of understanding. It is
necessary, therefore, to comment on the neglected situation of
emotion.

The Neglected Situation of Emotion. The situations of
human interaction are phenomenological constructions; that is,
they flow from and out of the inner and outer streams of consciousness of individuals and their associates. All experience is
situated. Situations envelop, enclose, and capture individuals.
Situations anchor individuals in the world. All situations contain historical halos that connect them to previous situations.
And situations are forward-looking, for they throw people into
the future, into actions that have yet to be intended, let alone
attempted. People can never be free of situations, for they are
never free of time, and time is realized situationally.

Emotions are situated self-feelings. The situation of emotion is brought vividly alive in and through emotion. Paradoxi-

cally, however, the emotional stream of consciousness freezes time, space, and being into a single slice of emotional experience. Faulkner, (1981, pp. 289-290) offers a moving illustration from his short story "The Bear": "As he looked up the wilderness coalesced, solidified—the glade, the tree he sought, the bush, the watch, and the compass glinting where a ray of sunlight touched them. Then he saw the bear. It did not emerge, appear; it was just there, immobile, solid, fixed in the dot dappling of the green and windless noon, not as big as he had dreamed it, but as big as he had expected it, bigger, dimensionless against the dappled obscurity, looking at him where he sat quietly on the log and looked at it." Time, space, and being stand still in emotion's frozen situation. Feelings are attached to such situations, often after the fact. The situations of emotion become a part of the individual's emotional biography. They occupy spaces, like paintings on a wall, in the person's emotional memory.

Situations are neither objective nor subjective phenomena. They occur and exist, rather, in the interface between the person and the world-at-hand. Granted, situations occur in *places,* or settings, but the places of situations are where people are being themselves so as to carry on new transactions with the world-at-hand.

This place where I am now, or where I was then, is the place of my situation. This place occurs to me in the order and arrangement of things as they appear to me now and appeared to me then. This chair, this table, this typewriter, the large windows to my right that look out over the snow, the view to the left, onto the street and the winter trees, the room I am in, the green plants, the cedar chest, the country music that is in the air—this is the place where my situated interaction with the world-at-hand occurs. That situated interaction, that confrontation, is my melding with and into the world. It is in me and in the world. I embrace that which surrounds me, as it envelops me; we are one, as in an indissoluble synthesis, or unity.

When I came into this place, I left another place, and that other place, with my situated presence there, provides a horizon against which my current thoughts, emotional consciousness, and inner and outer streams come together, are sketched and lived. I came to this place, where I am now, with a past—a past of past feelings toward myself and this place and a past full of feelings. By acting in this place, by being-in-it, I change it and me. I enter into the situation and it enters into me. We (the situation and I) become one together, a moving being, or a moving presence-in-the-world: the Situation and I.

The situation of emotion always exists ahead of the person as a space to be filled with emotional consciousness and emotional action. I embody and fill this situation with my thoughts, my actions, my feelings, my posture, my gestures, my sounds, and my movements. The words that I write and read spill out of my consciousness into the situation and become the traces of lived experience that I give to this situation and it gives to me.

Although the situation always exists ahead of me, the person, at the same time the situation of emotion *exists alongside* me as a part of the emotional stream I am experiencing. The situation becomes me, illuminating things through my actions and thoughts. I am alongside that which is ahead of me, for while I act in this situation, these actions that I have just produced exist just behind and next to those I am moving toward. They are part of what I am doing now and provide the context for understanding what is coming next. My situation is simultaneously behind me, alongside me, and in front of me.

In my situation I illuminate the projects that I am pursuing, for my actions define my purposes-at-hand, and these always lie ahead of me, as part of the situated "doings" I am doing, as I move forward toward them. In emotional consciousness, and in emotion's situations, I pursue emotional purpose, or emotional intentionality, hoping to achieve, through my actions and in my embodied consciousness, an emotional expression and display that meet or fulfill my purposes-at-hand. In the situation I declare and experience my emotionality. Emotion's meanings are situated accomplishments, given through my actions and thoughts in the situation. These meanings always lie ahead of me, to be captured, if at all, after specific action has occurred.

There is no privileged emotional situation that I can sit atop so as to compare different situations. There is only the situation of emotional consciousness and emotional behavior I am currently occupying. I can realize only one situation at a time—my own—and this is biographically unique to me. The situation can be understood only from within, as my situation. In this sense the situation is "eminently concrete" (Sartre, 1943/1978, p. 703).

The emotional situation defines all that emotion, consciousness, and the person are at a given moment in time and space. Emotion and the person are given a sense of permanence in the situation. As frozen moments, memories and actions in time and space, individuals refer back to their situations as objective markers in their emotional biographies.

The Temporality of Emotion. Emotions are temporal phenomena. The temporality of emotion belongs to the person's inner and outer streams of experience. Although single emotional experiences appear to have beginnings and ends, they actually occur as a succession of events within the continuity of time in the ongoing stream of experience (Husserl, 1913/1962, p. 217). Inner phenomenological time is continuous and circular, wherein the future, the present, and the past constitute a continuous temporal horizon against and in which the person's emotional consciousness is experienced and accomplished. In the circular horizon of temporality, which engulfs individuals and their consciousness, the future moves toward them, the present is alongside them, and the past pushes the present forward. Emotional consciousness takes root in this circular horizon of temporality, perhaps first attaching itself to an event, a person, a thought, a goal, a feeling, a fear, or a joy. The temporality of emotional consciousness becomes circular, internally self-reflective, and encased within its own experiential boundaries. The future, the present, and the past all become part of the same emotional experience. What is felt now is shaped by what will be felt, and what will be felt is shaped by what was felt. When in the emotionality of emotional consciousness, the person cannot draw a firm and steady chronological line between past, present, and future. Nor can people give clear meaning to an event until they have moved through it, and are able to look back on it, as an occurrence involving them. Such lines and meanings can be drawn only after the emotional experience has been lived. Then it can be dated, situated, interpreted, and fixed on a calendar; but not so during its lived occurrence.

The Person. The inner, temporal life of emotional consciousness must be interpreted from within the lived experience of the person. The subject of the "person" must now be addressed. Two levels of analysis (which do not necessarily correspond to linguistic levels) will be maintained in the following section: the phenomenological, or deep, level and the taken-for-granted, or surface, level. At the taken-for-granted level, persons are assumed to be "real," substantial beings, with fixed inner personalities. On the phenomenological, deep level, persons are processes in the world, who think they are "real" and substantial. At the deep level, persons *are* the moral self-feelings they feel and attach themselves to.

The person is that being already present in the world, ahead of itself, aware of itself, and capable of expressing and acting on that being, awareness, and presence (Heidegger, 1927/ 1962). The person is a worldly phenomenon, a moving presence in the world. The person is evident in accomplishments, doings, saying, declarations, talk, and gestures. Phenomenologically a person is a feeling, thinking, accomplished structure of practices embodied and located in the world. To the person is attached a body of biographically connected and disconnected feelings, thoughts, pleasures, experiences, and actions. Some of these experiences are disavowed; others are held too closely. Some of them, persons call their own; others, they disclaim.

The person appears and emerges as an embodied, situated structure of experience in the world. The person exists in the intersection of the inner and outer streams of experience called the world. Analysis of this thing called person works outward from the body and its practices to the everyday social world.

A self is at the center of what are called persons, *at the taken-for-granted, everyday level.* This self, which individuals call their own, or "themselves," is always just ahead of or just behind the person, situated in the circular horizon of temporality. The self is a part of both the inner and outer streams of experience of the person.

A circuit of selfness joins the person to the world in an indissoluble synthesis of being, action, meaning, and consciousness (Sartre, 1943/1978, p. 155). Sartre states: "Without the world there is no selfness, no person; without selfness, without the person, there is no world. . . . It would be absurd to say that the world as it is known is known as mine. Yet this quality of 'my-ness' in the world is a fugitive structure, always present, a structure which I live. The world [is] mine because it is haunted by possibles, and the consciousness of each of these is a possible self-consciousness which *I am*. It is these possibles as such which give the world its unity and its meaning as the world" (1943/ 1978, pp. 157-158).

The self, that reflective part of themselves that individuals call their own, or their personality, is not a substantial self located in consciousness or in persons. The self, the person, lies in the world, always thrown and ahead of itself (Heidegger, 1927/1962, pp. 72-73). The self is the "I" of the "I-am-in-a-world" or "in-the-world" (Heidegger, 1927/1962, p. 368). The self is a worldly phenomenon. *The self, the "I," is not a thing but, rather, a process that unifies the stream of thoughts and experiences the person has about himself around a single pole or point of reference* (Sartre, 1957, p. 60). The stream of thoughts and experiences that are unified and threaded around the self, the "I," or the "person" is frozen in time and space into actions, states, and qualities that are objectified and made an autobiographical part of the person through reflection (Sartre, 1957, p. 60; Schutz, 1964, p. 288; James, 1890/1950, vol. 1, p. 332).

"I'm not Stiller!," Max Frisch's (1958) protagonist states, over and over again, after he has been imprisoned and asked to write his life history. He says:

> I'm not Stiller!—Day after day, ever since I was put into this prison, which I shall describe in a minute. I have been saying it, swearing it, asking for whisky, and refusing to make any other state-

ment. For experience has taught me that without
whisky I'm not myself, I'm open to all sorts of
good influences and liable to play the part they
want me to play, although it's not me. But since
the only thing that really matters in my crazy situation (they think I'm a missing resident of their
little town) is to be wheedled and to guard against
all their well-meaning attempts to shove me into
somebody else's skin, to resist their blandishments
even if it means being downright rude—in a word,
to be no one else than the man I unfortunately
really am—I shall go on shouting for whisky the
moment anybody comes near my cell. . . . Today
they brought me this notebook full of empty
pages. I'm supposed to write down my life story—
no doubt to prove that I have one, a different one
from the life of their missing Herr Stiller [pp. 3-4] .

The "I" of "I'm not Stiller" unifies and binds together
an experience and a denial of a person in the world; the "I"
does not refer to an isolated subject but, rather, expresses the
consciousness and presence of the person called Stiller. The "I"
expresses, too, at the everyday level, the conviction that inside
the skin of this peson "called" Stiller, is a real person who is not
Stiller! In saying "I" the person, in every case, is referring to
himself—to a particular, real person located in the here and now
of the world.

However, the real person is always just out of reach, always just ahead of the person, or located somewhere in the distant or not so distant past. Searching to find himself in the present, the person is always at a loss. The "who-ness" of the person,
the "who" of the "who am I" always lies out of immediate
reach, often wholly lodged outside the person in the world. In a
fugitive way, the person tries to catch himself through this fleeting "I." The person, as Heidegger (1927/1962, p. 368) states,
has fallen into the world and "flees" in the face of itself (himself) into the "they": "When the 'I' talks in the 'natural' manner, this is performed by the they-self. What expresses itself in
the 'I' is that Self which, proximally and for the most part, I am
not authentically. When one is absorbed in the everyday multi-

plicity and the rapid succession of that with which one is concerned, the Self of the self-forgetful 'I am concerned' shows itself as something simple which is constantly selfsame but indefinite and empty. Yet one *is* that with which one concerns oneself" (p. 368). That with which one concerns oneself is the everyday doings and practical accomplishments one calls one's own. These doings and accomplishments, situated, embedded, personal practices, fill the gaps and holes in the person's life, giving a sense of purpose and meaning to the daily round of activity. It is in these practices (to be considered later) that the concerned self loses itself and becomes self-forgetful, giving itself over to its practices and to the practical scrutiny of the "they." The "they," those indefinite others of the social world, of whom one is a part, enter into the person's idle talk, chitchat, and everyday discourse (Heidegger, 1927/1962, pp. 211–219). The person hides within this discourse, fleeing and seeking to find herself in such talk and in those practices she shares with others.

However, the natural way in which the "I" of the person enters into everyday discourse is not the "I" of the phenomenological person. Underneath this everyday "I" is the "I" of the *moral person,* which expresses a "specific *modification of self-consciousness*" (Heidegger, 1975/1982, p. 132). This is the "I" of a person who feels, has feelings, feels herself feeling, and has dignity, self-respect, self-responsibility, and an inner sense of moral worth (Heidegger, 1975/1982, pp. 135–137). Moral self-consciousness is at the core of the person; it is this self-consciousness, not the public "I" of natural everyday discourse, that defines the person's true being as a mental being in the world (Heidegger, 1975/1982, p. 132).

The morally self-conscious person has self-feeling, whose basic structure involves (1) having a feeling for one's self, (2) feeling this self-feeling, and (3) revealing the moral self through this feeling (Heidegger, 1975/1982, p. 137). The feeling person, the person in emotional consciousness, feels herself in emotion. This feeling is distinguished from indiscriminate and spurious feelings, such as boredom, fleeting fatigue, irritation, mock anger, or pretended joy and happiness. This moral feeling is felt to the core of the person and radiates throughout inner consciousness.

The essence of the moral feeling of the moral person is respect for the moral law of the everyday lifeworld. This moral law embodies the core features of human nature, as upheld by social structures and culture. Such matters as honor, respect, freedom, dignity, love, shame, the ritual, the sacred, the civil, and personal responsibility are embodied in the moral code of the person and society (Shils, 1975; Durkheim, 1912/1973; Heidegger, 1975/1982; Sartre, 1981; Riezler, 1950; Cooley, 1902/1956; Scheler, 1913/1970; Geertz, 1973). By subjecting himself to a respect for this moral law, the person gains self-dignity. This dignity obligates a responsibility for self in the world. In yielding to this moral code persons bring that respect to themselves. This internalized self-respect, which comes from yielding to an external law in the world of daily affairs, constitutes the inner essence of the moral person.

Faulkner (1981, p. 295), in the closing of "The Bear," has a father speak the following lines to his son. They embody the conception just described of the relation between the person and the moral codes of society. "His father was watching him gravely across the spring-rife twilight of the room; when he spoke, his words were as quiet as the twilight, too, not loud, because they did not need to be because they would last. 'Courage, and honor, and pride,' his father said, 'and pity, and love of justice and of liberty. They all touch the heart, and what the heart holds to become truth, as far as we know truth. Do you see now?' " These truths, which refer to the human passions, or the emotions, must be seen as standing in a complex relation to the person and to society. They suggest that society is an underlying moral concern. They refer to the fundamental bonds that join humans to one another, these bonds being both emotional and moral. That they are emotional and moral and involve complex interrelationships between more than one emotion suggests that the primary connections that join individuals to societies are themselves moral and emotional. (This point will be developed in detail in the Conclusion.)

These truths point to universal features of human nature,

as these features are given in such values as justice and liberty, pity, courage, honor, and compassion for others. They reference truths, or feelings that are deeply felt by the person—truths, that is, that touch the heart. In this sense Faulkner is suggesting that they lie at the inner core of the moral person. These principles are not given; they must be learned through emotional experience. Furthermore, their meanings must be revealed to the self so that the self becomes attached to them. In this way the person is connected inwardly to these external, eternal truths. That connection, to repeat, is established through the interpretations that individuals give to their emotional experiences. *Emotionality connects the person to society.*

The phenomenological, deep self of the person is given, then, in and through the feelings of moral respect and care for self and for others. The person is that being who cares for its own existence, and feels that caring, through moral self-consciousness (Heidegger, 1927/1962, pp. 370-380). In moral feeling the person finds his personal dignity. The person is a moral agent, the means to his own ends.

As moral agents, the agents of their own morality, persons feel their feelings at and to the core of the "who" of the "who-they-are." Feelings felt in this deep, self-conscious fashion cut to the core of the person. What is phenomenologically decisive in these feelings is the uncovering and revealing of the person to herself. These feelings announce themselves and make their presence felt by the person. By feeling these feelings, persons come to know themselves deeply and phenomenologically.

Faulkner (1965, pp. 434-435) offers an example of the feeling felt in the inner essence of the morally self-conscious person.

> Then the time came to go on. He was glad of it in a way; a man can get tired, burnt out on resting like on anything else. . . . But then a man didn't need to have to keep his mind steadily on the ground after sixty-three years. . . . He thought *I'm free now. I can walk any way I want to.* . . . A little further along toward dawn, any time the notion struck him to, he could lay down . . . he could af-

ford to risk it; to show how much he dared risk it,
he even would close his eyes, give it all the chance
it wanted. . . . But he could risk it. . . . And in fact,
as soon as he thought that, it seemed to him he
could feel the Mink Snopes that he had had to
spend so much of his life just having unnecessary
bother and trouble, beginning to creep, seep, flow
easy as sleeping; he could almost watch it.

Challenges to the inner, moral essence of the person
evoke a moral self-consciousness of heightened emotionality.
For if, as argued above, persons are the emotions they feel and
value most deeply, then a moral affront to the person awakens
these emotions. This point is evident in the following incident.

I was a week on the new job. This bastard
comes by in his truck and gives me the finger.
"Hey, 'fairy,' getting any lately? Whatsamatter,
ain't you a man?!" I stood there. Just because I'm
new, they think they can get away with anything.
I walked up to him, really steaming. I just held my
fists beside me and said "Hey, fucker, get off my
back. You say that again and I'll lose my job and
you won't be able to ever work again!" We went to
the foreman. Now we work on different sides of
the plant and don't see each other anymore [Field
conversation, twenty-eight-year-old male, Emotions Project, winter 1981].

Sexual identity lies near to the core assumptions held by the
person about himself or herself (Lindesmith, Strauss, and Denzin, 1978, p. 510). In this episode a challenge to the man's sexual identity provoked near-violent emotional action.

As the reflective subject of her own thoughts, feelings,
and actions, the person is continually attempting to maintain
that stream of activity she calls herself and to give it a sense of
sameness, continuity, organization, permanence, "sensibility,"
respect, and "my-ness." Yet there is no permanent outer substance to the person, or to the self, only movement that ema-
nates outward from her body and its practices. The person,
though, claims permanence for what is changing.

The person is a constantly changing, shifting, emerging, reflective, and unreflective stream of intersubjectivity that arises out of and from the inner and outer streams of experience in the world. The interiority of the person is to be found in the inner, embodied stream of experience, as reflection is turned inward, on the self and consciousness. The subjective interior of the person, minded, embodied inner consciousness, occurs in the circuit of selfness that attaches the person to the world-at-hand. The world is in consciousness, just as consciousness is in the world. The interior, intersubjective life of the person is a worldly phenomenon. The person can never be free from or out of the world.

A person is a shell, an encasement, a container full of holes to be filled with activities, doings, practices, accomplishments, relationships, meanings, feelings, thoughts, and projects (Sartre, 1943/1978, p. 781). As an ongoing temporal and situational accomplishment, the person claims and gives a semblence of order to himself and his activities through commitments, personal names, and identities. Others confer order on the person by consensually identifying him within a mutually understood universe of discourse (Stone, 1962; Strauss, 1959).

Persons are defined and define themselves in terms of the things, accomplishments, achievements, and material possessions they surround themselves with (James, 1890/1950). These accomplishments, doings, and relationships overflow the thing called person and fill the holes of nonbeing and nothingness that this palpable container encases (Sartre, 1943/1978).

The body of the person is her instrument in the world. The body provides the means for doing the things the person does and lays claim to. The person's body situates her in the world, making her and her practices visible and accessible to the doings, accomplishments, and gazes of others. The person acts, feels, and speaks through and with her body. The body talks for her and is her embodied consciousness and presence in the world.

Interpretive study moves outward from the human body and its practices to the everyday social world. The practices of the person must now be considered, especially those that are emotional.

The Person and Emotional-Interpretive Practices. The activities of the person may be studied as interpretive practices, for they involve the practiced doing of such activities as sign making, tool making, knowledge making, sound making, and product using and consuming. These doings are interpreted, evaluated, and judged by the person and by others—hence the term *interpretive practices.*

The interpretive practices of the person involve a constitutive core of recurring activities that must be learned, taught, traced out, coached, felt, internalized, and interiorized, as well as expressed and exteriorized. They must be practiced over and over. They become a part of the taken-for-granted structures of activity that surround and are ingrained in every individual. They require special discussion, for the emotionality of the person attaches to these interpretive practices.

Practices operate at two separate levels: the practical level, the actual doing of the practice; and the interpretive level, the evaluation and judgment of the practice. Interpretations of practices involve criteria of judgment, rules of relevance concerning how and on what a practice may be practiced, and tacit understandings concerning how the person is to do the practice, when, with whom, and under what circumstances.

A practice may be embodied or disembodied. An "embodied practice" involves the use of the body or parts of the body. Tool using and music making are embodied practices. The thinking of a thought may not be. A "situated practice" is located in a particular locale or social situation; it requires the situation for its accomplishment. A "personal practice" is a practice that a person lays periodic or permanent claim to. Personal practices involve a sense of personal ownership, or "my-ness." They belong to the person and are often taken as being the embodiment of the person.

An "embedded practice" is a practice that is often embodied, always situated, and lodged in the practices of others. Embedded practices are attached to something or to a local social situation. These practices require the presence of certain, often tacitly recognized properties, things, or events for their accomplishment. These things, which may be tools, other persons, or certain activities, are noticed when they are missing or when they become problematic (for example, break down). They may be called the taken-for-granteds in the situation. They are, however, in the situation and are part of the embedded practices that are accomplished in the place of the situation. An "accomplished practice" is a practice that has been completed to the satisfaction of its practitioners.

An "emotional practice" is an embedded practice that produces for the person an expected or unexpected emotional alteration in the inner and outer streams of experience. Such practices may be recurring—for example, lovemaking, eating, drinking, exercising, working, or playing. Emotional practices place the person in the presence of others and often require others for their accomplishment. Emotional practices are both practical and interpretive. They are personal, embodied, and situated. Unlike purely cognitive practices, which are taken for granted and not emotionally disruptive of the flow of experience, emotional practices make people problematic objects to themselves. The emotional practice radiates through the person's body and streams of experience, giving emotional coloration to thoughts, feelings, and actions.

Any practice may become emotional, for all that is required is a transformation in the consciousness of the person out of the taken-for-granted into the world of emotional consciousness. The interpretations of practices are emotional because practices are central to the person's embodied conception of herself in the world. To criticize and evaluate a practice is to criticize and evaluate the person who lies behind the practice. Hence, practices lie at the emotional core of these "recurring constancies" that people claim as their own.

In the circuit of selfness, the practices of the person become the "possibles" that give the world a sense of "mine" and "my-ness." In the possibles of the practice, a world of doing that haunts and eludes the person is grasped and molded into concrete doings and accomplishments. The person claims ownership of these doings. The world becomes the person to the extent that practices produce actions that can be reflected on and claimed. The practices of the person produce things that are extensions of the person. In these practices the person is disclosed and revealed. Heidegger (1975/1982, pp. 159-161) observes:

> Each of us is what he pursues and cares for. In everyday terms, we understand ourselves and our existence by way of the activities we pursue and the things we take care of. We understand our-selves by starting from them because the Dasein finds itself primarily in things . . . as the Dasein gives itself over immediately and passionately to the world, its own self is reflected to it from things. . . . It is surely a remarkable fact that we encounter ourselves, primarily and daily, for the most part by way of things and are disclosed to ourselves in this manner in our own self. . . . Let us take a simple example—the craftsman in his workshop, given over to his tools, materials, works to be produced, in short to things with which he concerns himself. . . . Certainly the shoemaker is not the shoe, and nevertheless he understands *himself* from his things, *himself*, his own self . . . the self of our thought-lessly random, common, everyday existence, "re-flects" itself to itself from and out of that to which it has given itself over.

We give ourselves over to our practices, and in these practices we find ourselves.

We understand and interpret ourselves in terms of our daily doings and emotional practices. The everyday meaning of the person is to be found at this level. We lose ourselves in the everyday world. This level of self-caring is "inauthentic self-understanding," which is genuine and actual, but not authentic in terms of the "extreme possibilities" of the ultimate meaning of the individual's existence (Heidegger, 1975/1982, p. 160).

Situating the Person. Every person embodies, in a situated fashion, the historical and cultural epoch that he is born into and lives through. Each person is, to quote Sartre, a "universal singular" (1981, p. ix), for each individual sums up in his lifetime a segment of human history. And in their slice of history and their projects, individuals reproduce the epoch they are a part of. To understand people, then, requires that they and their projects be situated within a particular moment in lived historical, world time. The emotions they feel, the projects they undertake, the people they associate with, the moral codes they embody, the agreements they make, the situations and places they pass through, and the world they call their own must all be placed within the specifics of a given historical-cultural epoch.

A person is a biological fact, the consequence of a chance occurrence, the meeting of a certain body and "psychosomatic reality" with a certain social milieu, a certain mother, father, peer group, social world, and family structure (Sartre, 1981, pp. 48-51). The person emerges from a particular family as a social unit, from a primary group of intimate others and associates who indelibly impress on her a biographical structure that will never be permanently shaken or let loose of.

Individuals are haunted by this past, by this childhood that they have inherited. Their lives can be understood only in terms of this total situation that they embody and inherit—their historical and cultural epoch, the biological facts of their existence, the social milieu they were thrown into, the childhood they lived. Individuals, then, are products of chance and, at the same time, the sum of their projects, intentions, and practices.

To grasp the significance of emotionality for the person would require the situating of emotional experience within that lifetime the person calls his or hers.

The Person in Summary. The person is that moral being, already present in the world, ahead of itself, occupied and preoccupied with its everyday doings and emotional practices, capable of feeling, acting on, and interpreting the meanings of its actions. Two levels to the person are distinguished: the everyday, surface, practical level, in which persons act "as if" they were real, substantial personalities, and the underlying, deep, phenomenological level, in which individuals are conceptualized as ongoing moving processes. At the core of the moral person lie respect and dignity. The self of the person is a process in the world, a process that in everyday discourse is unified and threaded around actions, states, and qualities that the person attempts to make an autobiographical part of himself through reflection.

The world of the person is haunted by "possibles"—by

actions and purposes that elude and always stay ahead of the person's grasp. Through situated, embodied, personal, emotional practices, people attach themselves to the world, laying claim to a part of the world as their own.

Two modes of self-understanding can be described in addition to the everyday and the phenomenological. At the level of inauthentic self-understanding, individuals lose yet find themselves in the world of practices. At the level of authentic self-understanding, the deeper, underlying moral and existential meanings of the person are to be found. At this level, the meaning of the person as a moral, caring being is identified.

The emotionality of the person is located in emotional practices and in the moral codes the person submits to. In submitting to these moral codes, the person attains an inner sense of self-respect, dignity, and responsibility. The emotionality of the person can thus be seen to have a double structure—the first deriving from the emotional practices the person constructs, the second from the moral codes the person embodies and draws into her inner fabric of meaning and being.

The who of the person is haunted by the past, a past that finds its nexus in the sociality and social interactions of the individual. This past, which is embedded in individuals, provides a frame of reference against which their current engagements in the world can be judged.

Emotional Associates. At the beginning of this chapter I said that an emotional experience "plunges the person and his associates into a wholly new and transformed reality—the reality of a world that is being constituted by the emotional experience." The nature and character of those others who share in the person's emotional experiences must be briefly indicated. An emotional associate will be defined as the person or persons who are, in some fashion, drawn into the emotional world of experience of the individual. They may be witnesses to the experience, coproducers of and participants in the experience, or people with whom the person shares the experience after the fact. They may be intimate significant others (Sullivan, 1953a, 1953b), orientational others (Kuhn, 1964), situation-specific others (Denzin, 1966), contemporaries of the person (Schutz and Luckmann, 1973), persons in a "we" relationship with the person (Schutz and Luckmann, 1973), distant, "theylike" others (Heidegger, 1927/1962, 1975/1982), or complete strangers, significant only by virtue of their copresence to the person (Schutz, 1964). Emotional associates or others often stand in a close relationship to the person's emotional practices. They may be coparticipants in the emotional practices of the person, focal interpreters of the practice, or the recipients of the products that come from the practice.

Regardless of the personal relationship between the person and the emotional associate, the associate is a significant emotional other because his presence in the individual's emotional experience is and becomes a significant part of the meaning, order, and significance of that experience. Emotional experiences are social experiences and require the presence of others (real or imagined) for their occurrence.

The emotional other stands in the same relationship to persons that persons stand in relationship to themselves. That is, the other is a moral other, also an embodiment of the moral codes the person adheres to. To act and feel in the presence of the emotional other is to have one's feelings revealed and mirrored in and through the feelings and actions of the other. An emotional bond unites the person and the emotional associate, for they together have shared in or lived a common emotional experience. They have emotionally grown older together (see Schutz, 1964, pp. 159-178).

Emotional Reality. Emotional consciousness has a lived "realness" that is not doubted by the person. The emotional experience radiates throgh the person's stream of consciousness and is felt in and throughout the body. The reality of emotion is held to be true by the person. This reality, to the degree that it remains uncontradicted and not doubted by the person, is "believed and posited as absolute" (James, 1890/1950, vol. 2, p. 289). Hence, a cardinal feature of emotion emerges: During its occurrence emotional experience is lived as absolute reality by the person. As such, emotional consciousness crowds out doubt and disbelief. Individuals are engulfed by the emotionality of the experience they are in. This lived reality of emotion cannot be easily displaced. It grips one's attention and sweeps one along and through its own inner motion, tension, and organization.

Emotional reality projects itself on the person's field of experience and finds its realization in that field. Emotional consciousness becomes captured by the person's belief in it, and as in a dream or in hysteria, the individual is caught in the reality of the experience-at-hand. This consciousness of emotion is captive to itself and tends to perpetuate itself. As the reality of emotion builds, the person, too, is moved by the emotion and becomes a captive. He is heightened and moved by the very emotion he is feeling. The man who flees a fire in fright becomes more frightened the faster he flees (Sartre, 1939/1962, pp. 79-80).

Emotional reality would not be so all-absorbing if it were not so deeply believed in by the person and if it did not have the characteristic of sweeping the person along through its inner trajectory. In emotional consciousness one finds oneself transformed into an emotional object and into a world of lived experience over which one appears to have little direct control. For, once underway, emotional consciousness must run its own course through and in one's inner and outer streams of consciousness. All emotions, Sartre (1939/1962, p. 80) observes, evoke the appearance of the same world, whether cruel, terrible, bleak, joyful, or depressing—that is, all emotions appear within a world made emotional. And this world that is evoked takes on qualities that are believed in. As if magically, consciousness is transformed into the world of emotionality. The person, too, becomes an emotional project and object in emotion's lived reality. What is lived, in emotion, is the person's inner and outer meanings to self and to others. Individuals and their inner meanings are at issue in emotional consciousness. There is a world of emotion.

The World of Emotion. Sartre states that "we have to speak of a world of emotion, as one speaks of a world of dreams or of worlds of madness" (1939/1962, p. 81). A social world is a separate province of reality in which certain things are believed in and held to be true, and other things are disbelieved and disregarded. Each social world, or province of reality, has its own style of meaning, being, and existence, its own taken-for-granted practices, its own moral codes, and its own special criteria of truth and verification. Each world, whether the world of immediate sensations, dreams, fantasy, work, play, the supernatural, religion, science, madness and vagary, phantasms, or everyday life, embodies certain epistemological and ontological assumptions (James, 1890/1950, vol. 2, pp. 287-293; Schutz, 1964, pp. 135-136). Epistemological problems include "how we know anything" and "what knowing is." Ontological problems concern such matters as what a person is and what sort of world this is (Bateson, 1972, p. 313).

The world of emotion is a separate province of reality that derives from—indeed, is embedded in—the everyday-life world, yet stands distinct from that world. The world of emotion is distinct because inner meanings and feelings are revealed in this world, while they are hidden and glossed over in the taken-for-granted world. Furthermore, the world of emotion cannot just be walked away from, as a person can when she leaves one sector of the everyday-life world and enters another place and situation. The world of emotion shatters the everyday-life world and renders its meanings and assumptions inoperative and problematic.

The world of emotion is symbolically indirect, for the meanings given to objects in the world of emotion often cannot be gleaned from their surface appearances or from their everyday, taken-for-granted meanings. The indirect symbolism of the world of emotion must be traced back into the biography and personal history of the individuals who occupy that world at any given moment.

The symbolic structure of the world of emotion is laden with subtlety. These meanings are often not directly accessible to the person. They exist out of the person's awareness (Stone and Farberman, 1981). Nor are these meanings readily apparent to the person's emotional associates. The emotional experience must be interpreted by the person and his or her associates, and often the meanings thus obtained must be conferred on the experience after it has occurred. After the fact, the symbolism of the event becomes apparent, as the meaning of the mention of a death, a person's name, a political figure, a crime, or a past accomplishment of oneself is thrashed out and fitted into the emotionality of the experience and the person. In short, each person is a symbolic structure of latent and manifest meanings, and these meanings can be understood only by grasping the person's biographical structure and situations.

The world of emotion "refers to what it signifies . . . what it signifies is . . . in effect, the totality of the relations of the human reality to the world" (Sartre, 1939/1962, p. 93). The reality that is lived within the world of emotion totally grips and encompasses the person, constituting a separate and unique indissoluble synthesis of the person with his world.

The world of emotion is emotional. The "rational" structures of everyday life are radically altered in this world. Out-of-the-ordinary occurrences are common, including character assaults, disjointed speech, inappropriate dress, refusal to follow ceremonial rules of conduct, trancelike states, and hysteria. In this world people pursue emotionally pragmatic actions in the attempt to gain definitions of the situation that cannot be or will not be given through normal practices.

In the world of emotion, the person collapses the barriers of time and space. The person attempts to grasp in a single instant what will be given only bit by bit, over time, in the real world. For instance, the anticipatory joy a man feels while awaiting the arrival of an old friend overcomes him. He cannot stand still, he makes innumerable plans that are forgotten. He cleans his house, calls friends, cancels appointments, and engages in endlessly time-consuming tasks, in an attempt to make time pass faster. He is caught in the excitement of the emotion. He is in the world of emotion. He becomes uneasy, nervous, and jittery. Until the object of his emotion (his friend) arrives, she is still not his. By singing, humming a tune, racing madly across town to buy an item for an elaborate meal, rearranging furniture, hanging pictures, picking flowers, and even becoming irritable, he attempts to symbolically realize and possess the object of his emotional consciousness—his friend.

But even when the friend arrives, she will make herself

available only one step at a time, "through numberless details" (Sartre, 1939/1962, p. 72). It will be impossible for the man to grasp his friend instantaneously, completely, as a totality. However, in emotional consciousness the man "tries . . . to realize the possession of the desired object as an instantaneous totality" (Sartre, 1939/1962, p. 72). Symbolically and emotionally the man embraces and consumes the other, thus realizing his emotional consciousness in a single instant. Emotional consciousness collapses time, annihilating the distinctions between the past and the future, into a single instant in the present.

Sartre (1939/1962, pp. 84-85) contends that the world of emotion is governed by the laws of magic. There is an existential structure to the world that is magical. This magical structure, Sartre argues, appears when the rational structures of the world collapse. Magical structures replace deterministic activity when ordinary dealings with the world no longer work. Emotional consciousness is transformed, and it transmutes the deterministic world into a magical world. Sartre offers the following example: "This face that I see ten yards away behind the window may be lived as an immediate, present threat to myself. But this is possible only in an act of consciousness which destroys all the structures of the world that might dispel the magic and reduce the event to reasonable proportions. . . . In reality, the window and the distance are seized *simultaneously* in the act of consciousness which catches sight of the face at the window. . . . This aspect of the world is an entirely coherent one; this is the *magical* world. Emotion may be called a sudden fall of consciousness into magic; or, if you will, emotion arises when the world of the utilizable vanishes abruptly and the world of magic appears in its place" (1939/1962, pp. 88-90).

Although Sartre nowhere (to my knowledge) clarifies in any detail the meanings he intends for *magical*, it is clear that the world of emotion confers qualities on persons, places, and things that would not be conferred in the everyday world. In the world of emotion, people seize the objects of their emotional consciousness and indissolubly unite themselves and their consciousness with those objects. In the everyday world, they keep a distance from their objects, employing a detached utilitarian attitude in their attitudes and practices. Not so in the world of emotion.

In the world of emotion, the circuit of selfness is permeated with emotionality and feeling. The person, as an embodied structure of feeling, is in-the-world emotionally. This emotionality shatters the emotional consciousness of the person's associates, thus rendering real the other person's emotions.

Edward Albee (1962, pp. 230-232) reveals the shattering nature of the world of emotion in the closing lines of his play *Who's Afraid of Virginia Woolf?*

George: All right. Well, Martha . . . I'm afraid our boy isn't coming home for his birthday.

Martha: Of course he is.

George: No, Martha.

Martha: Of course he is. I say he is!

George: He . . . can't.

Martha: He is! I say so!

George: Martha . . . (long pause) . . . our son is . . . dead. (silence) He was . . . killed . . . late in the afternoon . . . (silence) (a tiny chuckle) on a country road, with his learner's permit in his pocket, he swerved, to avoid a porcupine, and drove straight into a . . .

Martha: (rigid fury) YOU . . . CAN'T . . . DO . . . THAT!

George: . . . large tree.

Martha: YOU CANNOT DO THAT!

Nick: (softly) Oh my God. (Honey is weeping louder)

George: (Quietly, dispassionately) I thought you should know.

Nick: Oh my God; no.

Martha: (quivering with rage and loss) NO! NO! YOU CANNOT DO THAT! YOU CAN'T DECIDE THAT FOR YOURSELF! I WILL NOT LET YOU DO THAT!

George: We'll have to leave around noon, I suppose . . .

Martha: I WILL NOT LET YOU DECIDE THESE THINGS!

George: . . . because there are matters of identification, naturally, and arrangements to be made . . .

Martha: (Leaping at George, but ineffectual) YOU CAN'T DO THIS! (Nick rises, grabs hold of Martha, pins her arms

behind her back) I WON'T LET YOU DO THIS, GET
YOUR HANDS OFF ME!

George: (As Nick holds on; right in Martha's face) You don't
seem to understand, Martha; I haven't done anything.
Now pull yourself together. Our son is dead! Can you
get that into your head?

Martha: YOU CAN'T DECIDE THESE THINGS.

Nick: Lady please.

Each of the key terms in the definition of emotion—
stream of consciousness and *experience, situation, time, person,
emotional associate, reality, world*—has now been clarified and
elaborated. It remains to consider the structure of emotional experience.

The Double Structure of Emotional Experience. The phenomenological structure of emotional experience has two basic
elements: a core, or essence, to the emotional experience, as
named and recognized by the person within the terms of everyday language (for example, anger, fear, joy), and encircling
spheres of feelings, thoughts, memories, and emotions that surround the core of the experience. The spheres of emotional consciousness that encircle the core of the emotional phenomenon
may be termed the horizon of the emotion (Husserl, 1913/
1962, p. 413; James, 1890/1950, vol. 1, pp. 258-259). There
are layers, levels, and forms of emotional consciousness that we
experience as we move into a particular emotional consciousness such as anger, fright, jealousy, ressentiment, or joyfulness
(Arnold, 1960a, pp. 169-192; Izard, 1977, pp. 123-129). Furthermore, there are emotions we experience as a consequence of
having experienced a particular emotion—for example, happiness after depression, exhaustion and fatigue after fear, emotional boredom after victory. The double structure of emotion
refers to this twofold passage through an emotion's horizon to
its core and then the passage out from the core, forward through
an often new emotional horizon into a new stream of consciousness. The experiencing of a particular emotion takes the person
into and through other emotions. Thus, the person moves into
emotions and then out of them, passing in both directions in

and through different streams of emotional consciousness. The emotions we pass through on the way to or from a particular emotion may overtake, dilute, or redefine the emotional consciousness we are approaching.

Every movement to the core of an emotional experience must be understood as a new movement, to a new core, for the horizon of the emotion is continually changing, just as the meanings associated with the core of the experience are changing. As James (1890/1950, vol. 1, p. 186) remarks, our language lacks the words and subtleties that would permit a new meaning to be given to each reexperiencing of a common or similar emotion. Although we repeat our emotional experiences over and over again, however, they are always experienced against the horizon of the experiences that came before. That is, every emotional experience carries elements of earlier experiences with the emotion in question. Consider the following description of anger.

> When I get mad and angry, especially at my wife, I feel humiliated. I remember my father, when my mother used to get mad at him. She would yell and scream at him when he would come home drunk. He would sit at the kitchen table and hang his head and cry, and then go off to bed. The next day they would have a fight, all over again, only this time he would yell at her, over a little thing. I don't like to get mad, I'm afraid of [anger], and I hate myself when I get mad. Afterwards I am always embarrassed. Then I get resentful toward my wife, especially. If I keep this inside me, we have a fight all over again [Field conversation, forty-five-year-old chemist, Emotions Project, fall 1981].

The complex double structure of emotion is evident in this man's description of his anger. The inner core of anger for him is colored by the horizon of meanings he carries toward his father, himself, and the fights between his parents and by his own attitude toward his wife. Anger anticipates for him a host of other feelings and emotions: humiliation, fear, and hate. His experienced anger produces other feelings—loathing of himself, embarrassment, and resentment toward his wife.

Individuals, then, do not experience emotions as single slices of experience. Rather, emotional consciousness is a complex structure of related, interrelated, at times complementary, and at other times conflicting and contradicting feelings, thoughts, and emotions. An understanding of any emotion must place the emotion within the person's emotional stream of consciousness. The horizon of meanings and emotions that surround a particular emotion may be more important for an understanding of that emotion than the emotion itself.

> Contrary to the general assumption, the first days of grief are not the worst. The immediate reaction is usually shock and numbing disbelief. One has undergone an amputation. After shock comes acute grief, which is a kind of "condensed presence" —almost a form of possession. One still feels the lost limb down to the nerve endings. It is as if the intensity of grief fused the distance between you and the dead. Or perhaps, in reality, part of the one dies. . . . One must grieve, and one must go through periods of numbness that are harder to bear than grief . . . there is a temptation to self-pity. . . . Courage is a first step, but simply to bear the blow bravely is not enough. . . . Remorse is another dead end, a kind of fake action. . . . It is a beating oneself in a vain attempt to make what *has* happened "un-happen." Remorse is fooling yourself, feeding on an illusion, just as living on memories, clinging to relics and photographs, is an illusion. . . . As the reader will see, I am familiar with the false roads: stoicism, pride, remorse, self-pity, clinging to scraps of memory. I have not named them all; they are legion. I tried most of them. The fact that, in our case, horror was added to suffering does not change its fundamental character [Lindbergh, 1973, pp. 212-215].

In these words Ann Morrow Lindbergh summarizes the complex structure of experiences she experienced on the kidnapping and murder of her son, Charles Lindbergh, Jr. Her account reveals an additional feature of the double structure of emotional experiences—namely, that a sequence of closely related emotions may be felt around the core of an emotional event. As the feelings around the core of the emotional event change, they replace earlier feeings, and each feeling becomes *the* feeling of the event for the person. Importantly, the experience is felt as a sequence of feelings. Each feeling is both a part of the total experience and an experience in its own right. As a consequence, the emotional meanings of the original event are lost through and in the course of subsequent experiences. Yet each subsequent feeling-experience has meaning only in its relation to the original event.

The Essence of Emotional Experience

The essence of emotional experience can now be stated: *Emotional self-feeling is the essence of emotional consciousness.* In emotional experience persons find and feel their innermost moral feelings as persons. In these inner feelings they locate and feel themselves as distinct moral objects. This inner moral feeling is carried by the person into and through the everyday-life world. It is felt, also, in the other social worlds and provinces of reality in which the person participates. This inner moral feeling provides a landscape of inner and outer feeling against which the person's life experiences are projected, judged, interpreted, and evaluated.

People return over and over again to the world of emotion and emotional associates, for in that world they find and experience an inner sense of themselves that can be given nowhere else. An emotional, moral, feeling self lies at the core of the person, and that core can be realized only in emotional consciousness and in the worlds of emotion.

The world's sense of "my-ness" for the person is affirmed and given in and through emotional consciousness. The world and essence of emotion are neither rational nor deterministic. Perhaps, as Sartre argues, emotional consciousness is founded on magical behavior, on incantation, on sorcery, on the uncanny, and perhaps there is a magical quality to the world that governs interpsychic relations between individuals in society (Sartre, 1939/1962, p. 84). Perhaps, too, when the world presents itself as unrealizable, emotional consciousness does abase itself and "abruptly transmutes the world in which we live into a magical world" (Sartre, 1939/1962, p. 84).

But whether emotional consciousness is founded on magic and abasement is not central to the argument at hand. Emotional consciousness gives the person something the deterministic, everyday, taken-for-granted world does not. In emotional consciousness people find and locate themselves as distinct moral objects.

Summary

Emotional consciousness has a double structure: an inner phenomenological dimension and an outer interactional dimension. These two elements are united in the person's emotional stream of experience. Emotional consciousness is directed toward itself and the person as its own objects of consciousness. This mode of consciousness is intentional, continuous, sensibly organized by the person, felt as a single "pulse of subjectivity," and characterized by the categories of awareness termed firstness, secondness, and thirdness.

The process of experiencing an emotion also involves a double structure of experience and emotional movement—to and from a core emotion, through a horizon of encircling spheres of interrelated emotional forms. The feeling of an emotion involves a threefold process: (1) having a feeling for one's self, (2) feeling this self-feeling, and (3) revealing the moral self in and through this feeling. The feeling person feels the self in emotion.

Unreflective and reflective emotional consciousness can be distinguished. In unreflective emotional consciousness the person is completely contained within emotional experience. In reflective emotional consciousness the person situates himself biographically in the emotional experience and reflects the emotion onto himself. He attempts to guide, direct, and interpret the emotion as he is experiencing it. Reflective emotional consciousness may be focused on the past, the present, or the future. Five distinct emotional forms are noted: (1) reconstructed emotion, which flows from backward-looking reflection, (2) altered emotion, which is produced by forward-looking reflection in the present, (3) directly lived emotion, uninterpreted, and following from unreflected emotional consciousness, (4) redefined emotion, which redefines previously felt emotions through reflection from the standpoint of the future, the present, and the past, (5) spurious or pretended emotion, which represents an attempt to reproduce socially an emotional feeling that occurred in the past.

The neglected situation of emotion always exists ahead of the person, as a space to be filled with emotional consciousness and emotional action. People embody their situations with feeling. Time, space, and being are frozen in the emotional situation. An emotional situation becomes a part of the person's emotional biography.

The temporality of emotion belongs to the person's inner and outer streams of experience in what is termed the circular horizon of temporality. In this horizon of time the future moves toward the person, the present is alongside her, and the past pushes the present forward. Emotional consciousness is rooted in the circular horizon of temporality.

The person is defined as that moral being already present in the world, ahead of itself, occupied and preoccupied with its everyday doings and emotional practices, capable of feeling, acting on, and interpreting the meanings of its actions. Two levels to the person—the everyday practical and the underlying phenomenological—are distinguished. These levels, which are not conceptualized as linguistic structures, are also termed surface and deep (Cicourel, 1981). A circuit of selfness and self-feeling attaches the person to the world and the world to the person.

The emotional experiences of the person are lived in the company of emotional associates, in the social world of emotion. The reality of that world is not doubted, and it is taken as absolute reality by the person and his associates. The world of emotion is distinct from the everyday taken-for-granted-world and has its own symbolism.

The essence of emotion exists in the inner, self- and moral feelings the person experiences in emotional consciousness. How emotions are felt and lived in the everyday world is the next topic of discussion.

Chapter Four

Emotion as Individual Experience

Fyodor Dostoevsky, in *Crime and Punishment* (1866/1950), offers the reader a thick phenomenological description of the layers and levels of lived emotion that Raskolnikov experiences as he prepares to murder Alyona Ivanovna.

> Drawing a breath, pressing his hand against his throbbing heart, and once more feeling for the axe and setting it straight, he began softly and cautiously ascending the stairs; listening every minute. . . . He was out of breath. . . . "Am I very pale?" he wondered. "Am I not evidently agitated? . . . Had I better wait a little longer . . . till my heart leaves off thumping?"
>
> Recalling it afterwards, that moment stood out in his mind vividly, distinctly, forever; he could not make out how he had had such cunning, for his mind was as it were clouded at moments and he was almost unconscious of his body. . . .
>
> His hands were fearfully weak, he felt them every moment growing more numb and more wooden. . . . A sudden giddiness came over him.

He had not a minute more to lose. But as
soon as he had once brought the axe down, his
strength returned. . . . He was in full possession of
his faculties, free from confusion or giddiness, but
his hands were still trembling [pp. 68-69, 71, 74,
80].

Raskolnikov's lived emotion permeates his stream of consciousness. The experience comes in "scraps and shreds of
thoughts . . . swarming in his brain." His presence both outside
and inside Ivanovna's flat finds him trembling, going numb, trying to pull himself together, drawing himself up, trying to appear calm and not agitated. Within his body he trembles, his
heart throbs violently, he feels weak. Afterward he is "almost
unconscious of his body." He reveals himself to himself through
these feelings." "Am I very pale?," he asks. "Am I not evident-
ly agitated?" His very temporality as a person in the midst of
committing a crime is revealed through his emotionality. His
emotionality is both inside him, in his trembling body, and in
the act that lies in front of him, which is about to be done. It is
as if he were part of the very emotionality that is making him
emotional and out of control of himself. Yet, in order to control himself, he must move forward into the act that is making
him emotional. Finally he can stand it no longer. "He slowly
put his hand to the bell and rang." In that act he momentarily
seizes control of himself and of the act that is producing his loss
of self-control. Once he enters the flat, it is as if time and feeling had stopped for him. "He pulled the axe quite out, swung it
with both arms, scarcely conscious of himself, and almost without effort, almost mechanically, he brought the blunt side down
on her head" (p. 71). Later, leaving the scene of the murders,
"he was only dimly conscious of himself."

This description of lived emotionality reveals the four
"feel-able" structures of feeling. Raskolnikov feels the sensations of his body (his heart trembling). He feels fear and appre-
hension and doubt (intentional value feelings). He feels his overall body in a state of agitation. He has feelings for himself as a
person who is about to commit a murder ("Had I better wait a
little longer . . . ?"). These structures of feeling may be respec-

tively termed sensible feelings, intentional value feelings, feelings of the lived body, and feelings of the self and moral person.

Dostoevsky's account of Raskolnikov's feelings provides a foundation for the analysis of the structures of lived emotion, the topic of this chapter. *Lived emotion* refers to the actual emotional experiences that are felt, embodied, interpreted, and expressed by the person. This feature of emotionality has not been given detailed examination in the current literature on emotions. Scheler's (1916/1973) account of the lived body and the stratification of emotional life points in the directions my analysis will follow, as do the recent works of Scheff (1979), Hochschild (1979, 1983), Shott (1979), Charmaz (1980), Finkelstein (1980), and Kemper (1980, 1981).

The dynamic, processual elements of lived emotion are to be contrasted to "emotional abstracts," or "emotion-image ideals"—that is, to emotion in the abstract. Emotional abstracts stand midway between the knowledge of a feeling and the actual feeling of a feeling, or an emotion. An emotional abstract is the knowledge of fear, shame, guilt, anger, or embarrassment for example, as a feeling that might be felt, not the actual experiencing of such an emotion in an interactional episode (see Sartre, 1943/1978, pp. 435-436; Izard, 1977, pp. 125-126).

Preliminaries

The essence of emotionality lies in its inner moral meanings to the self of the person. These inner feelings are constantly changing, in the process of being revealed to the person. Persons and their meanings are constantly changing as well. In their feelings persons are feeling selves, having a feeling for themselves in the feeling that is felt. In having a feeling for or about something, whether that feeling is an overall state of agitation or the feeling of the heart trembling, the person has, at the same time, a self-feeling, in which the self is revealed to the person as a feeling self. "In this self-feeling a mode of becoming revealed to oneself" is made evident (Heidegger, 1975/1982, p. 132). In moral feelings the moral self-consciousness of the person is revealed. Raskolnikov revealed himself to himself as a moral, acting being capable of killing another person.

How the person lives, experiences, expresses, and interprets emotionality must be examined. Social, cultural, and physiological factors certainly influence and condition the display of emotion, but they do not lie at its inner essence. The meaning of emotionality lies in what is revealed to individuals through the feeling of their feelings.

This thesis will be explored through an examination of the following assumption: "Emotional life is characterized by an internal stratification that incorporates the structures of the person's lifeworld into a meaningful grammar of emotional expression and interpretation." This grammar can be uncovered through an inspection of the layering of emotionality, which moves outward from the physical body to the lived body and to the lifeworld that surrounds the person. These layers constitute the structures of lived emotionality that the person experiences.

Emotion's Body

The phrase *emotion's body* borrows directly from David Sudnow's *Talk's Body* (1979). The importance of the human body for the study of emotion is not disputed, for emotions are embodied experiences. What is disputed, however, are the interpretations to be brought to the study of the body. Investigators who emphasize the physiological and chemical transformations that accompany some emotional forms contribute little to a social phenomenological analysis of the emotions, for they sever the body from the lived consciousness of the person.

The lived body is owned, cared for, and dressed by the person. It is an extension of the person's presence in the world. Although it can be seen by others, it cannot be totally grasped and seen by the person. As a corporeal being, the lived body appears in the world and declares itself through the senses, the perceptions, and the streams of experience that are the person. The body is an expressive, instrumental, affective embodiment and extension of the person's inner and outer streams of experience. It consists of structures of behavior, feelings, and movements that are uniquely the person's. The body is an expressive-gestural system that receives and perceives sensory experiences and embodies and expresses those perceptions. Individual consciousness is interwoven in the world through the person's embodied conduct (Merleau-Ponty, 1968). The structure of the person's embodied conduct involves the integration of the lived body with the person's inner and outer streams of experience. The body is both a reflected-on and a taken-for-granted object in this integration.

The body, while occupying time and space, does so with meaning, for it is an extension of the person (Heidegger, 1975/ 1982, p. 203). The lived body is a temporalized spatial structure. That is, the person's spatial movements, locations, and relocations can be understood only as movements within time. The person's bodily locations in time and space are marked by the distinctions of before and after, right and left, front and back, side to side, and near to far (Heidegger, 1927/1962, p. 143). The body does not fill up space in the same way that other real, physical things do or a piece of equipment does. The person takes space *in* and determines her own locations, making room for herself as she moves about and draw things near (Heidegger, 1927/1962, p. 419). The lived body is in space but understands itself temporally and relationally.

The physical body of the person is a certain structure that has its own laws of governance. It is capable of being defined from the outside. The interior body of the person, including the glands, organs, nerve endings, and nervous system, can be seen by others but never by the person, except indirectly, as on a screen or in x rays. The interior body is the setting for the person's sensible feelings. The person's interior consciousness can be grasped and understood through reflection, but the interiority of his body can be neither seen nor so conceptualized.

The person has a circular relation with his body, for what he defines in it—a pain, a sensation—comes to take on specific localized meanings as it is interpreted. Once interpreted, the meaning of this interior thing, or process, changes. What begins as pain in the interiority of the body is defined as an illness and, if diagnosed by others, may be defined as a disease (Sartre, 1943/1978, p. 466). This may produce self-pity on the person's part (Charmaz, 1980, p. 129). For the interiority of the body to be grasped by the person, it must be understood as a fact of consciousness, both reflectively and unreflectively (Sartre, 1943/ 1978, p. 404).

Two levels of the body may be noted: (1) the body-for-the-person, as it is known physically, physiologically, and phenomenologically as the arena for lived experiences, and (2) the body-for-others, as it is known by others as an object and an ensemble of activity in the lifeworld (Sartre, 1943/1978, p. 471). The body-for-the-person is at once the original physical body of the person and a phenomenological presence in the world that embodies within a single structure the person's inner and outer streams of experience. The body-for-others is gazed upon, inspected, interpreted, and taken as an expressive extension of the person's inner phenomenological life. The person's moral claims to respect and dignity are gleaned from and determined by the appearances he makes before others (Goffman, 1959; Strauss, 1959; Stone, 1962; Maines, 1978).

The body-for-the-person provides an anchoring in the world and is a point of reference for which no other referential locus exists. (In other words, no other person can occupy the space each person's body takes up.) The person cannot stand behind herself and see herself seeing herself. As a corporeal thing, the body can present itself in manifold shapes and forms as "one and the same thing" (Heidegger, 1927/1962, pp. 124–125). That is, the body is an expressive, moving structural schema of action that embodies its own shapes, movements, and forms. It is that entity that is always immediately with the person, yet the body itself is unable to interpret any of its parts or movements, nor are the bodily senses able to convey to the person any sense of meaning or being.

The lived body is a corporeal schema for lived experience. It is a structure of lived experience, a repertoire of choreographed actions, movements, and feelings involving touching, hearing, seeing, feeling, speaking, and interpreting (Merleau-Ponty, 1968, p. 256).

The lived body is said to be carried by the person, and with a certain sense of grace, carriage, character, and style; as such it becomes a body-for-others.

This body has a worn everydayness—a manner of appearance that indicates growth, decay, decline, health, illness, cheerfulness, despondency, and presence. The person's moods and feelings are worn as extensions or expressions of her lived body. Feelings, too, have a worn everydaynesslike quality. This inhabited, everyday quality of the body is made visible through the person's expressions and actions. The person is known by others as the performer of intentional acts, not as an object, but as an ensemble of embodied action. The body-for-others is given through the intentional actions of the person.

Persons, as Plessner (1970, pp. 35-36) observes, have a threefold relation to their bodies. They *are* their bodies; they are *in* their bodies; and they are *outside* their bodies, looking in on the interior life they experience from within. The world appears to the person only through the eccentric position this threefold relation to the body affords. The person is not just a living body or only a body. A stance that reconciles this relation between having a body and being a body, from both the outside and the inside, must be developed (Plessner, 1970, p. 37). Laughter and crying are two emotional forms that break through our eccentric structures of experience. In each experience the world overwhelms us. Through laughter and tears we reestablish a relationship with that which we cannot control.

Emotion's Lived Body

The lived body is the locus of the person's feelings and presence in the lifeworld. It provides the point of reference for all lived emotional experience (Merleau-Ponty, 1968, p. 256). The lived body has a fourfold structure. First, it is a physical body for the person, known as a source of feelings, sensations, and embodied actions. Second, it is a lived presence for the person, known phenomenologically in the inner stream of consciousness. Third, it is an enacted ensemble of embodied actions for others. Fourth, it is an ensemble of moving action for the person. These four structures may be respectively termed the physical body, the lived-phenomenological body, the enacted body for others, and the enacted body for self.

The private and public bodies known by the person are not the same private and public bodies known, glimpsed, and understood by others, nor is the body that is felt by the person the same body whose experiences and actions are felt and experienced by others. The sensations that occur within my inner body are purely private and unfeelable by others; and whereas others may observe and inspect the interior workings of my body, I can seldom do so directly.

Each of the four forms of the body provides a distinctly different mode of lived emotion. As indicated earlier, these modes are (1) sensible feelings, or feelings of sensation, (2) feelings of the lived body, felt and expressed by the person, (3) intentional value feelings that are felt in the phenomenological stream and throughout the body, and (4) feelings of the self at the everyday and morally deep levels of the person.

Stratification of Lived Emotion. There is a stratification to one's emotional life that refers to the depth and level of one's feelings. This structure moves inward to the lived body and outward to the self in the world. This structure, or layering of feelings, is not static, for what occurs on one level has implications for feelings on another level. This stratification schema corresponds to the structures of one's entire emotional and personal being-in-the-world. Each of these levels of feeling will be treated in turn.

Sensible Feelings. Sensible feelings are given in particular parts of the lived body as sensations or states. They lack intentionality. Raskolnikov's heart "throbbed more and more violently." He could not stop its throbbing, just as a person cannot stop the pain in a cracked rib. Sensible feelings are related to the person in "a doubly indirect manner" (Scheler, 1916/1973, pp. 330-331). They are given as a part of the body, which is the person's, but they are not attached to the self of the person, as an intentional feeling of joy or elation would be. "It is not related to the lived body as a part of body-consciousness" (Scheler, 1916/1973, p. 331). A sensible feeling is felt, but there is no emotional remembering, no "refeeling" of the feeling, although a halo of emotional memory may surround the feeling experience. After the murder, Raskolnikov "was almost unconscious of his body." *During the emotional experience, however, the sensible feeling is acute and deeply felt in the physical and lived body.* Raskolnikov felt his hands growing more and more numb, his strength draining away. These sensible feelings were part of the lived emotional experience. Sensible feelings cannot be altered by the intentional feelings. Raskolnikov could not stop his heart from beating so violently. Sensible feelings are endured, felt during their presence, to the extent that I bring them into my inner stream of consciousness. They are, however, not mediated by intentional feelings; that is, I do not bring a feeling of pain into existence in my body. Sensible feelings appear in the lived body as a consequence of habit, routine, accident, and other factors outside my immediate stream of consciousness. However, a feeling that has frequently occurred in the person's body in connection with certain objects, situations, events, or persons may become routinized and symbolic of these external objects. For example, a person recognizes the onset of an illness by the appearance of a particular pain (Scheler, 1916/1973, pp. 257-259).

Sensible feelings are felt and given to the person through intentional focusing on the body (and its parts) as a structure of ongoing lived experience. When such intentionality occurs, the body (and its felt parts) becomes an enlivened structure of meaningful, feeling experience. Sensible feelings are not immediately lived reflectively. They may simply be experienced as a part of the person's current activity. Such feelings have their own temporal structure, which is outside the person's control (Sartre, 1943/1978, p. 437; Maines, 1983). They draw on the person's physical lived body and on his consciousness yet appear to exist somewhat independent of reflective consciousness.

When apprehended reflectively, sensible feelings are named and given objective qualities. They are "felt" in consciousness. They have their own time, seriousness, intensity, duration, internal signals, rhythms, and inner and outer meanings (Sartre, 1943/1978, pp. 436-447). Outward, conventionalized modes of expressing the feelings are given by the person, thereby rendering the happenings of her inner, private body accessible to others (Lindesmith, Strauss, and Denzin, 1978, p. 543).

Others cannot enter into a person's sensible feelings, nor can the person anticipate the feelings or share them in an immediate fashion (Scheler, 1916/1973, p. 240). These feelings can be given only as having been felt by the person. That is, they are the person's feelings. There is no "immediate 'feeling' of these feelings in others, only a [judgmental] knowledge of someone else's" feelings (Scheler, 1916/1973, p. 240). Others can, however, *reproduce* their own similar situations with the feeling and "reawaken" a "vague" continuing of the feeling in themselves. But there is no "sensible sympathy" (Scheler, 1916/1973, p. 240). Others can, through contagion, appear to take on one's sensible feeling.

Pain, Consciousness, and the Body-for-the-Person. In order for the person to act on his body and give it meaning, it must become a part of his consciousness. It must be given to consciousness through intentional focusing on the body as a structure of ongoing lived experiences. When such intentionality occurs, the body comes alive; as with a high diver, all of the body, its limbs, and their movements, and all of the person, including his thoughts and feelings, become part of a single synthetic experience. The body becomes a conscious structure, a part of the person's lived consciousness.

An examination of pain, a sensible feeling localized in the lived body, will reveal how the body-for-the-person becomes a part of the person's consciousness and will indicate additional dimensions of lived emotion in the body-for-the-person.

A person who experiences a pain in a part of his body— his eyes or his lower back or his rib cage—is already engaged in a situated activity in the lifeworld. His body is given to him as a point of departure for that activity. He may be seated reading a book, playing a round of golf, or trying to move a piece of furniture. The activity he is engaged in is given as "motionless movement across a movement in his consciousness" (Sartre, 1943/1978, p. 437). At the moment that he is acting, a pain is given. He finds that his eyes are hurting, or his back is aching, or a bruise over his rib cage pains him. The pain is indicated by and through the activity he is engaged in, and it is located in a particular part of his body. The pain is lived as a part of immediate consciousness. The pain is not immediately lived reflectively, nor is it even named in consciousness. It is simply sensed at the levels of firstness and secondness as being a part of the activity the person is currently doing. The pain is not lived by others, it is lived and experienced by the person. The pain has its own temporal structure, apparently beyond the person's control; it comes and goes at its own intervals, with its own intensity and its own levels of felt pain. The person cannot control it, although he may appear to be able to control its comings and goings by interrupting or modifying his ongoing activity. The pain, however, is not located in objective space and time. It temporalizes itself within the psychic, or lived, body. It is lived within the corporeal structure of the body and is subordinated to the total structure of the body. It is lived in the back, the eye, or the rib cage and is perceived as being a part of the person's lived experiences at the moment. It becomes a fact that must be dealt with, both in consciousness and in the body.

The pain, as illness or injury, draws on reflective and unreflective consciousness and on the person's body and activities for its own lived meanings. It exists somewhat independent of consciousness and the lived body yet requires both for its existence. In this sense it joins these two structures of experience. It has a passivity and a unity, an interiority and spontaneity, an individuality all its own (Sartre, 1943/1978, pp. 440-441). It has a melodiclike structure, with rhythms, sharp jabs, twinges, followed by lulls, dull pulsations, silences, and absences. The ensemble of twinges, feelings, and pains is given as the illness (Sartre, 1943/1978, p. 442). Across each pain the person experiences the entirety of the illness. The pains are given as a whole; the illness is purely lived as a totality. There is no distance between the pain/illness and reflection; they are united in a single experience. The presence of the pain/illness fastens in the person's consciousness and becomes a lived presence for him.

At the unreflective level, the *body* is in pain. At the reflective level, the illness is distinct from the body; the *person* is in pain. Now that the illness is named, it takes on its own existence. It comes and goes from the body at will, or so it may appear to the person. The illness becomes the person's illness and feeds on the body and consciousness. Yet it has an active passivity: It cannot be started and stopped by the person. The illness is nourished, Sartre (1943/1978, p. 443) argues, by a passive environment—namely, the person's passivity toward the occurrences in his body and his consciousness.

This passive, interior environment is the psychic body of the emotion (James, 1890/1950, vol. 2, p. 459; Sartre, 1943/1978, p. 443). When a lived emotion radiates through the person's body during an anxiety attack or in acute fear, the emotion is felt as an embodied state and may appear to have a purely bodily cause. The psychic body becomes a sounding board for the emotion (James 1890/1950, vol. 2, p. 471). The psychic body supports and records the durations and intensities of the emotion. While it is apparently passive on the face of such intense emotion, the body reverberates and builds upon the emotionality that is felt. It does not appear, however, to initiate such occurrences. It records sensations, movements, and feelings. Nor does the mind directly produce these occurrences and feelings. As with seasickness or intense nausea, every experience that is felt augments the sensations of being sick. Consciousness reveals and displays itself through the body and the mind of the person as being in the state of nausea or seasickness.

Following James (1890/1950, vol. 2, p. 459) it may be assumed that the nervous machinery is labile in one emotional direction or another, such that any emotional disturbance will engender the "particular complex of feelings of which the psychic body of the emotion consists" (James, 1890/1950, vol. 2, p. 459). The upsurge of the emotion is felt immediately in the body, whether this be in heightened blood pressure, an attack in breathing, a sudden shakiness, a loss of voice, or an overall sense of physical weakness. These sensations appear, as if magically, inside the arenas and organs of the psychic body. Emotionality is felt and experienced against these currents and sensations that move through the psychic body.

The psychic body is the person's point of reference in the world. As that world impinges on the body, the interaction between the body and the world is felt and fused in the inner stream of bodily consciousness—in the psychic body. This modality of the lived body is the perpetual basis or source of possible meaning, action, feeling, and expression for the person. For when emotionality radiates through the psychic body a new way of being-in-the-world is signaled.

The consciousness that experiences and becomes aware of illness or pain within its psychic body directs itself to those occurrences in a feeling, emotional manner. The person adopts an attitude toward the pain that is felt, perhaps hating it, enduring it, or rejoicing in its presence in her consciousness (Fagerhaugh and Strauss, 1977, pp. 92-93; Charmaz, 1980, p. 139).

The psychic body provides the materials and the substance for all the occurrences and phenomena of the mind or the psyche. This body is suffered, endured, and experienced as the contingent space wherein the emotional life of the person is experienced. Its existence reveals an indifference to the person's mental life. Yet the body creates, as Sartre (1943/1978, p. 444) states, a psychic space for itself that is under the melodic and structural organization of the mind. This body is the perpetual field of possible action for the person's inner stream of consciousness (p. 444).

The object that is reflected on through pain is illness. Pain defined as illness is distinct from consciousness. Although it appears in and through consciousness, pain remains semipermanent or constant, while consciousness changes. As a passive spontaneity that comes and goes in the person's consciousness, illness is magical (Sartre, 1943/1978, pp. 441-442). There is an uncanny animism to illness. It is given as a living thing that has its own habits. There is a special sense of recognition about illness. Unlike a lasting emotion, such as anger, which leaves objects of attention even after the feeling has been felt, when illness returns it is announced by the return of pain. This pain is then synthesized into the total experience of the pain/illness/injury syndrome that has returned. But when illness disappears, it does so entirely, unlike emotional attitudes that leave residues and intentional meanings. Illness leaves physical traces, such as scars and limps. These are not reconstituted as abstract emotional ideals like anger, fear, jealousy, or rage but, rather, appear or are remembered as particular lived feelings.

Illness that is reflected on by others (the body-for-others) may be defined as a disease. Such a determination includes, along with the pain and the illness, their causes, which can be diagnosed, treated, and cured. At the level of disease, the body becomes an object for others and is given to them in and through the disease (Sartre, 1943/1978, pp. 466-467).

To summarize: With pain, the lived body becomes the object and subject of the person's and others' consciousness. Initially pain is experienced as a part of the lived body and is located in the situated practices of the person at the time that it appears. This pain is at first private, unnamed, and known only to the person. It is lived within the total corporeal structure of the body. When it is reflected on, it becomes an emotional object that combines physical feelings of pain with emotional definitions. As a part of lived experience, pain or illness exists alongside the person's consciousness and his psychic body. It is localized in the body and lived as a particular conscious fact. It has a facticity—a realness—that is both in consciousness and in the lived body. At this level there is no distance between the feeling of the pain and the consciousness of the pain. They are united. This phenomenon that draws on the psychic body and on consciousness for its existence and meaning has magical/ animistic qualities and appears to be governed by its own laws of appearance and disappearance, duration, intensity, and quality. In this respect it has a great deal in common with emotion.

Feelings of the Lived Body. Feelings of the lived body, or lived feelings, are termed vital feelings by Scheler (1916/1973, p. 335). They cannot be reduced to sensible feelings, for they are feelings of the lived body, or the body ego, and are a part of total body consciousness (Plessner, 1970; Meinong, 1972). These feelings are captured by such labels as "nausea," "sorrow," "sadness," "hung over," "despair," "joy," or "happiness." They are, however, accompanied by complexes of sensible feelings. Raskolnikov felt forgetfulness, blankness, dreaminess, weariness, and emptiness after the murder. His lived body embodied his consciousness. Particular feelings in his body were felt as a background to his total lived feeling.

Feelings of the lived body express the minded intentionality of the person, and in them the person feels a peculiar value content in her lifeworld (Scheler, 1916/1973, p. 339). She feels dread, nausea, joy, or sorrow in and through her body, and this feeling permeates her affairs with emotional associates. Such feelings are not localized in the body or in a particular part of the person's consciousness.

James Joyce (1976, pp. 395–396) offers the following account of Stephen Dedalus about to vomit: "He flung the blankets from him madly to free his head and neck. . . . He sprang from the bed, the reeking odor pouring down his throat, clogging and revolting his entrails. Air! The air of heaven! He stumbled towards the window, groaning and almost fainting with sickness. At the washstand a convulsion seized him within; and, clasping his cold forehead wildly, he vomited profusely in agony. When the fit had spent itself he walked weakly to the window and lifting the sash, sat in a corner of the embrasure and leaned his elbow upon the sill. . . . He prayed." Sensible feelings fuse with a total state of mind, synthesizing the sensations of the lived body into a single, drawn-out act of vomiting. The self of Stephen, including the attitudes he holds toward himself, are expressed in the actions Joyce describes. This emotional experience radiates throughout his inner and outer streams of experience.

The embodied feelings of the lived body express an orientation to the interactional stream of experience. Hence the feelings of the lived body are accessible to others. They furnish the foundations for socially shared feelings (Scheler, 1916/1973, pp. 338–339). Others are able to share vicariously in the person's feelings. This is not true of sensible feelings.

In the feelings of the lived body there are genuine recollections of feelings, whereas with sensible feelings there are only feelings of recollection (Scheler, 1916/1973, p. 339). The person, however, is not able to reproduce the feeling that was previously felt; what is generated is a new feeling, or moment of emotionality.

The meanings and values of events and persons that surround the person are given through lived feelings. In the anticipation of an event or object, the person feels a feeling before she is given the phenomenon; this is not true for sensible feelings. Before entering Alyona Ivanovna's flat, Raskolnikov felt the meaning of the event that was about to occur. His pulse quickened. He was out of breath. He felt pale and agitated. He was worried about how he would appear to Ivanovna. Her emotional meaning and the emotional meanings of the act he was about to commit were given in these prefeelings that radiated through his lived body. Lived feelings point to what is about to come, and as with Stephen, they may generate, in a self-fulfilling fashion, sensible feelings, which reinforce and quicken the person's feelings of anticipation or revulsion. In Scheler's terms, they are spatial and temporal feelings of distance. Lived feelings communicate an emotional definition of the situation that moves outward and encompasses those who are in the person's presence. (See "Enacted Emotionality" in the Introduction to Part Three.")

Intentional Value Feelings. Intentional value feelings are given as intentional objects of feelings and are independent of subjective emotional states (Schutz, 1968, p. 163). In an emotional feeling the person feels a value quality. Intentional value feelings anticipate (or remain after) actual emotional experience. Feelings of sadness, anger, or joy remain while subjective emotional states, sensible feelings, and lived feelings change. Value qualities are not feeling states, although a value or a meaning can be given in feeling. Value qualities are external to actual lived emotional experiences. Such emotions as anger, fear, resentment, love, hatred, and loathing are intentional value feelings that remain after the specific experience of anger, fear, resentment, love, hatred, or loathing. (Some have termed these "sentiments"; see Shibutani, 1961; Turner, 1970.) Value feelings are part of the person's interpretive framework and exist as orientations toward the world, independent of specific interactional experiences (see Chapter Six). Intentional value feelings are moral values that the person holds toward herself and her sensible, lived, and inner moral feelings. All feelings are given intentional meaning, if reflected on by the person. The feeling of a feeling, however, must be distinguished from the meanings given to the feeling, for a pain can be suffered or enjoyed, depending on the meaning it is given.

Intentional value feelings are felt in the phenomenological stream of consciousness, not in the lived body immediately and directly. Others can feel and hold the same value feelings as the person. They are feelings toward something objective, outside the body—namely, values or meaning states. Emotion's body has associated with it certain recurring intentional value themes that refer to conditions and forms of emotionality, such as being attractive, not being in pain, or being in control of one's emotions. These are socially shared value conceptions of "intended" emotionality. These kinds of feelings are not given as factual states of the body, as in the location of a particular pain. Rather, they arise from meanings directed by the person to himself as he is located in the circuit of selfness in the world. Intentional value feelings intend their own objects— namely, values (Scheler, 1916/1973, p. 257-263). Accordingly, they are capable of accomplishment or fulfillment. That is, a person may intend to feel a particular way, and this intention may be given to her by others. On grief Durkheim observes: "One weeps, not simply because he is sad, but because he is forced to weep. It is a ritual attitude which he is forced to adopt out of respect for custom . . . independent of his affective state. Moreover, this obligation is sanctioned by mythical or social penalties. . . . Therefore in order to square himself with usage, a man sometimes forces tears to flow by artificial means" (1912/1973, p. 43). Raskolnikov attempted to intentionally control his sensible and lived feelings as he climbed the steps to Ivanovna's flat and was barely able to do so.

Because values can be intentionally felt and accomplished, or fulfilled in the person's inner and outer streams of consciousness, they are "in principle understandable" and can be vicariously experienced and reproduced by others (Scheler, 1916/ 1973, p. 258). Sensible feelings and lived feelings cannot be so reproduced, although another can imaginatively reconstruct the memory of a pain or remember the feeling of an experience of nausea or deep resentment or hatred. Intentional value feelings

—the feeling of sorrow or of ressentiment—can be understood by others, while sensible feelings of the lived body are subject only to observations by others (Scheler, 1916/1973, p. 257).

The value qualities in value-affair complexes promote certain emotional reactions or feelings, which are expressed in the value that is felt. These complexes of meaning and value form constellations of understanding that can be grasped by the person and by others, independent of particular emotional experiences. Thus, if a value demand is unfulfilled, a person may suffer. He may be sad because he "cannot be happy about an event to the degree that its value deserves" (Scheler, 1916/1973, p. 258) or because he cannot be as sad as the death of a friend demands.

Intentional value feelings point to only those experiences in which the value that is intended can and does appear. This feeling may come on the person through reflection that objectifies what has been felt—sorrow, fear, sadness, anger, embarrassment. *Feelings that receive values are intentional feelings* (Scheler, 1916/1973, p. 259). Values are the basic phenomena of emotional intuition and understanding. The ultimate thesis of phenomenology, that "there is an interconnection between the essence of an object and the essence of intentional experience," is given in the examination of these feelings (Scheler, 1916/ 1973, p. 265). The values that are felt by the person cannot be explicitly created or destroyed through experience. They exist independent of actions.

Intentional value feelings are feelings in the presence of a norm, or a value. The norm or value that defines a feeling, as when a person suffers grief at the loss of a loved one or feels joy, depression, or anger, is personalized by the person. That is, the value is fitted to the peculiarities of the person's emotional situation. However, the norm always lies ahead of the person, and any actualization of the norm is surpassed by its ideal. The value, or ideal meaning, of the intended value feeling is out of the person's reach—if not unattainable, certainly unexpressible in concrete, lived emotional experience. Sensible feelings and feelings of the lived body cannot capture and perfectly reflect these feelings.

The very living of a feeling annihilates the ideal that is intended. The suffering, rage, or sorrow that is felt and lived is never exactly what is felt and embodied in the ideal, or value, that is sought in the feeling. Value feelings are always ahead of the person, yet lived in the present. Past refeelings of them can never fulfill the ideal that is sought. And when people speak of the feeling they feel, what they speak of is never exactly what is felt. "What we call 'noble' or 'good' or 'true' suffering and what moves us is the suffering which we read in the faces of others, better yet in portraits, in the face of a statue, in a tragic mask. It is suffering which has *being*" (Sartre, 1943/1978, pp. 141-142). The suffering that has being is frozen in a fixed expression that embodies the value ideal which individuals internalize and attempt to reach in their own lived emotional experience. The feelings expressed in the portrait, in the voice of another, in a face, in the lines of a singer's song, are presented, seen, and heard by individuals as objective statements and realizations (expressions) of their own feelings. These expressions did not await the person's coming or feeling in order to be felt and expressed. They express the person's feelings better than the person can express them. These expressions are pure; they do not suffer from extraneous detail, flawed intentions, intoxication, or lapses in memory. These idealized expressions are not discolored with imperfect, marred, interrupted experiences of the feeling.

We are haunted by our intentional value feelings. What we feel and express is never adequate. The ideal always eludes us. We suffer our idealized feelings in silence, yet chatter away incessantly and inwardly about the feeling and ourselves. We brood over a feeling, we relive it, drink to it, mull it over, replay it. We reexperience the situation in which it occurred and play out alternative ways we might have acted. We make plans for the future, anticipating what we will say if the object of our feeling should offer us a second opportunity. We endeavor to get even with the person who has hurt our feelings and will do so by hurting the other's feelings.

Seeking an external mode of expression for our internal feelings, we act, at times, violently, passionately, clumsily, with

rage, tenderness, bitterness, kindness, or even envy. These in-
articulate actions and emotional expressions are like broad,
heavy brushstrokes that aim to delicately express our inner feelings. We find that it is better to feel and express our feelings in
silence.

The meaning of the self that feels is *value*. Value has the
double characteristic of being and not being (Sartre, 1943/1978,
pp. 143-144). That is, value does not have to be present in reality in order to exist as that which is possible. Values are possibles. The reality of an intended value lies ahead of the person,
just as persons lie ahead of themselves, as actions and expressions yet to be undertaken and accomplished. The person exists
as possibilities.

Every value-oriented act is a surpassing of what has been
and a moving forward to what has not yet been, "a wrenching
away from the person's own being toward—" (Sartre, 1943/
1978, p. 144). Emotion, feeling, and value haunt every act of
the person, for the person is free to value and to feel and also to
value or not value what is felt (Mayfield, 1982).

Feelings of the Self and the Moral Person. Purely self- and
moral feelings of the person (psychic, or mental, feelings) originate in the inner stream of consciousness—in the ego, or self, at
the everyday and phenomenological levels. They do not have to
first pass through the givenness of the lived body, as sensible or
lived feelings. They arise out of internal self-reflection, reflection on the self. Self-feelings make the selfhood of the person
an intentional object of value consciousness. The person intentionally draws his focus of attention into and onto himself as a
distinct object in the inner and outer streams of experience. A
quality or value of the person is felt in self- and moral feelings,
and these feelings may permeate the lived body.

Moral feelings permeate all features of the inner stream of
experience and are evident in the person's manner and comportment in the world-at-hand. They are distinguished from purely
self- or psychic feelings, for they are not states of consciousness.
In true bliss and despair, and even in cases of serenity and
"peace of mind," all ego states are absolute feelings, not conditioned by external value complexes (Scheler, 1916/1973, p.

344). The person's entire being radiates with moral feelings, and these feelings are not conditioned by the presence or absence of particular classes of emotional associates. The total person is given in these feelings, and there is a charisma, or presence, to the person. These feelings take root in the value nature of the person. They are not feelings that can be directly produced by the person, nor do they derive from particular values, lived emotional experiences, or sensible feelings as such (Scheler, 1916/ 1973, p. 344). Moral feelings join the person with others. They embody the connection that obtains between the person and her society. As Chapter Three suggested, these values define the moral worth of the person.

The Feelings in Summary. Four classes, or modes, of feeling have been identified. They have the following defining characteristics.

Sensible feelings are extended and located in the body. Others cannot share in them—they are private. They lack intentionality. They are part of the body but not of the self. They cannot be refelt or altered by the person. They can become symbolic tokens of other events occurring in the person's inner and outer streams of experience. They have their own temporal structure, and they draw on the person's body and consciousness for their existence. Conventionalized expressions of their presence in the body are developed. Examples include the feelings of pain and hunger.

Lived feelings (feelings of the lived body) express a particular value content or meaning found in the world by the person. They are not located in a particular part of the person's body but are given in the total extension of the lived body as a unitary expression or experience. The meanings of events are given to the person through lived feelings, in advance of their actual occurrence; lived feelings point to what is coming. They are experienced as embodied bodily states, associated with particular states of consciousness and with the person's current location in the world-at-hand. Examples include fatigue, nausea, sadness, exhaustion, and joy or happiness.

Intentional value feelings are given as intentional objects of feeling, independent of subjective emotional states. They cannot be modified by specific emotional experiences; that is, values are external to emotionality. They are moral values that individuals hold toward their sensible and lived feelings. They are felt in the phenomenological stream of consciousness, not directly in the lived body. The experiencing of intentional values generates experiences that others can share and participate in—such values have public expressions. They are idealized feelings that are seldom perfectly felt or realized by the person. The values that lie behind intentional feelings are personalized by the person. Examples include the feeling of sorrow at a funeral and the feeling of anger at another after a particular instance of anger has occurred.

Self- and moral feelings originate in the inner stream of consciousness and in the circuit of selfness that connects the person to the lifeworld. They are typically not first given in and through the body as sensible feelings or lived feelings. They arise out of intentional reflection on the self as an object of consciousness—for example, shame. Moral values of the person are felt in these feelings. Moral (or spiritual) feelings encompass the totality of the person and are not given through body states, external values, or sensible feelings. Examples include despair, bliss, serenity, and awe.

Conclusions

Four levels of the body have been distinguished: the physical body, the lived phenomenological body, the enacted body-for-the-person, and the enacted body-for-others. These four levels correspond to the four types of feeling just summarized. Directly related to the four types of feeling are the three modes of emotional being: the inner stream of consciousness, the person's embodied presence in the interactional stream, and the lived body. Several conclusions can be drawn, as follows.

A firm distinction must be maintained between sensible feelings and all other feelings that the person may feel and experience. At least five distinct vocabularies are needed for the modes of lived emotion: (1) a language for bodily sensations and feelings, including pain and discomfort, (2) a language that refers to feelings about those feelings, including quality, quantity, and desirability (for example, "a great deal of painful pain"), (3) a language that refers to the feelings of the lived phenomenological body, including such terms as *exhaustion, fatigue, exhilaration,* and *satiation,* (4) a language that refers to feelings of the self, including disgust, shame, self-defeat, and pride, (5) a language that refers to the moral person—for example, *serenity, graciousness, character, élan, spirit, presence.* Accordingly, when speaking of emotion and feelings, it is necessary to distinguish clearly the mode and form of emotion and feeling that one refers to.

The term *lived emotion* might properly be confined to the feelings of the lived body and feelings of the self and the moral person, while the term *intentional value feelings* reference emotional abstractions, emotional ideals, not lived emotion as such (Sartre, 1943/1978, pp. 435-436).

Intentional value feelings appear to provide continuity and organization to the person's emotional and personal life, both with self and with others. These value feelings infuse, animate, and haunt lived emotions. Self- and moral feelings lie at the inner core of the person and his relations with others. Emotional attachment or grounding in the world-at-hand, whether deep or surface, fleeting or enduring, is rooted in the emotional situation and in the person's intentional value feelings, self-feelings, and moral feelings.

Emotional understanding, or the sharing in another's emotional experience, is confined to experiences that are given in one's outer stream of experience. Private sensations, sensible feelings, intentional value feelings in the abstract, and immediate feelings of the lived body cannot be immediately communicated to or publicly and easily shared with others. The largest proportion of the person's emotional experience, even if reflected on, is not made available to others. This is so because (1) others are not present when the person experiences them or (2) they are largely ineffable and unexplainable or (3) they reside inside the lived body and the inner stream of experience and are experienced as feelings of the lived body or (4) they are experienced and expressed silently by the person.

Chapter Five

Emotion as Social Experience

In the previous chapter I analyzed the stratification of emotional life. The point of departure was the individual and lived emotional experience. Analysis began by working outward from the physical body, through the lived phenomenological body, to the world of intentional value feelings, self-feelings, and the feelings of the moral person.

The sociality (Mead, 1982a) of lived emotion must now be considered. This raises the problem of emotional intersubjectivity. The following passage from Thomas Wolfe sets the central features of emotional intersubjectivity, the topic of this chapter.

> "Give him the stamps," Gant said.
> Mr. Crocker came rocking forward behind the counter, with the prim careful look that now was somewhat like a smile. "It was just that—" he said.
> "Give him the stamps," Gant said, and threw some coins down on the counter.

Mr. Crocker rocked away and got the stamps. He came rocking back. "I just didn't know—" he said.

The stonecutter took the stamps and gave them to the boy. And Mr. Crocker took the coins.

"It was just that—" Mr. Crocker began again, and smiled.

Gant cleared his throat: "You never were a father," he said.

"You never knew the feeling of a father, or understood the feelings of a child; and that is why you acted as you did. But a judgment is upon you. God has cursed you. He has afflicted you. He has made you lame and childless as you are—and lame and childless, miserable as you are, you will go to your grave and be forgotten!" [Wolfe, 1982, pp. 16-17].

Wolfe is suggesting that in order for two persons (the lost boy and Mr. Crocker) to enter into the same emotional point of view regarding a common object (the stamps), one of them must have participated in a field of experience shared by the other (being a child or being the father of a child). Lacking that commonality, no emotional understanding on the part of either party is possible.

Characteristics of Emotional Intersubjectivity

Emotional intersubjectivity is the interactional appropriation of another's emotionality such that one feels one's way into the feelings and intentional feeling states of the other. Emotional intersubjectivity is an interactional process that joins two or more persons into a common, or shared, emotional field of experience. Because the concept is central to the discussion that follows, it requires careful dissection.

At least since Husserl's formulations, intersubjectivity has been understood as the knowledge one subject has of another or of another's conscious states (Husserl, 1913/1962, pp. 149-152; Scheler, 1913/1970, pp. 5-7; Sartre, 1943/1978, pp. 301-400; Merleau-Ponty, 1962, pp. 346-365, 1963; 1973b, p. 49; Schutz,

1964, p. 70; Natanson, 1970, pp. 27-46). *Subjectivity* refers to a subject's knowledge of her own mental states. The *inter-* in *intersubjectivity* refers to the shared knowledge that exists between two persons. Merleau-Ponty's double phrase "The Intertwining—the Chiasm" perhaps better reflects what is intended (Merleau-Ponty, 1968, pp. 130-155, 214, 263). This intertwining twists, intermingles, inverts, reverses, crosses, and leads to an intersection of two emotional fields of experience into a single, indissoluble synthesis of two embodied persons *in* emotionality. The "rays" (Husserl) of the other's emotionality penetrate one's fields of experience. One's own emotionality, in turn, is reflected from those rays back to oneself and to the other. Emotional intersubjectivity refers to this reflective intertwining of rays of emotionality from one person to another and back again.

Intersubjective knowledge, knowledge that is known by two parties in a situation, is often assumed to derive from their common stock of knowledge and their taken-for-granted assumptions about themselves and the world (see Schutz, 1962, p. 116). My concern here is not with proving the existence of an alter ego intersubjectively. Rather, my appropriation of the term in connection with emotionality is intended to refer to (1) what two parties know about each other's emotionality, (2) how they gain that knowledge, and (3) how they act on it so as to (4) bring themselves into a shared or not shared field of emotional experience. Glaser and Strauss's (1967) concept of "awareness context" is close to what I have in mind, as is Mead's concept of sociality. (See below.) As I intend the term, *emotional intersubjectivity* refers to the cognitive and emotional alignment of selves in a common field of emotional experience.

Given these considerations, the following points are basic. First, this process involves the "pairing" or "joining" of two or more embodied selves into an intersubjectively constituted situation (Merleau-Ponty, 1973b, p. 49). That is, the emotionally intersubjective situation is objective, observable, taken for granted, and there for all selves to participate in.

Second, sociality (Mead, 1982a; Natanson, 1970, pp. 33-34, 47-67) lies at the base of the intersubjectively constituted situation. Selves take each other's attitudes, appropriate each other's point of view, engage in interior dialogues with each other, rehearse actions and social acts, judge their actions from the standpoint of each other, and make each other's experience their own. In turn, they share and engage in common fields of experience, thereby producing a social object that is common to both of them. The meaning of the selves that interact is located in the circuit of selfness that attaches each self to the other in the interactional field of experience.

Mead's principle of sociality (1936, pp. 65, 85; 1938, pp. 654-655; 1982a, p. 184) suggests that in reflective social conduct "the self as a social object enters the field of adjustment on the same basis as other objects" (1982a, pp. 184-185). Applied to emotionality, the principle of emotional sociality suggests that the self as an emotional social object enters the field of experience on the same basis of emotionality as does the other person's self. (See discussion below.)

Third, in emotional intersubjectivity the other reveals the person to himself, as a feeling subject in an intersubjectively constituted, interactional field of experience. The other's emotionality becomes a social fact, or social object, for the person. That emotionality is then acted on and given meaning (Mead, 1982b, pp. 9-13). Emotionality, like language, is not an entity. It exists only in and between feeling, thinking, acting, speaking/ interacting subjects (Merleau-Ponty, 1973b, p. 97). Consider Sartre's (1943/1978, p. 455) account of the perception and interpretation of anger: "These frowns, this redness, this stammering, this slight trembling of the hands, these downcast looks which seem at once timid and threatening—these do not *express* anger; they *are* the anger. But this point must be clearly understood. In itself a clenched fist is nothing and means nothing. But also we never perceive a *clenched fist*. We perceive a man who in a certain situation clenches his fist. This meaningful act considered in connection with the past and with possibles and understood in terms of the synthetic totality 'body in situation' *is* the anger." Sartre might have added that the anger that is seen in the other is also seen and felt as a part of the situation for the perceiving person. It becomes part of her anger or non-anger. She defines herself in relation to the anger that is perceived in the other.

Fourth, the sociality is emotional. Hence the term *emotional intersubjectivity*. That is, the social interaction that draws individuals together is grounded in the world of emotionality. That world, as argued in Chapter Three, is real, problematic, and experienced in ways that involve the emotion-taking attitudes. In such interactions individuals call out in themselves, and act on, emotional definitions and feelings of self. The principle of emotional sociality makes emotionality a processual social object that is drawn to and into the feeling selves of the interactional participants. Like other social objects in the situation, emotionality takes on new and different meanings as the interactants adjust and redefine their respective lines of action toward each another.

Fifth, emotional intersubjectivity, as the definition implies, refers to the problem of how we meaningfully enter into another's emotional world. Various terms, including *sympathy, empathy, imagination, role-taking ability, sympathetic understanding, introspection,* and *Verstehen,* have been used to describe all or part of this process (see Husserl, 1913/1962; Scheler, 1913/1970, 1916/1973; Cooley, 1902/1956; Engell, 1981; Merleau-Ponty, 1962, 1973b; Weber, 1946; Natanson, 1963, 1970). These terms, however, apply to only a part of the process of emotional intersubjectivity. Further, they are often used in reference to understanding or interpretation generally and not to the understanding of emotionality in particular (Engell, 1981, pp. 143-160; Abrams, 1953, pp. 53-56). These seemingly parallel terms will not be employed in this discussion.

Sixth, consequently, although emotional intersubjectivity can produce emotional understanding, sympathy for another, or an empathetic projection into another's feelings, it often does not. The emotional understanding and interpretation of another that emerge from the intersubjectively shared emotional situation may be complete or partial, erroneous or correct, suspected or pretended, spurious, reciprocal, or one-sided. One may also deliberately conceal one's feelings or fake an understanding of another's emotionality. Emotional understanding may be imitated, shared, or wholly absent in an interactional episode, as in the passage quoted from Wolfe earlier. Indeed, the absence of emotional understanding may be all that interactants understand about their recent transactions with another.

Seventh, because emotional intersubjectivity is an interactional process, two related problems are raised. The first concerns the question "How do individuals 'know' and 'understand' the emotional experiences, utterances, and actions of another?" The world of daily emotional life, though not wholly private, is not entirely public, yet individuals do enter into and interpret their own and others' subjective emotional experiences (Scheler, 1913/1970, p. 229; Schutz, 1962, p. 176). Merleau-Ponty (1973b, p. 45) comments: "We see, we perceive the feelings of others (not only their expression); we perceive them with the same certitude as our own feelings . . . it is impossible to confuse in other people the redness of shame with that of anger, heated arousal, etc. Perception takes us a long way into the comprehension of other people."

Emotional intersubjectivity describes the forms that these interpretations of the other's emotionality take and their consequences for action. Clearly the other's body must be taken as a field of expression of the other's inner experiences if one is to act on one's emotionality. Furthermore, one must be able to call out in oneself emotional attitudes and feelings that connect with the expressed emotionality of the other. In this regard Scheler's (1913/1970, p. 229) term *emotional evidence* is important. Merleau-Ponty (1973b, p. 47) observes: "One cannot become the other *really*, but one can become him intentionally. One can reach others through all the expressive manifestations by which they give themselves to us." The emotional manifestations and evidence present in the expressions of the other are the other's emotionality for us, in part at least.

The second question raised when emotional intersubjectivity is treated processually is "How are individuals interactionally affected by what they 'know' about or observe of another's emotionality?" Individuals do share feelings, imitate the feelings of others, infect others with their feelings, and enter into common emotional bonds and relationships with others. They inflict and force their emotions onto others, asking or forcing others to understand them. They also define themselves and their feelings in terms of the feelings of others. In these and other ways individuals take their information about the emotionality of others and draw those understandings into their own emergent emotionality and feelings of self. In such actions they join into the other's field of emotional experience. *How* these various forms of "emotional understanding" and emotional interaction are possible is a major problem this chapter examines. These are the problems raised by the concept of emotional intersubjectivity.

If emotions are interpersonal phenomena, then emotional intersubjectivity must be seen as a process that fundamentally shapes the fields of experience that draw individuals into one another's emotional presence. The *process* of emotional intersubjectivity structures the modes and forms of emotional understanding that emerge during the interactions of two or more persons. That understanding, in turn, shapes the nature of the emotionality felt by the person. This emotionality reveals individuals to themselves as particular kinds of persons, which will vary depending on the emotional intersubjectivity and emotional understanding that are experienced. They may feel self-pride, self-mortification, embarrassment, anger, rage, fear, or self-disappointment. This field of experience has both an inner and an outer side. The inner side of the field comes at the person, engulfing him in the emergent emotionality of the situation. This inner side is uniquely felt by each person. The outer side of the field is shared by both parties. They are objectively lodged in the field and in the presence of each other. They are both emotionally attached to the situation. Their selves are revealed through this attachment and through the emotionality that each feels and expresses to the other.

The temporality of this field pushes forward on the basis of understandings, misunderstandings, tacit assumptions, agreements, and checked, hesitating moves made by each party. The immediate emotionality that is lived cannot be overturned or reversed, although the intersubjective ground on which the interaction unfolds may be reconstituted, redefined, or even changed in midcourse. As that ground is changed, the field of experience changes. Shifts in understanding and meaning alter the form of emotional understanding that is experienced. In turn, the emotionality of the feeling selves changes.

This point may be grasped by returning to the end of the interaction excerpted above between the stonecutter and his son. Wolfe (1982, p. 17) describes the son's feelings as he leaves Mr. Crocker's store with his father:

> The stonecutter, the breath still hoarse in him, left the store, still holding the boy tightly by the hand. Light came again into the day.
> They walked across the Square, the sheeted spray of iridescent light swept out on them, the horse swizzled at the water-trough, and "Well, son," the stonecutter said . . . "be a good boy."
> And he trod his own steps then with his great stride and went back again into his shop.
> The lost boy stood by the square, hard by the porch of his father's shop.
> "This is Time," thought Grover. "Here is the square, here is my father's shop, and here I am."
> And light came and went and came again—but now not quite the same as it had done before. . . . He could not say, he did not know through what transforming shadows life had passed within that quarter hour. He only knew that something had been lost—something forever gained.

In the moment of reflective self-appraisal, the feeling self redefines itself, finding that its feelings and inner meanings lie in the fields of emotional interaction which it has produced and to which it has been a party.

Six categories of emotional intersubjectivity will be dissected. These are (1) feelings in common, or a community of feeling, (2) fellow-feeling, (3) emotional infection, (4) emotional identification, (5) shared emotionality, and (6) spurious emotionality.

These forms of emotional interaction are developed in Scheler's *Nature of Sympathy* (1913/1970, pp. 8-36), a general historical review of the idea of sympathy—"how the individual feels for other people . . . how he identifies with others" (Engell, 1981, pp. 143, 390). In this work Scheler reviews Lipps's theory of empathy, Freud's theory of identification, Bergson's theory of sympathy, Nietzsche's theory of fellow-feeling, and Schopenhauer's theory of pity. Engell (1981) offers an extremely useful review of the theories of sympathy, empathy, and the imagination that came to full development among the English Romantics, including Coleridge, Wordsworth, Hazlitt, Blake, Shelley, and Keats. Theories of empathic understanding were crucial to the development of Romantic literature, but they also occupied a central place in the theories of society and moral conduct of Hobbes, Leibniz, Locke, Hume, Kant, Adam Smith, Schelling, Schiller, Goethe, Fichte, and Herder. Spencer and Cooley developed in greater detail the position that emotionality is a key to understanding. G. H. Mead shifts this position considerably in his emphasis on the cognitive processes that underlie the taking of another's attitude. The more cognitive elements of understanding and interpretation find fuller expression in the works of M. Weber and A. Schutz.

In this work I take the position that emotionality is a basic component of meaning and understanding. This point will be developed in this chapter and in fuller detail in Chapter Eight. But first the problem of emotional understanding must be further analyzed.

Emotional Understanding

Emotional understanding, as indicated earlier, is an intersubjective process requiring that one person enter into the field of experience of another and experience for herself the same or similar experiences experienced by another. The subjective interpretation of another's emotional experience from one's own standpoint is central to emotional understanding. Shared and sharable emotionality lie at the core of what it means to understand and meaningfully enter into the emotional experiences of another.

Two terms are central to this process of emotional understanding: *interpretation* and *shared experience*. Interpretation precedes understanding and has as its meaning the phenomenological description of another's actions within a hermeneutic perspective that is meaningful to the person (see Heidegger, 1927/1962, 1977, 1975/1982; Gadamer, 1976; Ricoeur, 1981). Interpretation involves dissection of a unit of experience into meaningful segments that have an experiential bearing within the person's own frame of reference. The actions and conduct that are interpreted must be given a commonsenseness that renders the experience both plausible and understandable. Such an attribution requires a sense of immediate identification with the other and his actions. The person must realize that even though the experiences did not occur exactly as she herself has experienced them in the past, those differences are irrelevant for interpretive purposes (see Garfinkel, 1967).

Persons seeking to understand and interpret the emotional (and nonemotional) experience of another must make the other's experience their own and experience that experience from their own standpoint (Mead, 1982a). If they cannot appropriate the other's experience into their own experiential frame of reference, they are seeing the experience, if they see it at all, from the other's point of view, not their own. The other's experience must call out in the person experiences similar to those she has experienced. It is only on the basis of seeing the other's experience from one's own standpoint, as one takes the other's experience into one's own field, and interpreting that experience in terms of one's own experiences, that full emotional understanding and interpretation and intersubjectivity are possible. That is why shared and sharable emotionality are so crucial to full emotional understanding. The merging of shared experiences into a new, sharable field of experience joins two persons together.

If the person is not able to bring the other's experience into her own frame of reference, one-sided, empty, spurious emotional understanding may be produced. Such circumstances produce, at best, empathy, "projecting how another person feels and then identifying with that 'false' projection," or sympathy, "the imaginative feeling of identification with another human being" (Engell, 1981, pp. 157-158).

The emotionality that is shared or entered into may be directly coproduced by two or more persons, such that together they participate in the same or similar emotional fields of experience. Or, on learning of the experiences of another, a person may reproduce, reperform, or preperform (in anticipation) the emotional acts that generate the emotional experience of the other he wishes to understand. Such reproductions or preproductions of action and experience produce in a weakened or remembered form the experiences of the other. On the basis of these productions the person can vicariously participate in the other's emotionality.

These productions of another's feelings or emotional experience do not imply or require participation in the other's experience (Scheler, 1913/1970, p. 9; Cooley, 1902/1956, p. 138; Smith, 1892). It is possible to understand another's emotional experiences without participating in them. One has merely to produce in oneself the feelings and experiences of the other. Vicarious, or indirect participation can produce understanding if one takes the other's experiences as a point of reference for one's interpretive actions. As noted above, one must be aware of the other's body and self in the emotional situation. One must also have a stock of knowledge and a language that is shared or sharable with the other. The basis of a reciprocity of perspective must exist or be generated (Schutz, 1964, pp. 120-121). Without these conditions, emotional intersubjectivity and emotional understanding are not possible.

On these conditions Scheler remarks: "But one who 'understands' the mortal terror of a drowning man has no need at all to *undergo* such terror" (1913/1970, p. 11). In the process of understanding, what is understood need not be experienced as real (Scheler, 1913/1970, p. 11). The person merely has to imagine its realness for himself.

Knowing or being aware of the other and having an experience similar to his do not necessarily produce emotional understanding. One can, in "emotional infection" and "emotional contagion," duplicate the behaviors and outer experiences of another without meaningfully entering into his inner field of emotionality, as in the Jonestown mass deaths of 1978.

These two exceptions considered, insight into the experiences of others can be simply given when their bodies are treated as fields of expression of their inner emotional experiences. On the basis of such emotional evidence, the other's joy, fear, shame, anger, or embarrassment can be perceived in his voice, his facial expressions, his gestures, and his language—in short, in and through his embodied presence in the interactional situation (Ekman, 1973). "It is *in* the blush that we perceive shame, *in* laughter joy" (Scheler, 1913/1970, p. 10).

Emotional Versus Cognitive Understanding

However, it is not through emotion that emotional understanding first appears. On this point the argument sides with Mead (1982a) and against Cooley (1902/1956) and the Romantic theorists of imagination (Engell, 1981; Abrams, 1953). Rather, the other's embodiment of lived emotion, his expression of intentional value feelings and feelings of self must be given, visualized, interpreted, labeled, and only then understood. Location in the field of embodied experience precedes emotional understanding.

Once in a field of sharable experience with the other, the principle of emotional sociality suggests that emotional understanding emerges as a social object that is a part of the interaction that attaches the selves of the participants to each other. Emotional understanding is a process. Its meanings change and shift as interaction proceeds. It enters the interaction process as a social object.

Emotionality is the basic feature of emotional understanding. That is, as understanding moves along emotional lines, emotionality is built into the interaction process. Self-feelings become attached to the selves that are interpreting and understanding each other. In this way understanding is filtered through emotion. As that emotionality is felt in the bodies of the interactants, a sense of "realness" and "authenticity" is experienced. Emotional understanding ratifies itself as it is felt. It is these felt feelings that give emotional understanding a depth of feeling that is not present in purely cognitive interactions, understandings, and interpretations.

Emotionality, then, is crucial to a form of understanding and interpretation that may be termed emotional or lived. Lived, or emotional, understanding is to be contrasted to purely cognitive understanding, which is devoid of feeling and emotionality. On this major point it is necessary to recall James (1890/1950, vol. 2, p. 452), who said: "What kind of an emotion of fear would be left if the feeling neither of quickened heartbeats nor of shallow breathing, neither of trembling lips nor of weakened limbs, neither of goose-flesh nor of visceral stirrings, were present, it is quite impossible for me to think."

Applied to understanding, James's remark might become "What kind of understanding of another's fear, anger, self-shame, elation, or guilt would be left if the self-feelings of inner fear and trembling, excited breath, clenched fist, or silent inner laughter were absent?" It would be a shallow, empty understanding, devoid of the self-feelings that draw interactants together in a shared field of common emotionality.

One must be able to grasp and inwardly feel for oneself the emotionality felt by the other. These inner feelings give authenticity and "realness" to the other's experiences. They are felt and sensed in a "shock of recognition" that attaches the two selves to each other. The other presents an experience that is his. As he tells his story, the listener feels her skin move, her brows knit, her pulse quickens, a nod of recognition appears to move her head, a smile of "knowing" crosses her face, tears perhaps come to her eyes, a tension moves through her shoulders. In these and in other physiological sensations of the lived body, she feels and understands the experience that is being presented by the other. These felt sensations fill out the purely cognitive meanings of the other's account and give it a grounding in lived, undeniably relevant emotional experience.

William James grappled with this point in his treatment of the subtler emotions. He states:

> In all cases of intellectual or moral rapture we find that, unless there be coupled a bodily reverberation of some kind with mere thought of the object and cognition of its quality; unless we ac-

tually laugh at the neatness of the demonstration or witticism; unless we thrill at the case of justice, or tingle at the act of magnanimity; our state of mind can hardly be called emotional at all. It is in fact a mere intellectual perception of how certain things are to be called—neat, right, witty, generous, and the like. Such a judicial state of mind as this is to be classed among awarenesses of truth; it is a *cognitive act.* As a matter of fact, however, the moral and intellectual cognitions hardly do exist thus unaccompanied. The bodily sounding-board is at work, as careful introspection will show, far more than we usually suppose [1890/1950, vol. 2, pp. 470-471].

Two ideal-typical forms of understanding can now be distinguished: emotional and cognitive. Clearly in everyday life the two forms blur together and interwine, for emotionality and cognitions are always interrelated and present in the person's streams of experience (James, 1890/1950, vol. 1, pp. 185-187). Further, thoughts interrelate with feelings. The person must cognitively interpret a situation as he builds up, checks, and calls out in himself inner self-feelings and thoughts. All emotionality involves, at least on the reflective (but not the pre-reflective) level, thoughts and cognitions about the feelings one is feeling. These cognitions, however, are thought *through* the veil of feelings, just as feelings are felt and thought through the screens of cognition.

Corresponding closely to these two forms of understanding are two parallel forms of interpretation, which also may be termed, provisionally, emotional and cognitive. Emotional interpretation is the phenomenological description and dissection of another's emotional acts within a hermeneutic perspective that is meaningful within a double structure of cognitive and emotional meanings and understandings. Emotional interpretation often proceeds monothetically—that is, as if at a glance—when the person quickly places the other within an emotional frame and acts toward him emotionally (Schutz, 1964, p. 172; Dilthey, 1900/1976, pp. 226-227; Husserl, 1913/1962, pp. 309-311).

Cognitive interpretation, in contrast, precedes polythetically, or step by step (Schutz, 1964, p. 172). In this interpretive mode the person moves, often carefully and slowly, act by act, word by word, through another's conduct, trying to unravel its precise sequence, the motives that underlie it, while understanding the diverse meanings the other brings to it. Cognitive interpretation places interactants in a situation in which they interact *with* another, building and intertwining their interactions with each other in a stepwise fashion. Emotional interpretation often involves an interacting-*at*-another mode of interaction in which the sequence of the other's actions is of less importance than are the emotional meanings given to her actions (see Denzin, 1980, p. 256).

Emotional interpretation builds to emotional understanding, just as cognitive interpretation leads to cognitive understanding. These are clearly ideal types, for in no empirical instance will cognitions and emotionality be cleanly sheared apart. However, their identification and clarification permits a firmer location of interpretive theory within current sociology. With few exceptions, the interpretive theory that has built forward from Weber, Mead, and Schutz through Cicourel and others has been cognitive interpretive theory (but see Dilthey, 1900/1976).

The major exception in this regard has been the work of Garfinkel, especially the early studies (1967), which revealed the underlying emotional terror that exists when the taken-for-granted structures of everyday life are suspended, destroyed, or radically altered. The bewilderment, outrage, frustration, anger, and fear that Garfinkel's students experienced when they violated the taken-for-granted assumptions of their households revealed the underlying moral and emotional commitments they held toward themselves as embodiments of that moral code. The shattering of those natural attitudes regarding "normal" everyday conduct cut to the inner moral core of these persons, as feeling selves.

Garfinkel's studies revealed the emotionality that lies behind the moral codes that are taken for granted on a daily basis. His research can be interpreted as pointing in the direction of an emotional, as opposed to a purely cognitive, theory of interpretation and understanding. In this regard, and perhaps without stretching the limits of interpretation too far, the works of Freud and Lacan also point in the direction of an emotional theory of interpretation and understanding. Both Freud and Lacan reveal that an interpretation of emotionality lies at the basis of an understanding of the person in the everyday world.

An interpretive theory that secures emotionality centrally in the two processes of interpretation and understanding may be termed, for want of a better phrase, *the emotional theory of interpretation*. Similarly, theories that locate cognitions centrally in the interpretive process will be termed *cognitive theories of interpretation*. The analysis of emotional intersubjectivity that follows moves from the emotional theory of interpretation. It assumes that *deep* meaning lies in emotionality.

This theory might, with qualifications, also be termed *the hermeneutic-emotional theory of interpretation*. Dilthey's development of Schleiermacher's theories of hermeneutics (Dilthey, 1900/1976, pp. 35-77, 258-260) and his discussions of interpretation and understanding (pp. 207-245) suggest that emotionality and empathy are basic to understanding. He states: "The basis of the human studies is not conceptualization but total awareness of a mental state and its reconstruction based on empathy" (p. 181). In another section he notes that "this state involved in the task of understanding we call empathy" (p. 261). The methodology of the understanding of recorded expressions, Dilthey terms hermenutics. He argues that *"the epistemological, logical, and methodological analysis of understanding is one of the main tasks involved in establishing the foundations of the human studies"* (p. 261). The present volume attempts to forward the understandings of understanding and interpretation. If understanding involves the grasping of the relation of a part to a whole, then the leap that moves from part to whole is significantly grounded in emotionality. This point will be developed in the Conclusion of this book.

Emotional Understanding of Another

Visualized feelings need not produce a shared emotional feeling. It is possible to visualize another's embarrassment or pain and feel no compassion for him. For one to understand another's embodied emotion—for example, his pain—one must see him as being in pain, and then one must reproduce the experience of pain. Such a reproduction does not lead one to share in the actual pain of another, although an understanding of his pain and the fact that he is feeling pain can be produced and understood (Cooley, 1902/1956, p. 138; Scheler, 1913/1970, p. 10).

It must be remembered that each person has a sphere of "absolute personal privacy which can never be given to us" (Scheler, 1913/1970, p. 10). Furthermore, each individual possesses selves that are distinctly his and rooted in his own stream of experience. All that can be grasped and understood about the other and his emotionality is "our view of [the other's self] as an individual conditioned as such by our own individual nature" (Scheler, 1913/1970, p. 10). That is, the limits of our understandings are set by the range of our interpretive emotional experiences.

In order for true, or authentic, emotional understanding to occur, two individuals must produce a common field of shared experience that they can enter into, each drawing, if necessary, on his own visualizations of the other's feelings, his own productions and reproductions within himself of a common feeling, and the common participation in this publicly accessible field of experience. Experience, to repeat, precedes emotional understanding.

The following conditions are set forth as processes that structure emotional intersubjectivity and emotional understanding:

1. The subjective interpretation of another's emotional experience from one's own as well as the other's perspective.
2. Shared and sharable emotionality.
3. An approbation of the other's perspective as one's own.
4. The merging of shared feelings of experience into a common field.
5. A production, reproduction, or coproduction of the other's emotional experiences.
6. Vicarious participation in the other's emotionality and visualization.

7. An awareness and visualization of the other's body as a field of expression for their experience.
8. A shared biographical situation, a common language and stock of knowledge.
9. Emotional infection and contagion.
10. Remembered emotionality.

In each of these conditions a different form of emotional intersubjectivity is present. In order to understand the emotionality of another, one may preperform, coperform, or reperform the emotional acts that generate the emotional experience of the other that one wishes to comprehend. Understanding, however, requires shared and sharable emotionality, which lies in the field of experience that surrounds each person.

A tacit thesis underlies the discussion and may be stated as follows: *Emotionality lies at the basis of social organization, for emotionality is the basis of understanding. Social organization is nothing if it is not routinized, taken-for-granted understandings.*

Because social organizations and social relationships are the arenas for the generation of common fields of experience, emotionality is grounded in the very conditions that promote social structures. As recurring fields of common interactional experience, organizations provide the contexts for the preperforming, coperforming, and reperforming of those social acts that underlie all emotional understanding. Accordingly, the analysis of emotional intersubjectivity should lead to new views on the phenomenological theory of social structure, social relationships, and social organizations (see Weber, 1978; Schutz, 1962, 1964, 1968; Schutz and Luckmann, 1973; Berger and Luckmann, 1967; Garfinkel, 1967).

The Forms of Emotional Intersubjectivity

If emotional intersubjectivity describes the various forms emotional understanding may assume, then feelings in common constitute the point of reference for the analysis that follows.

Feelings in Common. Consider the following examples:

Two parents stand beside the dead body of a loved child. They feel in common the "same" sorrow, the "same" anguish. . . . A's sorrow is in no way an "external matter" for B . . . as it is, for example, for their friend C, who joins them, and commiserates "with them" or "upon their sorrow" [Scheler, 1913/1970, pp. 12-13].

He lingers at the counter making talk with the waitress.
"What'll it be today?"
"Well, what do you have for me? You got some of that homemade potato soup? That's a good soup. We used to have that at home. Back in Michigan."
"Anything else today?"
"Coffee. My usual coffee. My mother won a prize at the county fair with her potato soup. She has a secret recipe."
"And what else? Some dessert?"
At a quarter of five, he is slowly eating his potato soup, his pie, and sipping his cup of coffee. . . . "I used to be a very busy person. I used to have plenty of friends." . . .
"The Executive's alright." "Now I just came here four years ago; but there are some older folks who *live* here" [Hochschild, 1973, pp. 137-138].

The parents standing beside the body of their loved child have a feeling in common. They feel sorrow over the death of their child. The feeling that is in common is not the same feeling for each parent, for each feels sorrow over his or her own loss. The sorrow is in common between them—not the specific content of the sorrow. To take another example, if a friend of mine were to die, I would feel grief as would her husband, but we would not be feeling the same grief. Our "shared" grief, though it has the same object, would not necessarily bring us closer together, for it has a different content, based on our different relationships with her. This feeling is external neither to A nor to B, as it is for C who joins them, just as the old man's loneliness in the second example is purely his, not the waitress's. The old man and the waitress and C who joins the two parents are not part of a feeling in common. The two parents feel their sorrow together. What they feel in common is both the same value feeling over the loss of the child and the same "keenness of emotion" in regard to that loss and its meaning (Scheler, 1913/1970, p. 13). The waitress and C do not hold the same meaningful value feeling regarding the loss of a child or loneliness, nor do they *feel* sorrow or loneliness. They commiserate, to the degree that they are willing and able, in the emotion of the other.

The sorrow, as the value feeling that gives meaning to the feeling of grief, is synonymous with the grief. They are, as Scheler argues, one and the same. They may be termed *embodied value feelings*. Only mental pain, anguish, or joy (embodied, lived emotion) can be conjointly felt and suffered together. Physical pain and sensory feelings cannot be shared, only commiserated with (Scheler, 1913/1970, p. 13).

Feelings in common place two or more persons in the same emotional field of experience. This field publicly joins their inner streams of consciousness in a common experience. They are acting on and feeling the same value feeling. Each is capable of visualizing the other's embodied feelings, and the emotions that each feels in his lived body are similar to those he sees the other expressing. The persons are feeling and acting in a common field of emotional experience. They share the same intentional value feeling and the same intentional feeling. True emotional understanding arises from feelings in common.

Fellow-Feeling. In fellow-feeling a common feeling, or feeling in common, is not present. The waitress and C in the examples above are acting on phenomenological facts that are not those of A and B and the old man. They are acting on another's suffering or loneliness, which is not theirs. The suffering of the parents or the old man's loneliness is apprehended through an act of understanding, or "vicarious feeling," and it is toward that fact that feeling is directed (Scheler, 1913/1970, p. 13). Fellow-feeling involves an intentional reference to the feelings of another and is felt simply as a feeling-for-him. In fellow-feeling there is a reaction to the state and value of the other's feelings —as these are visualized in vicarious feeling (Scheler, 1913/ 1970, p. 14).

A person may take pleasure in the pain experienced by another. This is a form of negative fellow-feeling, for the form of the feeling felt by the other is not the form felt by the individual. Positive fellow-feeling joins two common value feelings (Scheler, 1913/1970, p. 14). Thus, whereas a feeling in common joins vicarious experiential sharing with a value feeling, these two processes are separated in fellow-feeling. The basic element of fellow-feeling, the intentional reference to the feelings of another, is not present in feelings in common. Here the intentional reference is directed to a feeling that is *interactively* the same for both parties.

The emotional intersubjectivity that arises from fellow-feeling potentially places a distance between persons and promotes "delusive," or spurious, understanding. The same experience is not shared in fellow-feeling. Hence individuals can only partly enter into one another's emotional fields of experience.

The emotional intersubjectivity that arises from feelings in common is high, for the same experiential field is held in common. Such feelings promote the intense emotional interpenetration of two selves. Emotional bonding, attachment, and embracement may follow from deeply felt and shared feelings in common. This is not (necessarily) true for fellow-feeling.

Emotional Infection. Emotional infection, or emotional contagion, has the following characteristics: (1) there is no appearance of fellow-feeling or of feelings in common; (2) the process is largely involuntary yet reciprocal and self-generating in its effects on the individual; (3) it involves no directing of feeling toward the feelings of another person; (4) it does not involve participation in the other's experiences; (5) its defining feature is the transference of another's emotional state to the person, without thought, prior intention, or prior knowledge of the other's feeling states. Consider the following example:

> A lonely somewhat depressed man taking a walk in mid-evening along a snowy street chances to see off in the distance the lights of a neighborhood tavern. He walks to the tavern, enters a smoke-, voice-filled room, and sees a large group of apparent friends gathered around a piano singing

> "We Shall Overcome." He walks to the bar, buys a
> beer, lights a cigarette, leans against the bar, and
> watches. Slowly he begins to warm to the heat in
> the room. He feels his loneliness easing away. He
> takes off his winter coat, a smile crosses his face,
> he sits on the bar stool, looks to his right and his
> left, nods at those at the bar, orders another drink,
> "My name is Andrew," he says softly, and begins
> quietly singing along with the group at the bar
> [Novak, 1967, p. 12].

Andrew has been infected by the emotion in the tavern. He has
not entered into the concrete emotional stream of experience of
those in the tavern. Rather, their emotion has entered his
stream of consciousness, and without intending, he has taken
on the feelings in the room. There is no (or only slight) emotional intersubjectivity in emotional infection, although Andrew
may delude himself into thinking and feeling that he understands the mood of the occasion. Retrospectively he may define
the situation as one of intense warmth and companionship.

In emotional infection the other's feelings are experienced as a landscape against which one's feelings arise and
emerge. Scheler suggests that "for such contagion it is by no
means necessary that any *emotional* experiences should have
occurred in the other person. Even the *objective* aspects of such
feelings, which attach to natural objects, or are discerned in an
'atmosphere'—such as the serenity of a spring landscape, the
melancholy of a rainy day, the wretchedness of a room—can
work infectiously in this way on the state of our emotions"
(1913/1970, p. 15).

Even though emotional infection is involuntary and largely prereflective, the feelings that are felt gather momentum and
increase as the emotionality produced reproduces itself through
imitation and repetition. In large public gatherings infectious
emotion is intensified through circular interaction among the
participants (Blumer, 1978). "It is the infective process itself
that generates purposes beyond the designs of any single individual" (Scheler, 1913/1970, p. 16).

Emotional infection should not be confused with either

fellow-feelings or feelings in common. The processes of infection are not intentional, and they often operate outside the person's field of direct reflective awareness. Fellow-feelings and feelings in common are intentional feeling states, reflectively grasped by the individual. However, the process of infection may be consciously sought out. Bored, lonely, and depressed, a person may seek out interpersonal distraction, anticipating that he will be caught up in a different feeling state. "When someone says that he 'wants to see cheerful faces around him,' it is perfectly clear that he does not mean to rejoice with them, but is simply hoping for infection as a means to his *own* pleasure. Conversely, an awareness of possible infection can so create a *dread* of it, as is found wherever a person shuns melancholy places or avoids the *appearance* of suffering (not the suffering itself), by trying to banish this image from his field of experience" (Scheler, 1913/1970, p. 17). The old man, noted earlier, who eats daily at the same cafeteria and the depressed man who wandered into a neighborhood tavern were seeking to be emotionally distracted and infected by the feelings of others. That they would have preferred a deeper form of emotional intersubjectivity and meaning is perhaps obvious.

Emotional Identification. The act of identifying one's self with, or through, the self of another person is termed emotional identification. This form of emotional intersubjectivity has the following characteristics: (1) Like emotional infection, of which it is a special and heightened form, emotional identification is largely involuntary. (2) It involves the separate processes of locating in another person values and feelings that one identifies and takes on as one's own. (3) A submersion of the self in the other occurs. (4) The person may be totally despotized by the other, or (5) the self may be totally lost in the other (Scheler, 1913/1970, p. 18, terms these respectively idiopathic and heteropathic identification). (6) The occurrence of emotional identification, which is largely involuntary, appears in those feelings that are midway between sensible feelings of the lived body and the moral feelings of the person. "A man's *bodily* consciousness, like the individual essence of his *personality,* is *his and his alone*" (Scheler, 1913/1970, p. 33). Emotional identification thus stands between these two private sectors of the person's life.

Examples of emotional identification include the relationship between the hypnotist and the subject, that between movie and musical stars and their fans, certain forms of religious ritual, transference in psychoanalysis, heightened emotional infection and identification with group leaders in times of mass societal disorganization, and certain forms of "young," teenage "love."

In emotional identification the roots of one's individuality are lodged in the personhood of another. One is eclipsed by the person of the other and deprived of all one's rights as an individual. One is lost in and subsumed in the other. One lives, not in oneself, but in and through the other. As a consequence, emotional intersubjectivity is virtually absent in heightened emotional identification, for the division between the person (as subject) and the object of the person's feelings is annihilated. The vicarious production or rehearsal of the other's feeling is absent in emotional identification. The attempt to establish an intentional field of feelings, distinct from the person yet entered into with another person, is also absent in this mode of feeling. Understanding is not present, nor are the intentional sharing and acting on of common value states. The person is "lost" and adrift in the other.

Yet emotional identification is a pervasive and recurring form of feeling, as evidenced in the diverse examples given above. This form of feeling may have pernicious effects on the individual and the group, especially during periods of collective protest and social unrest. In such moments the person, though elevated above mundane preoccupations with herself, is caught in the condition of communal frenzy, such that her individuality and that of the community "go under together in a *single* passionate surge of collective activity" (Scheler, 1913/1970, p. 36).

Emotional Embracement. In emotional embracement, or shared emotionality, the intentional feelings of two or more persons are drawn together into a common and recurring emotional field, thereby producing the conditions of emotional and relational bonding. Emotional embracement has the following characteristics: (1) sharing of common emotional/personal experiences in which (2) common feelings were felt, (3) reproduction and reenactment of those common experiences, (4) vicarious and real sharing of those experiences, (5) reproduction of the feelings that were felt in those experiences, (6) generation and feeling of common feelings on the basis of those reproduced experiences and feelings, (7) production of new experiences in which similar and sharable feelings are felt and jointly participated in, (8) reciprocal lodging by two or more persons of their selves in this recurring emotional field of experience (Denzin, 1969).

In emotional embracement the selves, experiences, and feelings of two persons are joined into a feeling structure that is interwoven through the multiple layers of their respectively stratified emotional lives. The meanings of their sensible feelings, the feelings of their lived bodies, and their closely felt and held intentional value feelings of and for themselves as persons are understood and even vicariously felt by each other. With ease the individuals can enter into each other's mental and emotional life. Central to emotional embracement are emotional understanding and emotional sharing. But embracement, understanding, and sharing can occur only when a recurring, common emotional field of experience is produced and shared. Examples of this form of emotional intersubjectivity include long-lasting friendships, certain marriages, love relationships, and primary or intimate group relations.

In emotional embracement there is a merger of selves, feelings, and intentionality. The other is conceptualized and felt as a valued other. Particular feeling experiences such as fights and arguments with each other do not necessarily alter the intentional value feelings that obtain between the two persons—although such value feelings may be altered, as all terminated friendships or close relationships reveal.

Spurious Emotionality. Consideration of the sociality and intersubjectivity of lived emotion reveals the varying degrees in which emotional associates are able to enter into and participate in one's lived emotions. Others enter into one's mental and emotional life only to the degree that they can act on and interpret one's experiences as a field of expression of their inner and outer experiences. Against this expressive landscape feelings in common, fellow-feeling, emotional infection, identification, and embracement are sketched, felt, lived, and varyingly understood.

What cannot be directly lived or understood is another's inner bodily consciousness and inner phenomenological stream of consciousness. Nor is the inner moral essence of one's personality directly accessible to others. "A man's *bodily* consciousness, like the individual essence of his *personality*, is *his and his alone*" (Scheler, 1913/1970, p. 33). Zones of the person's experiences remain outside the awareness and consciousness of others. Emotional intersubjectivity encompasses only those experiences that the person and others can enter into vicariously, by reproduction, participation, imitation, memory, sharing, embracement, intentionality, or contagion. Pure or complete understanding of another's experiences, feelings, and thoughts is an impossibility. "Supposing we could get rid of all physical differences between human beings (including their essential here-and-nowness), and could further eliminate all qualitative differences in regard to their private objects of consciousness (including the formal aspect of these objects—in short the whole of *what* they think, will, feel, etc.), the individual diversity of their central personalities would still remain, despite the fact that the *idea* of personality would be the same in each of them" (Scheler, 1913/1970, p. 34).

Spurious emotionality, or spurious emotional understanding, arises in those situations when individuals mistake their own feelings for the feelings of the other and interpret their feelings as the feelings of the other. Psychologists call this egocentrism. Spurious emotional understanding is characterized by (1) an inability or refusal to enter into the other's field of experience and view that field from the other's perspective, (2) mistaken emotional memory, in which one confuses emotional memories and interprets an experience that is not the other's, (3) assuming that the other's pain or inner sensible feelings can be felt and understood, (4) applying the incorrect intentional value reference to a value feeling of the other—for example, shame or embarrassment in a situation the other feels pride toward, (5) imitating the other's actions and feelings without entering into a shared emotional field of experience with her, (6) acting on another's feelings while not having had the other's experiences, (7) assuming that the other's feelings toward self are the same as one would direct toward oneself were one to have had the same experience as the other—for example, assuming that one can feel another's hurt pride the same way she feels it, (8) viewing the other's experiences *only* from one's own standpoint.

In each of these conditions spurious emotional understanding, or spurious emotionality, is produced. Spurious emotionality is a constituent element of the natural lifeworld and provides a frame of reference against which the other modes of intersubjective emotionality are understood and underscored. That is, spurious emotionality is a normative structure of the lifeworld, suggesting that, even at the level of sociality, people seldom enter into one another's mental and emotional lives at anything below the most surface level.

If emotionality is the underlying basis of understanding, and if understanding lies at the heart of social organization, then the foregoing suggests that the direct expression of emotionality in social organization is rare. Furthermore, intersubjective understanding of another's standpoint within recurring social structures is also a rarity. The taken-for-granted structures of everyday life, as Schutz, Husserl, Weber, and Garfinkel have argued, make the accomplishment of practical institutional and relational doings unproblematic and unemotional. Individuals are left to their own doings and to the assistance of close emotional associates when problems of emotion, meaning, and intersubjective understanding are of concern.

Faulkner (1981, p. 346) offers the following interactional episode, a conversation between a pregnant daughter and her mother. Interpretation suggests that even among close emotional associates spurious emotional understanding is commonplace. Each of the characteristics of spurious emotionality listed above is given in this account.

"Oh, God, oh, God," her mother wailed, "what will become of us now? How can I hold up my head and meet my friends with a daughter at home in the family way? What can I tell them?"

"Why must you tell them at all?" Frankie repeated wearily.

"And who'll look after you? Who'll give you a home? Do you think any man is going to take your brat, too?"

Frankie looked at her mother a steady moment. "Do you still think that I am waiting for some rich bird to fall for me? Do you still think that, knowing me like you ought?"

Temporality

Each of the forms of emotional intersubjectivity must be understood as a temporal phenomenon. Temporality is basic to the internal structure of each. Each form is a temporal accomplishment, and each is differentially rooted in the past, the present, and the future. Feelings in common, for example, are based on events and associations from the past. Fellow-feeling emerges in the present. Emotional infection moves across the past, the present, and the future, although it is largely located in the present. Emotional identification is lodged in the present and the past in such a way that the person can move forward into the future only through the lead and actions of the other. Shared emotionality, or emotional embracement, encompasses all three temporal modalities. Here temporality is located between persons in the interactions that bind them together through time. Spurious emotionality is backward-looking, involving one's inability to understand the actions of another except on the basis of one's own past actions.

It is inappropriate to view these forms of emotional intersubjectivity in isolation. A person may pass through all or several of these modes in the same interactional episode. Or, as the consequence of a turning point in the interaction, she may move from one mode to another—from emotional identification to emotional embracement, from fellow-feeling to feelings in common, and so on.

Consider the following account. Four members of an Irish family are seated around a Thanksgiving dinner table, conversing. A car drives up in front of the house. The eldest son of the family, Don, aged fifty-three, gets out of the car with his new wife and child. As they begin walking up the steps to the front door, his brother Paul, aged forty-eight, gets up from the table and moves to the front door.

Paul: Picks up a large easy chair in the living room and moves it in front of the door, blocking the opening. Grinning and laughing, he says, "I'll get Don." He returns to the table and sits down, returning to conversation with the other family members.

Don: Comes to the front door, tries to open it, pushes it a few inches open, finds that it will not open. He exclaims, "What in the hell is going on!" Pushing harder, he moves the chair several inches away from the door and slides into the room, around the chair, his new wife and child crawling in behind him. "Who did this? It's not funny!"

Paul: As Don is shouting, Paul gets up from the table, runs to the chair and moves it back to its original place, and then slowly retreats to his seat at the table. He says, "I'm sorry, come on in, I was just playing a joke." He shakes his head.

Don: "Who in the hell is trying to be funny? That's not funny!"

Paul: "I did it, Don. It's just a joke. Don't get all heated up about it. Come on in and sit down, there's plenty of food left. For Christ's sake, calm down!"

Don: "Well, it's not funny!" Walks to the end of the table, near the window. Says to the other family members seated at the table, "By God, you always know where I stand. If Don's mad, you know it. By God, I don't keep that stuff inside." Laughing, he sits down. Others laugh with him. Shortly thereafter, he gets up, puts on his coat, and goes out to his car to get some suitcases. He is heard to remark, "That was great. I loved it. I feel better already."

Paul: (to the other family members at the table) "My God,
what's wrong with Don today? So he was a little late for
Thanksgiving dinner. What the hell, can't he take a joke?
I was just trying to be funny. I'm sorry" [Reported by
undergraduate sociology student, winter 1981].

In this episode the fields of emotional intersubjectivity
range across the following forms:

1. Fellow-feeling—evidenced in Paul's making Don's emotion-
    ality an intentional object of his feelings.
2. Feeling in common—presumably shared by the other family
    members at the dinner table in and through conversation.
3. Emotional infection—evidenced as Don's emotionality in-
    fected Paul's mood.
4. Emotional embracement—Paul's attempting to draw Don
    into a common, shared field of emotionality regarding the
    moving of the chair in front of the door as a joke.
5. Spurious emotionality—revealed in Don's interpreting
    Paul's actions from his own point of view and vice versa.

Spurious emotionality was the dominant mode of intersubjectivity, but these other forms were present as well. This suggests
that any interactional episode is "kaleidoscopic" with respect to
emotional intersubjectivity. That is, individuals feel their way
into the feelings of others in multiple ways. No fixed sequence
of feeling and understanding need be followed in order for the
multiple forms of emotional intersubjectivity to be present during an interactional exchange.

The feelings that interactants reflect to others and back
to themselves shift in tone, intensity, shape, and meaning as interaction unfolds. These shifting, reflected meanings alter and
modify the temporal understandings each interactant has of the
other. Understanding, as such, becomes a temporal phenomenon, subject to the shifting reflections of emotionality. Accordingly, it must be seen that few if any interactions stay, for their
lifetimes, within one dominant form of emotional intersubjectivity.

Conclusions

The meanings of the person that lie in emotionality have been located in the fields of experience that draw two or more persons together. Who the person is emotionally, to the self and to others, is determined in large part by the processes of emotional intersubjectivity. With each form of emotional intersubjectivity a different part (slice, layer) of the person is revealed. Thus, different versions and layers of the person are disclosed in and through feelings in common, fellow-feelings, emotional infection, emotional identification, shared emotionality, and spurious emotionality.

Adherence to surface rules of conduct (Goffman, 1971) increases the likelihood that spurious emotional intersubjectivity and emotional understanding will be produced. The deep, underlying meanings of the person will be glossed through the use of surface, interpersonal rituals. Interaction remains at the surface, "theylike" levels of the self. The deep meanings of the person are not displayed or felt in ordinary, everyday discourse.

Such interactions tilt intersubjectivity in the direction of cognitive interpretation. Emotionality, to the degree that it is felt and expressed, is constrained, shallow, and surfacelike. Interaction and communication proceed unproblematically and without deep pause or reflection.

Deep emotionality is buried, hidden, clouded, and distorted within the tiny, fleeting, ritual/emotional/cognitive exchanges that make up the daily round. Individuals come into and out of each other's presence, exchanging greetings, smiles, apologies, sympathies, and small talk about the weather and the economy and setting times for lunch, while they make minor requests of each other. Laughing, perhaps hurting inside, they take ritual leave of each other. In these small actions and others like them, individuals keep their emotionality from themselves and from one another. The consequence, of course, is that, to the degree that they adhere to the public ritual order, they fail to reveal their deeper meanings to themselves. A certain kind of emptiness is thus felt.

PART THREE

Two Studies
of Problematic
Emotionality

The analysis of emotional intersubjectivity in Part Two revealed the degree to which others may enter into, understand, and be influenced by a person's emotional experiences. The discussion of the structures of lived emotion peered inward on emotion as seen and lived by an individual. It is now necessary to place the study of lived emotion in an *enacted-interactive, interpersonal context.* To this end Part Three offers two studies of enacted emotionality. Chapter Six presents a social phenomenological analysis of family violence. Chapter Seven examines the emotionally divided self. Before turning to these discussions, some brief remarks on enacted emotionality are required.

Enacted Emotionality

Enacted emotionality is an intersubjective, interactive process that places the person in the presence of another and involves the articulation and expression of emotional definitions of self and the situation. In enacted emotionality individuals provide an emotional definition of themselves, which others may act on and take as an expression of their inner field of emotional and cognitive experience. Enacted emotionality produces an interactive web that draws others into and makes them a part of the person's inner (and outer) streams of emotional experience. A field of jointly felt emotional experience is thereby brought into existence.

Enacted emotionality is interactive and interpersonal, requiring both the presence and the interpretations (real and imagined) of others for its accomplishment. It is a continual and ongoing part of the person's presence in the world. To be present to others is to be present emotionally, if only as an emotional object. Enacted emotionality places the principle of emotional sociality into interactive practice (see Chapter Five). Emotional enactments are akin to emotional performances, if by *performance* is meant dramatic, moral action having a beginning, a middle, and an end (Goffman, 1959; Burke, 1945, 1950). They thus contrast with hidden inner emotionality, in which a person masks his or her emotionality and *attempts* to *not* present an emotional definition of the self.

The emotional definition that is provided in and through emotional enactment may pertain to any of the structures of lived emotion discussed earlier (see Chapter Four). However, the meanings conveyed in enacted emotionality must be given as belonging to the person and as being part of the person's lived experiences in the current situation. In short, they must be attached or attachable to the person so that others can make reference to the individual's mood, feelings, and emotionality at a particular moment in time. Furthermore, the person must, at some point in time, be able to bring his enacted emotions into his field of consciousness, although many of one's enacted emotions may for long periods lie outside one's awareness (Stone and Farberman, 1981, pp. 4, 24).

Enacted emotionality communicates an emotional definition of the situation that encompasses those who come into the person's interactional field. The feelings that a person feels and expresses about himself shape, influence, and reveal the feelings others feel about themselves and about him.

There is a tenacity to enacted emotionality that derives from its "lived realness" and undoubted seriousness. In the moments of its occurrence, enacted emotionality is believed. This livedness overrides competing definitions that would render the enacted emotion harmless, comical, frivolous, irrelevant, or misunderstood.

Others' misunderstandings of an enacted emotional definition of the situation may intensify a person's emotional line of action. Witness the following interaction. The participants are two parents and two teenage daughters. The younger daughter, Ruth, has overslept. Joan, the older sister, is taking her morning bath. Nick, the father, is going downstairs and Kate, the mother, comes out of her bedroom just as Ruth comes out of hers.

7:05 A.M.	*Nick:*	Good morning, Ruth. How are you? Can I fix your lunch for you?
	Ruth:	No! (Slams the door to her bedroom, goes to the bathroom.) Joan, are you still in here? You do this every morning! Hurry up! You're going to make us late!
	Kate:	Hi, Ruth. How are you this morning? Joan is almost done. Can I do anything to help you?
	Ruth:	No! (Returning to her bedroom, Ruth is overheard slamming drawers while she dresses.)
	Joan:	(Leaves the bathroom saying over her shoulder to Ruth's room door) Hi, Ruth.
7:30 A.M.	*Nick:*	(Continues downstairs, goes to the kitchen, begins making a lunch for Ruth, who comes into the room.) Hi, sweetie. Do you want an apple or an orange?
	Ruth:	No, we don't have time! (Leaving the house, Ruth slams the back door, gets in the back seat of the car, throws her bookbag in the back of the car and sits down.)

7:40 A.M.		(Kate and Joan leave the house. Nick puts Ruth's lunch in the back of the car. They drive off to school. Ruth doesn't speak until they get to the school.)
	Nick:	There's a lunch for you, Ruth. Have a nice day. Goodbye, Joan. See you later.
	Joan:	Bye, Daddy, bye, Kate.
	Ruth:	I don't want any lunch. We're late.
7:52 A.M.	Kate:	(to Nick) What was wrong with Ruth? She was certainly uncivil. Did I do something wrong?
	Nick:	(to Kate) I think she was grumpy and mad because she overslept. I don't know.

Two days later

	Kate:	(to Ruth) Why were you so mad Tuesday morning?
	Ruth:	It was your fault. You let me oversleep.
	Kate:	I'm sorry. What time do you want me to wake you up? When I get up?
	Ruth:	Yes. Sorry I was so grumpy. [Emotions project, spring 1982].

Here Ruth, in a bad mood because she overslept, refuses to enter into the offered lines of interaction of the other members of her family. The overtures to her intensify her anger at herself, which is interpreted by Nick, Ruth, and Kate as anger toward them. It is only two days later that an interpretation from Ruth is secured. Enacted emotion produces definitional ambiguity regarding the intentions, feelings, and moods of the individual. Such ambiguity can distort or reduce emotional understanding. Furthermore, the enacted emotion of one person may infect the emotional lines of action of another in ways that are neither reflectively conscious nor deliberate. In this family interaction Ruth's enacted emotion, despite its briefness, served to produce an emotional aura that terminated interaction and conversation among the other family members.

Observations

The processes of enacted emotionality have started to receive attention in the recent literature on emotion. Scheff (1979) and Hochschild (1979, 1983), in their analyses of emotional catharsis and emotion management, have contributed to an understanding of this process. Freud and Breuer's (1895/ 1966) studies of emotional hysteria, Scheler's study of ressentiment (1912/1961), Goffman's examinations of the performances and presentations of self (1959), of embarrassment (1967), and of the "insanity of place" (1971), and Gross and Stone's (1964) study of embarrassment also contribute to the study of this phenomenon. Strauss's (1978) studies of negotiation contexts suggest that emotions are enacted in emotional contexts where different levels of "awareness," power, and authority are obtained (Sugrue, 1982, p. 280).

Recent work by cultural anthropologists on ritual, drama, and symbolic forms also points toward the study of emotional enactment (Geertz, 1973, 1980, 1983; Turner, 1974, 1982; Perinbanayagam, 1982; Sahlins, 1981). This latter body of work, however, tends toward the analysis of cultural and symbolic forms in the abstract. Emotion and mood are often regarded as artifacts of cultural symbols and rituals. They are seen as springing "from certain circumstances but they are responsive to no ends. Like fogs, they just settle and lift; like scents, suffuse and evaporate" (Geertz, 1973, p. 97). It is insufficient to state, as Geertz does (1973, p. 81), that "not only ideas, but emotions too, are cultural artifacts." Such a position belies a structural view of emotions and emotionality and contributes only slightly to the interactionist phenomenological understanding of emotional enactment.

The social phenomenological analysis of emotional interaction, which is the basis of emotional enactment, has not received explicit attention in previous work (but see Stanislavski, 1936, 1949). It is to this topic that the two studies in Part Three are directed. The study of this feature of emotionality is intended as a prelude to a deeper understanding of emotionality in everyday life. The study of situations in which individuals and their emotions get "out of control" and "out of hand" (for example, in which people become violent, verbally and physically abusive, or emotionally withdrawn) should provide insight into their opposite, situations in which enacted emotionality is modulated and controlled.

The enacted emotions of the person, as given in the interactional stream, enter into the emotions and feelings of others. Consequently, enacted emotions become social, public commodities, or social objects. They enter the world of lived interaction. Even if not understood, the person's moods, feelings, and values infect and enter into the emotional life and streams of consciousness of others. Enacted emotions are interactional phenomena and never the sole possession of the person.

With these preliminaries in mind, the discussion now turns to the analysis of violence, the violent self, and the emotionally divided self.

Chapter Six

Family Violence

"I'm always afraid of any violence, even violent emotions."
—John Barth

The study of violence within families requires, as many authors have argued, an examination of the concrete nature of violent activities within family contexts (Gelles and Cornell, 1982; Gelles, 1972, 1979; Gelles and Straus, 1979; Straus, 1972; Steinmetz and Straus, 1974; Dobash and Dobash, 1979, 1982; Athens, 1980; Blumer, 1980; Wolfgang and Ferracuti, 1982; Thomas and Znaniecki, 1920). Such conduct, whether between siblings (Felson, 1982), between spouses (Gelles, 1979; Dobash and Dobash, 1982), or of parents toward children (Kempe and others, 1962), is situated, interpersonal, emotional, and cognitive activity involving symbolic interaction between two or more parties (Athens, 1980; Blumer, 1980; Denzin, 1983b). It entails emotional enactment wherein one person's emotional and cognitive definitions of an interpersonal situation are articulated and inflicted, symbolically (verbally) and physically, on another. Violent family conduct, encompassing both legitimate acts of force and illegitimate actions of violence (Goode, 1971), in-

167

cluding pushing, slapping, punching, kicking, knifing, shooting, or throwing an object at another family member (Gelles, 1972, p. 20), as well as rape, child abuse, aggravated assaults, murder, physical destruction of property, and verbal abuse, is situated, embodied emotional action. Such conduct calls for intensive study from the perspective of a critical phenomenology of embodied experience (Sudnow, 1979; Sartre, 1943/1978; Merleau-Ponty, 1973c, 1974; Denzin, 1982a, 1982b).

The study of family violence is basic to a phenomenology of embodied experience because of the centrality of violent embodied conduct to the family's organization. How people enact and carry out violent definitions of self and other in concrete situations is a problem that joins critical phenomenology with the more macro concerns of family sociologists and students of violence in general. More specifically, an examination of violence from within, as lived experience, should shed important light on the organization and display of violence in families, small groups, and societies. Violence, it appears, is a generic, basic feature of all recorded societies (Foucault, 1980; Collins, 1981, pp. 133-158; Giddens, 1981). Violent thought and action is present as a matter of course in the behavioral repertoires of socialized and unsocialized individuals. So is the capacity for nonviolence.

Indeed, the occurrence of violence in American families, as Straus (1972, p. 16) observes, appears to reflect "standard features of American society and patterns of family organization which can be found everywhere in American society." Violence is a permanent and pervasive feature of capitalist societies (Sartre, 1976, pp. 716-737; Giddens, 1981; Foucault, 1980). A society which promotes the ownership of firearms, women, and children, which makes homes men's castles, and which sanctions societal and interpersonal violence in the forms of wars, athletic contests, and mass media fiction (and news) should not be surprised to find violence in its homes (Gelles, 1979). Violence directed toward children and women is a pervasive feature of sexual divisions of labor that place females and children in subordinate positions to males (Dobash and Dobash, 1979; Straus, Gelles, and Steinmetz, 1980; Gilbert and Gubar, 1982; Kristeva,

1981; Marks and de Courtivron, 1980; Hartmann, 1982). Since violence is a pervasive feature of American society, how it is organized, felt, and experienced demands detailed study.

A phenomenology of family violence requires examination of the following topics: (1) emotionality, self, and violent conduct, (2) violent emotional enactment as symbolic interaction, (3) the structures of violent enacted emotion, (4) violent emotional action, (5) inflicted emotion, (6) spurious, playful, real, and paradoxical violent emotionality, (7) the interiority of violence within families, and (8) family repair and bad faith. A single thesis organizes my argument: *Emotionality and the self are at the core of violence.* If emotionality is understood as self-feelings, directed toward self or others, then violence can be understood only from the perspective of the self-reflective, feeling, violent individual (Athens, 1980). That self stands in a bad-faith relationship with itself (see Sartre, 1943/1978, p. 115). The structures of bad faith are embedded in the family of violence. Accordingly, an understanding of enacted self-feelings and bad faith is basic to an understanding of violence.

Emotionality, the Self, and Violent Conduct

The root meanings of *violence* include to treat with force, to abuse, to go after something, to pursue something, to go after something with force, or to regain something, often with the use of force. *Violence shall be defined as the attempt to regain, through the use of emotional or physical force, something that has been lost.* What has been lost is directly traceable to the self of the violent person. Consider the following account, by Ray Yarborough, a fictional character in Andre Dubus's (1983) short story, "The Pretty Girl." Ray rapes his ex-wife Polly and severely beats the man she slept with. He held his wife at knife point. He states: "They would call it rape and assault with a deadly weapon, but those words don't apply to me and Polly. I was taking back my wife for a while; and taking back, for a while anyway, some of what she took from me. That is what it felt like: I went to her place torn and came out mended." The self and its feelings are at the core of violent conduct. The self (see

Chapters Two and Three) will be defined as (1) all that the person calls his at a particular moment in time, including his feelings, his actions, his material possessions, his body, and his relations to others (James, 1890/1950, vol. 1, pp. 291–292), (2) the meaning of the person to himself as a distinct object and subject at any given moment in his existence (Heidegger, 1927/1962, p. 153), and (3) the meaning of the person's being to himself, as he turns back on himself in reflection and self-apprehension (Heidegger, 1975/1982, p. 159). The self of the violent subject is not in consciousness, but in the world of social interaction. It haunts the subject. Its meanings are given through violence. But the goal of his violent act always eludes him, even when he has the flesh of the other in his grip, her will and her freedom slip from his grasp.

What the self attempts to regain through violent means may include lost or threatened self-esteem, personal safety (in response to threats to the body), self-control, or control over another. Through violence one regains or tries to regain what the self has lost or has had threatened. This often involves self-deception.

If the self attempts to regain, through violent means, what has been lost or threatened, then the emotional feelings of anger, loss, rage, hostility, fright, and fear are central to the organization of violence. The violent self is a feeling self, feeling in and through violence a sense of outrage, a sense of loss, and a desire to regain. In the emotions of violence, the self of the person is revealed as a feeling, moral self that has been touched and affected at the foundations of its very being and selfness. The feelings of the violent person (and of his or her victims) have a threefold structure: (1) a sense of the feelings of violence in terms of awareness and self-definition, (2) a sense of self feeling the feelings of violence, (3) a revealing of the moral, or feeling, self and person through this experience (Heidegger, 1975/1982, p. 137).

The emotionality of the reflective, feeling self is basic to the study of the family of violence. The family of violence is a network of violent, feeling, reflective, interacting selves. An emotional climate attaches to every family. This climate, or "atmosphere of feelings," changes and takes on new forms as the moods and states of mind of the family members change. Emotionality and self-reflection are central components of the family of violence. The family of violence uses emotional and physical force to regain what it slowly loses through violence— the sense of intimacy, nostalgia, closeness, and "we-ness" that characterizes all primary groups (Cooley, 1902/1956; Wiley, 1980; Franks, 1976; Davis, 1979; Erchak, 1981).

Norbert Wiley (1980, p. 3) has suggested that in certain types of families and relationships "all selves are fully armored and protected from each other." In contrast to the families of schizophrenics, where pseudo communication and the pseudo sharing of intimacy may prevail, and where selves may be hidden and protected from one another through horizontal and vertical double binds (Wiley, 1980), in the families of violence few such barriers or shields exist. The selves and bodies of persons in violent families are nakedly exposed for the entire "world" of the family to see. Eugene O'Neill (1955, p. 27) observes a mother in a family of violence: "She stops short, overcome by a fit of acute self-consciousness as she catches their eyes fixed on her. Her hands jerk nervously to her hair. She forces a smile. 'What is it? What are you looking at? Is my hair—?' "

Violent Emotional Enactment as Symbolic Interaction

Violent enacted emotion is a subjective, interactive process that places the person (the family member) in the presence of another and involves the articulation and expression of an emotional definition of an interpersonal situation. In enacted emotion the individual provides a violent emotional definition of herself, which others may act on and take as an expression of her inner field of emotional and cognitive experiences. A violent emotional definition of the person is produced. She is regarded as dangerous, terrifying, harmful, abusive, no longer trustworthy, and out of control.

As symbolic interaction, violent enacted emotionality is (1) emergent and unpredictable in its consequences, (2) given

diverse interpretations and meanings as it is experienced and
reexperienced, (3) focused around the interiority and inner
meanings of another—a loved family member, most typically,
(4) temporally rooted in an interpersonal situation that is seen
as having got out of control, and (5) biographically, physically,
and psychologically consequential for all family members. (See,
for example, O'Neill, 1955, Acts 2 and 3).

Thomas and Znaniecki (1920, chap. 4) provide ten examples of family violence resulting in murders. Each example, in
varying degrees, has the features of enacted emotionality as
symbolic interaction listed above. Consider the following:

> *Woefil Snopczyski,* a bricklayer, fifty years
> old, was killed one Sunday morning in May at
> about 2:30 A.M. by Wadek Kowalski, outside the
> Kowalskis' home in Chicago. For several years
> prior to the murder the [Kowalski] family had
> kept a boarding house. Mrs. Kowalski testified that
> her husband often required her to have intercourse
> with other men. She stated that "several times he
> pulled a revolver and he wanted to kill me with an
> axe, too . . . he threatened me that I should do that
> kind of work . . . and he wanted to throw me out
> of a second-story window."
>
> The man who was with Snopczyski the night
> he was killed testified that when he was coming
> from his home the deceased was standing on the
> corner of Milwaukee and Division and he invited
> him to have a drink. While they were sitting on the
> corner Kowalski appeared and asked, "If you want
> intercourse, what's the use of hanging around here
> and looking for something else? You can come
> over to my home and have drinks and it will cost
> you less." Kowalski didn't say it was his wife.
> When the two men went to the house (at about
> 11:30 P.M.) only the woman and her husband were
> there. Kowalski brought out whiskey and wine and
> placed it on the table and he said: "Go ahead and
> drink." While the two were drinking the woman
> entered the kitchen. Kowalski said to her: "Well,
> why don't you go to him?" (the deceased). The de-
> ceased and the woman went into the bedroom.
> When she came back to the kitchen she gave her

husband a dollar. The man drank a second drink.
Snopczyski insisted that Kowalski's wife go with
him a second time. When the two returned the second time Mrs. Kowalski had money in her hand.
The man with Snopczyski reported that he said,
"Maybe you robbed him. How much did you get?"
She said: "No, I got two dollars . . . the first time
I charge a dollar because you shortly with me. The
second time it took longer so I charge two dollars."
The deceased said it was too much. "I said to the
husband: 'You had better return the dollar back
. . . (and on his refusal) I am going to fix you. I am
going for the police. . . . because you people are
pulling a person in here and want to rob them."
Snopczyski said: "Come on, we will go . . . over
there and complain." When Kowalski heard that,
he walked out first, followed by the deceased and
his wife. "I was still on the stairs and I heard a
shot and this Snopczynski says: 'I am shot.' "
[Thomas and Znaniecki, 1920, pp. 279-282].

Kowalski was arrested for murder some time later by the
Chicago police. Here, violent enacted emotionality arises out of
a triadic interpersonal interaction. The action was unpredicted,
focused around charges (perhaps a misunderstanding) leveled at
Kowalski's wife by the deceased and his friends. Its consequences included not only a murder but also the destruction of
the Kowalski family.

The unpredictable nature of the violent conduct in the
Snopczyski murder suggests that there is an inner side to violence and to violent self-definitions that is not seen by others.
That is, although violent conduct appears to be spontaneous
and volatile, it may have a long history in the violent individual's inner self-conversations regarding self, a close emotional
associate, and a recurringly problematic interpersonal situation.
In this situation it might be presumed that Kowalski experienced intense inner conflict over the situation he had placed his
wife in.

This murder, involving three persons, also suggests that
violent, intense interpersonal and psychological degradation was
inflicted on Mrs. Kowalski. Enacted violent conduct is triple-

edged, cutting back on victims, perpetrators, and their emotional, significant others.

The Structures of Violent Enacted Emotion

In violent emotional action individuals communicate a "framed," emergently violent definition of themselves and their associates. This entails a feeling that is felt by both the victim and the offender. Terror and pain may be felt on the one side, while guilt, satisfaction, and pleasure are felt on the other. A reflective process in which the act is defined, felt, and interpreted by both parties occurs.

The structures of violent, enacted emotion are fourfold, involving (1) an inversion of the everyday natural attitude regarding emotional action, (2) a circuit of selfness that connects violent individuals with their victims, (3) interpretive frames, and (4) interactional orientations to the world of family others.

The Natural Attitude of Emotionality. Three natural attitudes constrain and restrict the appearance of violent conduct in everyday life. The first is the illusion of the mood-neutral self, or emotionally in-control self—that people "express a mood somewhere in the middle range tending slightly toward euphoria" (Stone, 1977, p. 6). This illusion reduces the likelihood that out-of-control emotional selves will act violently toward family associates. Its violation, either by family members or by outsiders (Meisenhelder, 1979), can produce immediate feelings of helplessness, impending death, betrayal, self-violation, physical pain, and emotional nakedness.

The second natural attitude holds that moods, lived emotions, and intentional value feelings are situation-specific. That is, people are expected to fit their moods to the cognitive, personal, and moral tone of interactional occasions. Furthermore, violent actions are not expected to be a part of the interactional occasions in which the person is normally a participant.

Third, violence is, in the natural attitude, given an "other-worldliness," an "it occurs elsewhere" placement. That is, violence may occur in the lifeworld, but not in the lifeworld of this person or of this family. When it does appear, it produces immediate shock and the sense of betrayal noted above. Such appearances are given episodic notice and are not treated as "real" indications of the violent person's intentions, feelings, and attitudes. Should they become regular, they may be routinized by the victimized family members. Their causes may be lodged in the biographies and actions of the victims. That is, victims blame themselves for the violent actions another family member directs toward them.

Violent conduct ruptures the natural attitudes of emotionality. Violence places victims and their assailants outside the taken-for-granted structures of the world. Such conduct produces a sense of the bizarre, the unusual, the frightening, and the unknown. Violent conduct transforms family intimates into the categories of victims and assailants. Consider the following case of a man who attempted to "stomp" a fetus out of his former wife's abdomen.

In this case, which was presented to the supreme court of California, the court was asked to rule on whether an unborn but viable fetus is a human being (Marcus, 1982, pp. 161–163). The evidence in the case may be summarized as follows.

The petitioner and Teresa Keeler had obtained an interlocutory degree of divorce on September 27, 1968. They had been married for sixteen years. Unknown to Mr. Keeler, Mrs. Keeler was pregnant by a Mr. Ernest Vogt, with whom she had been living. Mrs. Keeler was in the third trimester of her pregnancy. Mr. Keeler had custody of their two daughters, aged twelve and thirteen. Mrs. Keeler had the right to take them on alternate weekends. On February 23, 1969, Mrs. Keeler was driving on a narrow mountain road in Amador County, having taken the girls home to their father. She met Mr. Keeler driving in the opposite direction. He blocked the road with his car and pulled her over to the side. He walked to her vehicle. He seemed calm. As she rolled down the window to hear him, he said, "I hear you're pregnant. If you are, you had better stay away from the girls and from here." Mrs. Keeler did not reply, and he opened the car door. She later testified that "he assisted me out of the car. . . . It wasn't rough at this time." Mr. Keeler then looked at her abdomen and became "extremely upset." He said,

"You sure are. I'm going to stomp it out of you." He pushed her against the car, shoved his knee into her abdomen, and struck her several blows in the face. She fainted, and when she regained consciousness, Mr. Keeler was gone. Mrs. Keeler drove back to Stockton, and the police and medical assistance were summoned.

She had suffered substantial facial injuries, as well as extensive bruising of the abdominal wall. Caesarean section was performed and the fetus was examined. The pathologist gave as his opinion that the cause of death was skull fracture with consequent cerebral hemorrhaging, that death would have been immediate, and that the injury could have been the result of force applied to the mother's abdomen. Penal code section 187 provides: "Murder is the unlawful killing of a human being, with malice aforethought" (Marcus, 1982, p. 163).

Although the court ruled that the penal code did not apply to Mr. Keeler, his violent actions toward his wife shattered the taken-for-granted status of their conversation on the highway and turned her (and her fetus) into the categories of physical objects and into the recipients of violence.

The Circuit of Selfness. A person is never free of emotion. Nor is one ever unattached from the world or too distant from potential violent actions that may be inflicted by family intimates, friends, or close associates. The circuit of selfness inevitably lodges the individual in the very violence he or she abhors.

Interpretive Frames. An interpretive frame reflects the person's current cognitive, moral, and personal attachment to herself and her present interactive situation. Such frames provide a framework for classifying fellow interactants into categories, or typifications, including whether the other who is confronted is a family intimate, a contemporary, a routine interactional associate, or a stranger. This frame also permits the classification of others in terms of gender identity, relational bondedness, biographical "nearness" or "farness," situational relevance for one's ongoing actions, and dangerousness to oneself. The "framed" classification of others is a temporal and situated process. Thus, particular categories of others are regarded as dangerous, near or far, and irrelevant or relevant to one's actions and safety de-

pending on the time of day and the places where they are met
or observed. Most people, most of the time, are temporally, and
perhaps spatially, near to others whom they regard as safe and
"undangerous." It is, of course, precisely those others who most
typically inflict violence. Violent others are frequently embedded in the circuit of selfness that attaches the person to her
family and to the world-at-hand.

A person may be attached to the world through two
modes, which Heidegger (1927/1962) has termed authentic and
inauthentic. Authentic attachment reveals a deep, sincere embracement of one's present situation. Inauthentic attachment
describes actions in which bad faith, role distance, and the
presentation of false selves predominate (Sartre, 1943/1978;
Goffman, 1959, 1961b). Violent conduct often appears under
the pretense of inauthentic attachment. That is, the violent individual pretends not to be about to engage in a violent action.
She appears to approach the person with authentic, sincere intentions in mind. When people are charged with violent conduct, they may contend that it was not their "real self" that
was acting. They make an appeal to an inauthentic mode of
being themselves. There is a seductiveness about violence that
catches victims off guard. This is so, in part, because the natural
attitudes toward emotional display work against doubt and suspicion of the family other.

Two modes of interaction in the world can be distinguished: interacting *at* another and interacting *with* another
(Denzin, 1980, p. 256). In interacting with another, a person
builds a line of action in a stepwise fashion with another, such
that their activities fit together in a mutual and reciprocal way.
In interacting at another (or against another), the other is transformed into an object, not a subject. Toward him the person directs wrath, anger, ressentiment, frustration, and perhaps physical violence.

Violent family conduct, it can now be argued, inverts the
everyday natural attitude regarding emotional display, for emotion breaks out in and during violence. In violence, a circuit of
interaction attaches individuals to the very violence they seek to
avoid. Violence, in turn, moves to the core of the authentic,

"real" self of the victim. Such conduct appears to implicate victims in a relationship in which they are interacted at, not with, even when they plead for reason.

The following account told by a ninety-one-year-old woman of how she was sexually assaulted and then robbed of her church contributions (Dey, 1982, pp. 1–2) displays these features of violent conduct. "Seated in a wheelchair and carrying a cane, the woman wept as she described in a strong voice the events of the evening of March 22. The victim told the . . . jury how she had gone to bed about 6:30 P.M. and was later confronted in her bedroom by a 'real dark-brown man' who possessed 'youthful, very strong arms. . . . I wasn't in bed very long until a human being appeared in the doorway,' the woman testified. 'I yelled for my son. I was frightened. . . . When I yelled, he came at me with both hands. I had a telephone at my bedside and I tried to reach for it.' " The assailant then grabbed her by the throat, tied her ankles, dragged her into the living room, and repeatedly sexually assaulted her. The victim testified that she asked her assailant "to pray to God and let me alone." She told jurors she placed money in the church contribution envelopes a month ahead of time. Her attacker ripped them open. "He sat at the front end of the bed. I could see his elbows moving and the scraps of paper on the floor," she said. "As near as I could tell, he was stuffing [the money] into his shirt."

Although this violent interaction did not occur between family members, it did take place in the woman's home, a presumed safe setting. Not only does the violence break the natural attitude regarding the place and display of violent conduct, it is directed toward the sexual body of a ninety-one-year-old woman. This fact amplifies the terrifying nature of the interaction.

Violent Emotional Action

The "with" and "against" interactional orientations join the person's actions and emotions with or separate them from the actions and feelings of others. In active emotional embodiment the bodies of the participants become instruments, or tools, or even weapons. In passive emotional embodiment one's body is a complementary extension of one's verbal and emotional lines of action. Violent embodied emotion involves the display, use, and articulation of the lived body in a negative, hostile manner. The negativity of the body may be passive or active. Just as persons hurl forth emotional anger with their voices, the silent, loud languages and actions of their bodies may speak more directly and more meaningfully than their utterances.

Athens (1980, pp. 49–51) presents an account by a man in his late twenties, with a violent self-image, who had committed forcible rape.

> I hadn't had any pussy for some time so I felt horny as shit. Then I started thinking about this girl I met at a party a couple of weeks ago. She was built thin but enough meat on her to throw it up to me good. She never acted interested in me, but I hear that her and the older woman in her building were giving up boatloads of pussy. I was drunk and my mind was on pussy so I headed for their place. (I found out from a friend where they lived.) When I got there, I noticed an older woman in her room with the door wide open so I went in and said hi. She asked me what I wanted. I said I wanted sex and decided to try to talk her into fucking first. But she said, "I'm not going to do anything like that with you," so I knew then that I was just going to take it. I said, "Yes, you are," and beat on her but she still wouldn't give open so I got the pipe . . . .

Here active emotional embodiment results in the physical abuse and rape of a woman. The woman is interacted at, not with. The natural attitude of emotional display is broken. She is treated as an inauthentic object that is an obstacle to the man's "authentic" sexual intentions.

Athens's (1980) seminal and highly instructive study of violent criminal acts reveals that violent emotional actions are often the *reflective* consequences of a violent actor's feeling that violence is necessary for physical protection, is the only appropriate action in a frustrative situation, or is called for because the other is defined as evil and as belittling the person. In each of these situations, which Athens respectively terms defensive, frustrative, and malefic, the attitudes of the victim and a generalized other are taken. In defensive situations a violent plan of action is judged to be the only means of preventing physical injury to self, to an intimate, or to one's reputation. In frustrative situations violence is judged to be the most appropriate "means of handling another person's potential or attempted blockage of the larger act the actor wants to carry out—for example, robbery, sexual intercourse, car theft" (Athens, 1980, p. 23). It is also a method for blocking or stopping an act another person wants to carry out—for example, calling the police. Forcible rape and murder are two forms of this line of violent emotional action.

The following factors are basic to violent emotional action:

1. The victim is seen as calling out the violent action in her actions toward the person: Violence is justified, and its source is in the other person.
2. A repertoire of violent conduct and violent thought is present in the violent actor's current mode of attachment to the world. That is, he knows how to act violently. He is capable of putting his body into an embodied stream of violent conduct.
3. Violent conduct is seen as a project that can be carried out and must be carried out *now.*
4. An inner moral core of the violent person is seen as having been affected by the actions of the victim; for example, he has been addressed profanely, he has been embarrassed, a close intimate has been attacked.
5. The individual is disposed to act, through self-indications and interactions, in a violent manner.
6. The individual perceives social support for his violent actions through the interpretations he attributes to significant others (Athens, 1980).
7. The victim's moral worth is denied, suspended, deemed irrelevant, or judged to be in need of physical attack so that

it will become more worthy—for example, a moral value will be beaten into him. Child abuse often involves such attacks. An abusive father reported, "I beat that son-ofabitchin' teenage son of mine till he cried. Now he knows what *honest* means!"

8. Alternative views of the violent action are denied and suspended. The moral, legal, and personal consequences of the violent action (for the person and the victim) are neutralized (Sykes and Matza, 1959).

9. Violence is now justified—indeed, demanded.

10. Once the violent action is underway, it assumes its own momentum and becomes all-absorbing. The person and the victim are indissolubly united in the joint production of the violent activity (Denzin, 1982b, p. 125).

In violence the perpetrator's emotions may flood over him, overwhelming him in a "blind rage," or he may act "cold-bloodedly" (Capote, 1965; Mailer, 1979). That is, he may control his violence and his emotionality, coolly inflicting pain and punishment on the victim. In either case—coolly or blindly—the person is drawn, through the circuit of selfness, into the violent activity and becomes a part of it.

Coldblooded violence deserves elaboration. Violent behavior may be free of inner emotional feeling for the perpetrator. Many of Athens's respondents reported little emotion during or after their violent activity. Their actions were carried out with the explicit intentions of producing harm, pain, and negative self-feelings in the victim. In such situations power over the victim is sought and may be obtained. Negative fellow-feeling, in which pleasure is taken in the pain experienced by another, may underlie the violent conduct (Scheler, 1913/1970, pp. 14, 22). Or the person may seek personal atonement and mercy from a violent act such as murder (Abbott, 1981, p. 70).

The emotional self-feeling that emerges from this conduct elevates the moral worth and dignity of the violent person at the expense (personal, moral, psychological, physical) of the victim. The victim's suffering provides the phenomenological cause and reward—the reasons for the violent act and the desired, sought-after feelings of the perpetrator. The moral value of the victim as a person is diminished, if not annihilated, in physically violent emotional activity.

Annihilation of the victim may, in fact, be the purpose of the violence. *In the inner temporality of violence all that is sought is the physical imposing of one's will on the will and body of another.* Time stops as the violent person produces a physical display of his violent thoughts on the body of the victim. Indeed, a major underlying motive for violent action is the fact that such conduct leaves a mark—an injury, a crippled, maimed body—as well as a damaged self. Where such marks are not made (and left), the violent act might well be judged a failure.

It is important to note that many violent actions are animated by mind- and mood-altering substances. Such chemicals appear to alter, if not remove, the normal restraints of the natural attitude regarding emotional-violent displays. Such chemicals also alter the flow of time in the stream of consciousness, giving rise to the feeling that time has stopped or has been both sped up and spread out during the moment of violence. Gelles (1979, p. 173) argues that people "will drink knowing that inebriation will give them an excuse for their violence." He suggests that the relationship between alcohol and violence is spurious. Gelles may be overlooking the fact that persons who are drawn to violence are also drawn to alcohol. Such persons seek the same experience in alcohol that they find in violence—namely, the regaining of a loss of self.

Inflicting Emotion

In physically abusive emotional behavior one person inflicts and imposes his emotional and physical definition of an interpersonal situation on another. In symbolically abusive conduct he draws emotional associates into his emotionally defined world. He inflicts his inner stream of feelings, values, and moods on another. He makes others his emotional captives. Taking them as hostages, he offers as a condition of release from emotional captivity acquiescence to his moods and feelings. He inflicts his emotions, in the form of punishments, on those closest to him. Rather than being physically attacked, the other is abused and attacked with and through emotion.

Three forms of inflicting emotion can be distinguished. First, emotional aggressors may inflict paradox and contradiction on their intimate (family) associates. They ask for love after they have pushed a loved child or spouse to the side. A mother asks her child for affection but flinches when the child gives her a hug. A father screams, "I didn't mean it! I don't hate you!" In each case the emotional aggressor places the victim in an emotional paradox, or a double bind (Bateson, 1972, p. 212; Wiley, 1980). Emotional confusion is produced, which is another form of emotional violence.

Second, through emotion the aggressor attacks the inner core of the other's integrity. This is often done through the emotional outburst—the direct attack on another's mood, self, and person. In the emotional outburst, an emotional line of action is hurled at the other. Consider the following:

> I went up to the sonofabitch and told him I hated him. He was standing there so smug and calm in front of a group of people at the party. I said, "You really screwed up my life. I hope you're happy. I got fired because of you. I've hated you for a long time. Now I just have pity. You miserable bastard. I hope you die and go to hell. You've fucked up everybody's life that you've ever touched. You're a miserable excuse for a human being. I don't see how anybody can stand to talk to you, let alone be seen with you" [Field observation, thirty-eight-year-old woman, April 1982].

The emotional outburst, like the physically violent act, transforms the other into an object, diminishes his moral and personal worth, and draws on a family (or personal) bond between the parties. The grounds for the emotional act are embedded in the biography that joins the two (or more) parties. In the outburst no dialogue is intended, nor is emotional understanding a goal. Emotional release is sought, and with release, vindication. Having suffered her feelings in silence, the person gets even by hurting the feelings of the victim. The harm and pain inflicted are felt to be justified. The person's own feelings have been hurt, at an earlier time, by the victim. By hurting the feelings of the other, the person attacks the victim's inner core as a person. After all, this is what emotional outbursts are all about—the moral and personal destruction of the other as a person. Hence, the person who symbolically inflicts emotion is as abusive as the person who physically attacks another, if not more so.

The third manner of inflicting emotion on a family member involves the use, often unwittingly, of "out of control" emotionality. Out-of-control emotions, including drunken outbursts, spurts of insanity, passive emotional withdrawals, and prolonged absences from the family setting (binges), introduce an insanity of place into the family (Goffman, 1971, pp. 335–390). Other family intimates are made to feel responsible for the insane, out-of-control member, while that member inflicts a reign of terror over the household. She is not responsible for her actions, because her emotions are out of control. She is, however, accorded a position of control, if only as a guise so that others may take greater control over her. Out-of-control emotions, when lodged in the actions of a single family member, radiate throughout the family, producing a jointly felt insanity. Emotional paradox and emotional outbursts merge into a solitary field of experience in which, to paraphrase O'Neill, each day is a journey into night and darkness. Violent, insane thoughts grip the entire family. Together and alone they live a nightmare of overt and suppressed violence.

The point to be drawn from this discussion of violent emotional actions and inflicted emotionality may be stated simply: The violent (and, by implication, nonviolent) emotions that a family member embodies and enacts are present in the actions of others. The actions of the other family members toward the violent individual call forth, as Mead (1934) suggested, the actions that are taken toward him. A field of violent experience that embraces all parties is thereby produced. In short, violent emotional conduct lies in the fields of experience that join intimates to one another through the interaction process. In this sense victims of violent attacks contribute to and often amplify the violence they receive. This is so because they are part of the very field of experience in which the violence occurs.

Spurious, Playful, Real, and Paradoxical Violence

Violent emotional and nonemotional interactions in the family are constructed not on the premise "This is violence" but, rather, on the question "Is this violence?" (See Bateson, 1972, p. 182, for a parallel set of questions for play.) The question asked takes several forms: (1) "Is this violence real?" (2) "Is this violence fake, spurious, or accidental?" (3) "Is this violence pretended and playful?" The underlying premise of violent interaction questions the violent and emotional intentionality of the initiating individual. That is, "Is what is happening here really violence or something else?" In answering the question of the realness of the violent conduct, paradoxical messages are often conveyed, and metacommunication and metainterpretation may be required. Bateson (1972, p. 189) illustrates this process in reference to animal behavior, where three types of message may be present and deduced: "(a) messages of the sort which we call mood-signs; (b) messages which simulate mood-signs (in play, threat, histrionics, etc.); and (c) messages . . . which resemble them. The message 'This is play' is of this third type. It tells the receiver that certain nips and other meaningful actions are not messages of the first type." A mood-sign is "an outwardly perceptible event which is part of the physiological process which we call a mood . . . the nonhuman mammal is automatically excited by the odor of another; and rightly so, inasmuch as the secretion of that sign is an 'involuntary' mood-sign" (Bateson, 1972, p. 178).

A triadic message structure involving mood-signs, simulated mood-signs, and discriminations between the two must be interpreted if the violent-emotional intentions of another are to be understood and acted on. If this is to be a violent interaction, then the victim must be able to discriminate among real, intentional mood-signs, simulated mood-signs, and nonverbal mood-signs (embodied actions) that contradict verbal declarations of intent.

For the message "This is real violence" to be conveyed, there must be no contradiction among the three message categories distinguished by Bateson. When there is contradiction, paradox, or confusion, then spurious, accidental, pretended, or playful violence may be defined as existing.

Spurious violence is false and often accidental, as when a family member makes an outward show of "violent" action toward another but does not carry through with an actual violent action. In spurious violence, nonviolence is intended. A mockery of real violence is produced. The person embodies a violent repertoire of behavior that she does not believe. Inwardly the outwardly violent family member is not taking herself seriously. However, her outer stream of behavior may lead others to believe in her actions and to act violently in response to an unintended violent action or utterance. Consider the following interaction between two teenage sisters who are going down a stairway in the family home at the same time.

Older sister: (Slips on the stairs, hitting her younger sister on the shoulder; her right foot catches the sister's heel, causing her to fall down the stairway.)

Younger sister: (Falls to the bottom of the stairs, gets up, runs up the stairs, hits her sister in the stomach, and shouts) I hate you! You hurt me! That's not funny! (Begins crying, runs out of the house.) [Emotions project, winter 1982].

Here a "mixed" episode of intended and unintended violence is produced. The older sister apparently did not intend to slip or to hit and trip her younger sister. The younger sister, however, did not interpret the messages as simulation or accident. She regarded them as real messages of intended violence and acted accordingly and in kind.

Spurious, false, and/or accidental violence is not to be confused with playful violence. In playful violence a family member tenders an intentional violent-emotional attitude or action in a playful manner. He would play at being violent if his family associates were to reciprocate in a playful manner. In playful violence the person indicates, through actions, utterances, and gestures, that a double or metamessage is intended. For example, the slap on the back that a father directs toward his teenage son is not a slap but a greeting, or sign of affection. Similarly, when a three-year-old child jumps on her father's stomach at 6:15 in the morning, she is intending neither to hurt nor to startle but, rather, to play. Should the father not interpret the action in a playful frame and act violently, by hitting the child, swearing, and stomping out of the bedroom, a violent episode would be produced out of playful beginnings.

In playful violence, seriousness is denied. A step "away from literal, habitual, and taken-for-granted reality is taken" (Lynch, 1982, p. 27). Playful violence is conveyed through the interpersonal interaction process in winks, smiles, shrugs, voice intonations, hand and shoulder movements, shifts in gait, and so on (Lynch, 1982, p. 29).

Real violence is intentional, believed in, authentic, doubted neither by the person nor by his family associates. In real violence the person embodies a violent line of action that he cannot willfully drop or walk away from once he has entered into it. Real violence grips the aggressor. He cannot get out of it as he pleases. Like real emotion, "it fades away by itself, but one cannot put a stop to it" (Sartre, 1939/1962, p. 76). Real violence radiates through the bodies of both the violent person and the victim. It is "naked emotion" with nothing held back. Its effects may be seductively intoxicating. There is a "sweetness" to its "madness." It is felt deeply in the inner stream of consciousness. Its reality crowds out other attitudes and beliefs. It totally destroys alternative definitions of the situation. In real violence the inner, moral, authentic core of the victim is attacked.

Physiological phenomena give the emotions that follow episodes of real violence an aura of genuineness. They are the "phenomena of belief" (Sartre, 1939/1962, p. 76). Although the physiological reactions to violence must be distinguished from violent behavior, they do provide a substratum of belief that gives violent experiences a believability and depth that are perhaps unparalleled. They combine with the violent behavior and the victim's emotional state of mind to produce a shattering experience that cannot be easily forgotten or easily overcome. Such episodes take on an obdurate existence in the streams of consciousness of the victim.

Violent individuals may, like their victims, find the memories of their violence intolerable. Consider the following account:

> The twenty-five or more women Gerald Stano says he strangled, stabbed, or shot stepped willingly into his car, and he says all were the victims of his drinking and fits of rage.
>
> "I would have to say alcohol would be the start," Stano told a reporter in an interview published Tuesday.
>
> "Beer and Jack Daniels would help . . . relieve one part of my mind, and the other part of my mind, the subconscious, would start to take over. I'd just start off going for a ride, just to relieve some of the tension for myself."
>
> "Instead," he says, "it would be directed at the young ladies in my car" ["Inmate Links Drinking, Murder," October 6, 1982, p. C9].

Stano, a former cook, motel clerk, and service station attendant who is serving three consecutive life sentences on guilty pleas of murdering three women, has confessed to killing at least twenty-five more in Florida. Described as being without conscience, Stano said he was attracted to women by "the way they set everything in motion when they go walking down the road." Most of them were wearing blue, his favorite color, and most had shoulder-length hair, he said. He said he got into arguments with the women, setting off his homicidal rages. The end result would be the death of a young lady. "Then I'd usually try to make it back in one piece to my apartment or where I was living at the time," he said. "That was a little bit like relieving the tension, but I would wake up in the morning with a heck of a hangover and go to work and not remember what had happened that night. Either I couldn't or I could but I didn't want to" ("Inmate Links Drinking, Murder," October 6, 1982, p. C9). Here violence traps the violent self.

Paradoxical violence combines and often confuses (for victims) spurious, accidental, playful, and real violence. In paradoxical violence more than one interactional meaning is communicated at once. In Bateson's terms the following paradox is communicated:

All the Messages Here are Untrue.

"I don't want to harm you."

"I want to harm you."

A contradiction is established if the first message is accepted. If the statement is true, it must be false. Similar conclusions hold for the other statements. If the first statement is "true, then all the others must be false; and vice versa, if the first statement be untrue then all the others must be true" (Bateson, 1972, p. 184). Similar paradoxes arise in families under the following circumstances: (1) A family member's embodied actions convey violence, but her verbal declarations of mood and intent contradict that message—for example, "I don't want to have to hit you and hurt you, but I have to." (2) A family member's playful acts are taken as conveying intended, real violence. (3) Serious, violent intentions are taken playfully, thus accelerating the violence, because the violent member demands to be taken seriously. (4) Spurious, false, or playful violence is believed in by others, when the person intends real violence. In this case the person may be locked into pretended violence when real violence is intended.

In each of these conditions contradictory violence-awareness contexts are produced. Misinformation is communicated, violent and nonviolent lines of action are thwarted, emotional and cognitive ambiguity appears. Wedges or gaps in the field of experience appear. Family members become trapped in emotional lines of action that are not intended. The interaction-awareness context moves action along the lines of pretension, suspicion, ambiguity, and denial (Glaser and Strauss, 1967).

The Interiority of Family Violence

The inner life of the family of violence revolves around recurring episodes of inflicted emotion, embodied violence, and emotional paradox. Violence, in its several forms, is a routinized feature of daily family life. The interiority, or inner side, of the family of violence may be approached through a discussion of the following topics: (1) the merry-go-round of violence, (2) the network of selves and identities that make up the family as a small primary group, (3) the uses and functions of violence, (4) the fields of experience of violence, (5) the situationality of violence, (6) the temporality of violence, and (7) the meanings and interpretations of violence.

The Merry-Go-Round of Violence. Interspersed throughout violence are efforts to restore family interactions to normality (see Gelles, 1972, pp. 58-70, 113-119). A merry-go-round of violence and nonviolence, emotional clarity and emotional paradox is lived on a daily basis. The family members are *on* and *in* a circuit of experience that seems vicious, endless, and inwardly spiraling. Promises are made and then broken in moments of outrage or violence. Amends are made. Lavish purchases are showered on victims. Outside help from family therapists, psychiatrists, clinical psychologists, ministers, and relatives is sought. The violent family member may be judged mentally ill and hence not responsible for his actions; or he may be judged to be willfully violent and dangerous. The causes of violence may be lodged in the family economic condition or in a spouse's job situation. Violence may be judged to be merely episodic and caused by out-of-the-ordinary circumstances, in which case patterns of attempted violence-denial and avoidance may be set in force.

Still, the violence will not go away. Long periods of normality are suddenly broken by an outburst of violence. The family cannot seem to get out of the cycle of violence, no matter how hard it individually and collectively tries. The slightest, seemingly trivial yet untoward act sets the violent family member off into a sequence of violent conduct.

If the family appears to be returning to normal, sudden

violent outbursts may be suffered in silence. A pattern of violence-denial is set in motion, for to admit to the reappearance of violence is to risk its undeniable return. Bruises and other physical marks are explained in terms of clumsy actions taken by the person. Their visible presence on the body of the victim serves to remind the offender that his last bout of violence left its mark. The denial of the violence may produce guilt and anger in the offender, thus laying the grounds for new violence.

Such denials place the family of violence in a collective state of bad faith (Sartre, 1943/1978, pp. 96-116). They deceive themselves into believing that the violence is not real or does not exist. It is their acceptance of not believing what they believe that places them in bad faith (Sartre, 1943/1978, p. 115). By acting as if they accepted what they do not believe, they disarm in advance all arguments that might reveal to them that they are deeply embedded in a violent situation that requires action. Their bad faith does not succeed in believing what they wish it to believe. It is precisely this situation that traps them, and at some level of reflection they all know this.

Violent acts are hidden inside the closed walls of the home (Straus, Gelles, and Steinmetz, 1980). Violence will not be reported to outsiders for fear of publicity. The violence remains a private family matter. Violence and bad faith continue. The following account illustrates this point:

Mrs.: I didn't want any of the neighbors to know that he was behaving that way . . . that's why I didn't have any neighbors. I didn't even call the police because I was afraid they'd put it in the paper [Gelles, 1972, p. 108].

In such circumstances original acts of physical violence are interiorized by each family member. The violence extends into every realm of his or her being. Physical violence produces inner turmoil, mental anguish, negative feelings for self, and doubt about one's meanings as a person at the deep, authentic level. It closes the family of violence in on itself. As the example above reveals, interactions with persons outside the family, if ever initiated, are terminated.

The Family as a Network of Selves. The family of violence is a network of selves attached to an ecological order of
spaces, places, and social objects. Selves seek hiding places, or
safe niches, and find excuses for not being in the same place as
the violent member. As the family withdraws into itself, it
draws apart internally. Patterns of member avoidance are set in
motion and routinized. The home becomes an empty meeting
place, devoid of warmth, intimacy, and safety. Members have
no safe place to hide, for the violent member seeks them out. Violence, after all, must be inflicted in an interpersonal field of experience (Toch, 1969). Consider the following accounts:

Wife: We'd stay away from home, me and the kids. I didn't
          want them there when he came home. We went to my
          parents', but he called and came over. He was mad
          'cause we weren't home. He hit me in front of my par-
          ents, tried to pull and drag me out of the house. He
          screamed at the kids. He blamed them for taking me
          away from him (Aged thirty-five, separated from hus-
          band of twelve years).

Wife: I went into the children's bedroom to sleep. He had
          been drinking and came into our bedroom shouting and
          swearing about how I didn't understand him and what
          was important to him. I thought he had gone to sleep.
          He stormed into the children's room, grabbed me out of
          bed, and flung me across the room. I couldn't believe it.
          It was like I was a rag doll. He cut his hand and blood
          got on my face. When he saw the blood on my face, he
          began to cry. He held me in his arms and asked me what
          happened. Then he just slumped against the wall and
          cried. I was afraid to do anything, and yet I wanted to
          do something (Aged thirty-two, married seven years,
          two children). [Emotions project, spring 1982].

The offender becomes a victim of his own violent actions. Even
offenders have no safe place to hide, for how can they hide
from themselves?

An internal identity structure built around violence appears in the family of violence. Dominance and submission patterns are produced. A wife may assume the identity of "family manager" because the violent father and husband cannot be depended on. This increases the tensions in the family. The wife may become a protector of her children, standing between them and a violent father. Older children may act as go-betweens, mediating between the violent parent and younger children. Younger children may become passive victims, unable to defend themselves; or they may become isolates, placed outside the circles of family interaction.

"Arbitrators" and "shields" may emerge in the family. The oldest children may take it on themselves to receive the violence intended for a mother or younger sibling. "Arbitrators" act as interpreters who read the moods and intentions of other family members. They may offer excuses for the untoward actions of a family member who provokes violence. Such members often internalize the violence intended for others. Other family members, often the nonproblematic parent, become "enablers" who attempt to soothe the violent emotions of the offender. They may unwittingly produce more violence because their actions can be read as attempts to control, manipulate, and take power away from the violent parent.

A constellation of identities, each drawn from the atmosphere of violence that surrounds the family of violence, is thus produced. Family managers, protectors, go-betweens, passive victims, arbitrators, shields, isolates, and enablers are identities and repertoires of action that are built on the "normal" family identities of mother, father, daughter, and son. The age-structured, sex-stratified authority structures of the normal family are absent in the family of violence.

Violence transforms the family into a different type of small, primary group (Cooley, 1902/1956). It is a small group characterized by schismogenesis (Bateson, 1972, pp. 64, 68-72, 108-111, 324, 333). The dyadic and triadic relations that make up the family of violence are characterized by symmetrical and complementary interactions. In symmetrical interactions the behaviors of two or more family members are regarded as similar and are linked so that more of the behavior by one member stimulates more of the same by another. The relationship is symmetrical in regard to these behaviors. Intimacy, violence, and love are instances of this type of behavior. In complementary interactions, the behaviors of two or more family members are dissimilar but mutually linked, so that more of one member's behaviors (for example, enabling, protecting, managing, arbitrating, shielding, isolating) stimulates more of another member's fitting-together behavior (for example, violence).

Bateson (1972, p. 324) suggests that "both complementary and symmetrical relationships are liable to progressive changes . . . of the sort called 'schismogenesis.' " Schismogenic change involves the progressive differentiation and increase of symmetrical and/or complementary behaviors such that the "breakdown of the whole system" becomes a likelihood (p. 68). Bateson illustrates this point with the case of complementary differentiation: "If, for example, the series O,P,Q includes patterns culturally regarded as assertive, while U,V,W includes cultural submissiveness, it is likely that submissiveness will promote assertiveness, which in turn will promote submissiveness. This schismogenesis, unless it is restrained, leads to a progressive unilateral distortion of the personalities of the members of both groups, which results in mutual hostility between them and must end in the breakdown of the system" (p. 68). If the patterns of interaction in a family include violence and its avoidance, then the reply to more violence, or more avoidance, is more violence and more avoidance. The fitting of these two patterns into a differentiated complementary structure with an extreme emphasis on either pattern destroys the family (see Erchak, 1981).

The ingredients of double binding are also present in the violent family (Bateson, 1972, pp. 206-207). That is, contradictory negative and positive injunctions are repeatedly invoked in a field of experience that cannot be escaped. The family is trapped in its own negative field of violent experience.

Families of violence are caught in double-binding patterns of interaction that increase hostility, conflict, and the collapse of the family as a unitary system of selves. The schismogenic process, in which violence is a central component, spins out of control. Violence, rather than being a single act, becomes a process over which no family member has apparent control.

Violent families, as small groups, are divided along the lines of intimacy, nearness, "we-ness," solidarity, and warmth, on the one side, and fear, rage, panic, and terror, on the other. The violent family is caught in a network of relationships that can self-destruct. The one-person, dyadic, and triadic relationships that makes up families are fractured in and through violence (see Simmel, 1950; Gelles, 1972, pp. 27–28; Butler, 1903; O'Neill, 1955; Albee, 1962). The fact that force appears to be legitimated in families merely contributes to the paradoxes that surround families of violence (see Stark and McEvoy, 1970).

The Uses of Violence. The interiority of violence turns its use into a means of making oneself clear and asserting oneself, which often requires a venting of hostility, anger, and frustration. Violence is also used as a means of "quieting" a situation, taking the initiative when on the defensive, and placing a distance between oneself and other family members. These uses of violence give it a double-edged quality, for it cuts both into the personal life of each family member and into the collective life of the family as a whole. The inner world of the family is fraught with ambiguity, guilt, hesitation, insecurity, and tendencies toward flight. A wish to not have things as they are is interwoven with a haunting desire for normality. The hovering, lingering sense that things might be different enters into every family interaction as an unstated background expectancy. Family interactions are sketched and lived against this hope. Family members strain and push themselves. They lie and deceive themselves into believing that things are getting better. They try to act "as if" violence were not in the background—or the foreground. "Being on edge" is a normal state of affairs for violent families.

Fields of Experience. The fields of experience that plague violent families engulf all family members, even those not directly involved in a violent episode; they exist as a constant and oppressive force. They inextricably and vividly connect the past with the future, in the lived, frightening moments of the present. These fields of experience are the family. That is, each fam-

ily member is part of the field of experience that he both abhors and produces. The inner side of this field of experience
comes at the family, surrounding them, yet it is perceived, in
part, as being outside them; and hence, while they are inside it,
it is seen as something that will be passed through. That is,
fields of experience are both discrete episodes of experience and
encompassing frames of reference.

Each experiential frame within the field of violent experience is seen as having its own inner logic, its own sensibility, rationality, order, and sense of sequencing. Although violence appears violent and irrational from the outside, from the inside it
has an intrinsic order and rationality. Each participant in a violent episode can "make sense" out of her own actions, pointing
to prior actions and events as plausible phenomenological causes
for her conduct. Fields of violent experience are seen as unalter-
able once the member is inside them. The flow of events that
the member is producing and experiencing moves at a patterned
rate that appears unchangeable. It must be accepted as obdurate
reality; as when an automobile goes into a skid, sliding off a
steep embankment, the violent events that are coming at the
person cannot be averted. If events in fields of experience appear to get out of hand, all that can be changed is the person's
interpretations of the events she is experiencing.

The Situationality of Violence. The situations of violence
are phenomenological constructions (see Wolfgang and Ferracuti, 1982, pp. 40, 110, 191, 248; Monahan and Klassen, 1982,
pp. 293–300; Gelles, 1972, pp. 93–118). There is no objectively
violent situation, only the situation of violence as experienced
by the family member. That situation occurs in the field of violent experience that encompasses the person at the moment.
The places of family violence are where members bring themselves or find themselves taken. Gelles (1972, pp. 94–98) suggests that family kitchens, living rooms, and bedrooms are the
commonest places for the situated violence that occurs in families. At an earlier time in the family's history, these were the
gathering places for warm, intimate interactions.

The violent situation is always just ahead of the victim,

yet also just behind her. She is part of the very situation that is doing violence to her. In that situation the process of violence is lodged. Violence is illuminated and lived in the personal situation of the victim and the offender. There is no privileged situation that the member can sit atop of, only the situation she is currently occupying and confronting. However, the situated experiences that occur in the family assume an obdurateness that will not go away. The family ceases to be a family in the minds of its members and becomes a situation to be escaped, avoided, or destroyed. It is a situation that exists in their minds.

The Temporality of Violence. The temporality of violence and emotionality is circular. The future, the present, and the past are vividly interconnected in violent emotional acts. The distinction between past, present, and future is blurred in the situation of violence. Time is both drawn out, as if in slow motion, and held still. In the blurred moments of violence everything happens at once. The emotions of fear, pain, self-denial, hatred, and dread burn into the person in a single instant. There is a searing "presentness" to the moment of violence. Its traces are felt deeply. Historically there is a sense in which all previous acts of violence are being relived in the present. The historicality of family violence lies in the future, not in the past. The past comes toward the person from the future (Heidegger, 1927/1962, p. 438).

Times between violence become problematic. Waiting for the violent family member to come home can be interminable. Minutes stretch into hours. Time both races forward and seems to stop. On the one side, as long as the family member is not home, violence cannot occur. However, the longer he is away from home, the greater the fear that something has happened to him grows, as well as the anxiety that surrounds the waiting for his return. The fear that violence will occur when he does return home increases the likelihood that his arrival will be met with anger, confusion, and hesitation. This, in turn, increases the likelihood that violence will be produced. To repeat, the person abhorring violence calls out violence in her own actions toward the offender.

Family Repair: Out of Violence

Trapped within an interactional world that feeds on violence, doubt, negative emotionality, physically abused bodies and selves, deceptions and lies, the family of violence appears to have no option but to destroy itself. This is so *if* the members remain inside the structures of bad faith that prevent the open disclosure of what is happening to them. Bad faith, whose first act "is to flee what it cannot flee, to flee what it is" (Sartre, 1943/1978, p. 115) must be replaced by good faith. Good faith, which wishes to flee the "not believing what one believes" by finding openness and being in the freedom of its own honesty, is free to choose its own ends. It seeks freedom, and freely chooses freedom, over bad faith's choice of not being free. The "coefficients of adversity" (Sartre, 1943/1978, p. 628) in my world, which are the limits or constraints I impose on myself, either trap me in my own nonfreedom or become vehicles for the expression of my freedom. The situations I confront are the contingencies of my freedom in the world. I can choose to be overwhelmed by these situations, or I can alter them. I can redefine them, I can change them. I can move out of them. But in every case I will be in the situation I confront—for I am my own situation.

So it is with the family of violence. They can collectively (and individually) redefine themselves, move out, or be overwhelmed and destroyed. But everywhere they go, they will constitute the situation they are in. To move out of violence requires a fundamental restructuring of the relationship the family of violence has with itself. The coefficients of adversity that violence sets before them can be destroyed, but not through violence. That is, the family can remove violence from their world by refusing to act in ways that promote and engender the schismogenic patterns they are trapped in. This requires open confrontation of violence, not willing submission to it. Patterns of nonviolence must be promoted. An open challenge to the violent member to be violent in the face of nonviolence must be made. The violent member must be made to see the destructiveness of his or her violence. The nonviolent, nonsubmissive action taken in the face of violence discloses to the violent member the very violence that controls his or her behavior. The violent self must be confronted by a nonviolent, noncompliant self. The nonviolent self must, in its moment of choice and freedom, disclose itself as a self who feels and who has feelings for the violent self. The violent self is thereby presented with choices. The violent member can choose to be trapped within violence, or he or she can be free to be not violent. Most important, the fact of that choice is made public and no longer hidden within the structures of bad faith. Furthermore, that member's violence is no longer embedded in the interactions that hold the family together; for by refusing to interact within the fields of violence that have previously obtained in the family, the nonviolent members reveal the violent member to himself as he is.

This standing up in the fields of violent experience and refusing to interact in a self-destructive fashion frees the nonviolent family members to pursue their choices. They can now be free of violence and free to find themselves. Making this option available to themselves, they also make it available to the violent member; for he is also free not to be violent—he is free to find alternative interactional ways of being himself.

By taking a stand in the interactional fields of the family, the nonviolent members reclaim their home for themselves. They bring new meanings into the situations of the family. They disclose themselves to one another as feeling persons. They must, however, take a stand for their own freedom. Only by so doing will they move out of the violent selves and social situations they have been trapped in for so long. Such actions will also free the violent member from her violence. If she chooses to be violent, the greatest price of all will be paid, for she will have only one person left to turn violence toward—herself.

This road out of violence is threefold. First, each family member must reexamine his or her place in the violent network of selves that defines the family situation. Each member, in his or her way, has been violent. These symbolic, emotional, and physical patterns of interaction must be exposed and altered.

Second, the member who has been defined as the producer of the family violence must reexamine his or her relationship to the family and to himself or herself. This person's attention must be focused on the self, not on the other family members, just as the other family members must focus on themselves, not on the "violent" member. Each member must learn to find the self that is his or her own and that has been lost in the interactions that have thus far obtained in the family.

Third, the family must learn how to interact nonviolently. They can do so only by focusing on themselves as individuals. The home must be redefined in terms that promote nonviolence. Old memories attached to violent places must be replaced by new memories and new experiences that draw the members back together, to one another.

These three lines of action hold the promise of removing the coefficients of adversity and destruction that violence has imposed on the family of violence. New coefficients of freedom and choice can replace the old structures that have trapped and destroyed the family. The meanings of this new choice cannot be estimated, for freedom's possibilities cannot be charted. What is promised, however, is the regaining or the attaining of a mode of family existence that allows each family member to find himself or herself in a network of interacting selves who are nonviolent and not afraid of one another. Warmth, intimacy, "we-ness," and solidarity, sown from the seeds of nonviolence, emotional understanding, and emotional embracement, can replace the nightmare of terror that previously captured and held the family of violence.

Chapter Seven

The Divided Self

"An emotion can only be overcome by an emotion."

—Spinoza

The phenomenology of the emotionally divided self requires analysis, for the self of the violent person is emotionally divided. The emotionally divided self has been described as a self against itself, as a "belle ame" (beautiful soul), as a false self-system, as a self trapped within its own bad faith, as a self without objective existence, as a self that is torn apart internally, as a self that feels emptiness and nothing. The emotionally divided self is a disembodied self (see Chapter Two; Lacan, 1968, p. 44; Laing, 1965, pp. 65-119; Wilden, 1968, pp. 284-292; James, 1904/1961, pp. 143-159). Self-estrangement (Hegel, 1910, pp. 508-513), self-loathing, and self-destructiveness are key features of the emotionally divided self. Characteristic feelings include guilt, anger, anxiety, fear, trepidation, dread, self-despair, suspicion, self-irritation, exasperation, a loss of self-hope, a splitting of the self from the body, an inability to communicate with others, and extreme withdrawal. Suicidal thoughts are not uncommon. Resentment toward the past and fear of

both the past and the future are overwhelming temporal orientations. The present is experienced as oppressive. The subject
withdraws from the present into himself. A temporal vacuum
engulfs him.

Such subjects have been treated in the psychiatric literature under various terms, including *affective disorders, schizophrenia, psychosis, manic-depression,* and *pathological destructiveness* (Laing, 1965; Sullivan, 1956; Spitzer and Denzin, 1968;
Cockerham, 1981). The earlier literature variously used the
terms *psychopathic* and *sociopathic* to describe such individuals. Violence toward self, in the form of self-destructive actions and thoughts, is frequent. Violence toward others, through
emotional violence, inflicted emotionality, symbolic withdrawal, and physical attacks, is also common.

This self places in stark dimensions the underlying thesis
of this work that self-feelings lie at the core of emotionality.
Discussion will be organized around (1) the structures of the
emotionally divided self, (2) the emotionality of the divided
self, and (3) collapse and repair of the emotionally divided self.

Consider the following examples of emotionally divided
selves. The first is a twenty-six-year-old male.

> Whilst in this state of philosophic pessimism
> and general depression of spirits about my pros-
> pects, I went one evening into a dressing-room in
> the twilight to procure some article . . . when sud-
> denly there fell upon me without any warning; just
> as if it came out of the darkness, a horrible fear of
> my own existence . . . and I became a mass of quiv-
> ering fear. After this the universe was changed for
> me altogether. I awoke morning after morning with
> a horrible dread at the pit of my stomach, and with
> a sense of the insecurity of life that I never knew
> before, and that I have never felt since. . . . It grad-
> ually faded, but for months I was unable to go out
> into the dark alone. . . . I have always thought that
> this experience of melancholia of mine had a reli-
> gious bearing. I mean that the fear was so invasive
> and powerful that if I had not clung to scripture-
> texts like "The eternal God is my refuge," . . . "Come
> unto me, all ye that labor and are heavy-laden," . . .

"I am the resurrection and the life," . . . I think I
should have grown really insane [James, 1904/
1961, pp. 138-139].

"Only towards the end of his life did William James admit that
[this] case was really his own" (Matthiessen, 1947, p. 217).

A forty-two-year-old insurance salesman:

> For days I couldn't leave my new apartment.
> I felt that the world was looking through me. Peo-
> ple would stare at me on the sidewalk. I would
> wait to go out until nobody would be on the street.
> I couldn't sleep at nights, for fear of the darkness. I
> refused to talk to my wife about my fear. She would
> ask me why I wasn't going to work and I would
> scream at her to leave me alone. When the tele-
> phone would ring, I would leave the house. At
> night I pulled all the curtains closed so nobody
> could see in. I kept the lights turned off. I felt so
> guilty I couldn't bear to think of my dying grand-
> father, whom I felt I had to see before he died. I
> never did. When he died, I hated him for dying be-
> fore I could talk to him. My mother called once
> and I cried when I heard her voice. She asked me
> what was wrong. I hung up on her. I hated her.
> Soon I hated and feared everybody. I took to
> drinking heavily to escape and to kill the fear. I
> couldn't go to work because they were talking
> about me. When I spoke before groups of people,
> they could see through me. I felt empty. I resented
> who I had become. I feared every day. I kept going
> back to when I had been normal in my head, but I
> couldn't get back there. People came to me and
> said, "What's wrong with you? You're not your old
> self." I couldn't talk to them. I said I was just fine,
> maybe having a bad day. It would be all right to-
> morrow, I said. I didn't want to be around people.
> I pushed my family away. All I wanted to do was
> escape. It never got better until I got to where I
> couldn't leave my bed and I finally sought help. I
> hated my body [Field conversation, Emotions
> Project, fall 1981].

All the elements of the emotionally divided self are present in these two cases. A fear of self, others, and the unknown and a sense of being disembodied, hollow, empty, and transparent to others are given in both accounts. A fear of being overwhelmed and trapped by time is also present. Withdrawal into the self is apparent, yet the self appears to have no attachment to the outside world (see Laing, 1965, p. 80). A sense of longing for something that has been lost—sanity, control, being normal —is also evident. In both cases there is an internal reflectiveness regarding the stream of consciousness and the circuit of selfness that attaches the person to the world, yet the circuit of selfness has been broken.

The snapping of the circuit of selfness that attaches the subject to the world is well described by Seymour Krim (1961, p. 113) in "The Insanity Bit."

> In the summer of 1955, when I was thirty-three, the thousand unacknowledged human (not literary) pressures in my being exploded. I ran barefooted in the streets, spat at members of my family, exposed myself, was almost bodily thrown out of the house of a Nobel Prize–winning author, and believed God had ordained me to act out every conceivable human impulse without an ounce of hypocritical caution. . . . I needed an excuse to force some sort of balance between my bulging inner life and my timid outer behavior, and I chose the greatest and most comforting symbol of them all. He (God) was my lance and my shield as I tore through the New York streets acting out the bitter rot of a world-full of frustrations that my human nature could no longer lock up. I was finally cornered on the fourteenth floor of the St. Regis Hotel by two frightened friends and another brother; and with the aid of handcuffs seriously-humorously clipped on by a couple of bobbies, I was led off to Bellevue, convinced all along that I was right. I tolerated those who took me away with the kindly condescension of a fake Jesus.

A break with reality and the emotional enactment of inner compulsions are characteristic of the emotionally divided self. Such bursts of insanity are believed to be expressions of a "real" inner self.

Consider the following case, in which emotions are used as a wedge between the person and the world.

> I kept people from me by laughing. I would break out in uncontrollable laughter at business meetings. Everyone would look at me and not know whether to laugh with me or at me. They would look away. I would go down the street laughing at the stop signs, at people's babies, at cars and buses. I would go home and close the door to my room, get a drink, and start to cry. I'd think that a shot of whiskey would make me happy. The more I drank, the sadder I got.
>
> I went to see my mother. I told her I was unhappy. And then I suddenly started to laugh, uncontrollably. This went on for months [Field conversation, twenty-five-year-old graduate student, spring 1982].

In the following case prescription drugs (Valium) and alcohol are used by an emotionally divided self in an attempt to find inner peace.

> I thought I was normal. My nerves were bad. I knew that. That's why I used the drugs. They would level me out. The vodka made me glow inside, made me feel good with myself. I was always mellow. I thought I was handling my responsibilities at work. I was a supervisor. At home my family never complained. They always asked me if I had taken my medicine. When I would get depressed or angry or yell at the kids, my husband would ask me if I needed a drink. I started to drink more. I went to another doctor and he gave me a prescription for Librium. Now I had two medicines for my nerves and the vodka for when I felt depressed and down. . . . I kept getting more depressed. I couldn't get high or happy. I couldn't get mad. I couldn't feel. It was like I didn't have any emotions; just the compulsion to take my medicine and have a drink. My family would be celebrating a birthday and I

would stay in the other room. I stopped going out
of the house. I wouldn't answer the phone anymore. I wanted to be happy and couldn't be [Field
conversation, forty-one-year-old business executive, fall 1982].

Finally, consider the following violently divided self:

I'm not violent when I don't drink. I'm a
peaceful person. I just have this emptiness inside
me. There's nothing in me. I'm hollow and full of
holes. When I drink, I get strength. The holes fill
up. I'm not afraid anymore. I get mad at myself
for being so down at myself. I get mad at other
people who don't have holes inside them. I resent
them. Why can't I be like them? When I get to
thinking like that, I want to hit somebody. Police
cars make me mad. I give them the finger on the
street. I'll come home a little tight. My wife'll say,
"You had too much to drink." I'll get mad. She
says I hit her, I never remember. I feel guilty and
full of hate the next day. All I can think about is
why is it this way [Field conversation, forty-three-
year-old career military officer, fall 1982].

In violence the subject fills a gap in an otherwise empty inner
self. Yet the violence is negative and loathed. Externalized violence, in the form of hitting out at others, is negatively internalized in the form of self-loathing, self-estrangement, and self-
degradation. The emotionally divided self has neither an inner
nor an outer reality that holds firm. Everything is loose, from
the center of the self to its outermost edges. Indeed, the edge
between inner and outer reality may be indistinguishable. Emptiness and nothingness have no boundaries for the self. They are
nothing.

The Structures of the Emotionally Divided Self

Four structures of the emotionally divided self may be
distinguished: others, self and body, situations, and temporality.

Others. An examination of the foregoing cases of emotionally divided selves indicates the following features of the others who populate the person's world. First, they are near to the subject, as intimate, warm points of reference, even sources of stability, yet also distant, as vague, unnamed "others." Second, they are threats because they are so near. Third, the other's perceived "normality" or stability is threatening. Fourth, the other is a source of resentment, anger, and guilt. Feelings from the past are directed to the other. An aversion to the other is felt and sensed, yet the subject cannot be free of him. She feels a debt of emotion toward him. If he dies before the debt is repaid, resentment is added to guilt as a feeling that binds her to him. Fifth, feelings are "emptied out" on or at the other, often through violence, withdrawals of affection, or inward obsessive dwellings on the other's emotions and expectations for the person.

Sixth, feelings of "they-self" are drawn from the other (Heidegger, 1927/1962, p. 154). The subject *"fails to hear* its own Self in listening to the they-self" (Heidegger, 1927/1962, p. 315). The self feels, sees, and hears itself through the voices and the eyes of the other. It stands stripped of clothing, naked to the gaze of the other (Sartre, 1943/1978). The other sees through the subject. He is hollow inside. He has "fallen" in his own eyes and in the eyes of the "they-other." The subject becomes indistinguishable from the "they-self." These others are indefinite. They haunt the subject with their presence in the world. The "they-other" is given the qualities of emotional solidity, calmness, serenity, security, and a sense of superiority that makes him feel inferior to it. The subject attempts to take on the moods of the other and fails. This failure places a double wedge between the subject and himself and between the subject and the others of the world. He is driven, in his own eyes, which are the appropriated eyes of the other, further into the empty interiority of the self. Acts of violence draw him out into the world. The use of chemical substances such as prescription drugs and alcohol is sought as a source of strength. Elevated moods fill the emptiness the subject feels on the inner sides of his self. Resentment is an overwhelming emotional attitude toward the other (see Scheler, 1912/1961).

Seventh, the other or others who dominate the world of the emotionally divided self may be from the subject's immediate situation (employers, interactional associates, family members, and the like), or they may reside in the distant past (see Lemert, 1962). Laing (1965, p. 98) insists that the "other . . . must in the first instance always be the mother, that is, the 'mothering one.' " This is not necessarily so, for the other may be a vague, undifferentiated "they-other." Regardless of biographical origin, the other overwhelms the subject, setting (in the subject's eyes) impossible standards. The subject tries to win the approval of the other, to be a "good" self in the other's eyes, but finds this impossible.

The other may be imitated, copied. The other's mannerisms are interiorized. Others are, in H. S. Sullivan's terms (1953a, pp. 167-168), "personifications" who become part of the subject's false self-system. This false self-system interiorizes the other as a negative significant other. The subject hates the persons he imitates, yet he complies with their perceived wishes. One of Laing's patients (1965, p. 98) observed that he was "a response to what other people say I am." Emotionally divided selves translate into action other people's definitions of who they are. They seem unable or unwilling to move forward in terms of their own self-definitions. The self that complies with the wishes of the other is perceived as a false, or inauthentic, self.

A basic split in the self-system of the subject occurs. Outwardly she complies with the wishes of others. Inwardly she rebels. Outwardly the behavior of her false self appears normal. Yet this is a façade (Laing, 1965, p. 99). She perceives herself as living a lie. Inwardly she feels intense anxiety, hatred, fear. (These emotions will be elaborated below.) There may be momentary liftings of the veil of normality. In an emotional outburst her "truer" inner self is exposed to the world and to those others who dominate her. Such outbursts may take the form of violence toward herself and others. She feels captured within the very skin of her body. She feels that she is a captive of the other. In an insane outburst she will pour out accusations of persecution, directing her vengeance toward the other who has forced the compliance of her false self. She will declare that the "alien" other has been trying to destroy her. She will claim that the other makes her do things she does not want to do. She may argue that the other is driving her insane. (The other makes similar claims.)

As more features of the other are interiorized into the false self of the subject, hatred for the other increases. The secret, inner self of the person hates the public, normal self of the other that has come to inhabit her body. She also hates her inner self.

Paraphrasing Cooley (1902/1956, p. 184), a "negative looking-glass self" relationship is established between the subject and the other. Positive attributions from the other are interiorized negatively, thereby contributing to the negative inner view of self held by the subject. A hatred of the other is "focused on the features of him which the individual has built into his own being" (Laing, 1965, p. 104). Still, the assumption of another person's personality gives the inner self a sense of security. The subject has a way of not being himself publicly. Thus the other is both a shield and a sword for the divided self. The subject can hide inside this identity of the other.

Self and Body. Recalling the extended definition of self given in the previous chapter (that the self is all that the person calls his, including self-meanings and reflective self-appraisals), it can be argued that the emotionally divided self is fractured into multiple selves that add up to nothing. In the first case presented in this chapter, James speaks of becoming a mass of quivering fear. He had no center, only a sense of massive insecurity. A pit of emptiness was at the base of his stomach. In the second case, an acute sense that an older, more normal self had been lost was felt. The new self had no pieces that could be fitted together. It was not a new self. It was nothing. In the third case, the "bulging inner life" that wanted out had no point of reference. Laughter kept the self of the fourth case intact.

The emotionally divided self lives two lives, one that is inner and perhaps fantasy-based and one that is outer and perhaps real. Sartre (1948, p. 165-166) observes:

> We can recognize two distinct selves in us:
> the imaginary self with its tendencies and desires—

and the real self. There are imaginary sadists and masochists, persons of violent imagination. At each moment our imaginary self breaks in pieces and disappears at contact with reality, yielding its place to the real self. For the real and the imaginary cannot coexist by their very nature. It is a matter of two types of objects, of feelings and actions that are completely irreducible.

Hence, we may think that individuals will have to be classified in two large categories, according to whether they prefer to lead an imaginary life or a real life. . . . To prefer the imaginary is not only to prefer a richness, a beauty, an imaginary luxury to the existing mediocrity in spite of their unreal nature. It is also to adopt "imaginary" feelings and actions for the sake of their imaginary nature . . . it is not only an escape from the content of the real (poverty, frustrated love, failure of one's enterprise, etc.) but from the form of the real itself.

The imaginary self is an inner, hidden self. It lives in fantasy. It may be, as Sartre observes, violent and inwardly destructive toward others, perhaps killing them in fantasy. The imaginary self dissolves and disappears when it has contact with reality. The subject withdraws from his imaginary self, allowing others to define who he is and who he will be. The real and the imaginary cannot coexist in the same moment.

Sartre and Laing suggest that the emotionally divided self lives an imaginary life that is split, or dissociated from the real world of real others. In the world of imagination and inner fantasy, the subject perhaps lives a full, rich life of embodied feelings, pleasures, and desires. She escapes from a harsh world of impoverished, frustrated emotionality. In her imagination she may dare to take chances she cannot or is not willing to take in the outer world. For the emotionally divided self, the world of emotion and the world of fantasy merge into one. These two worlds gather strength in the inner world of the divided self and crowd out the demands and exigencies of the demanding external world. In this inner world one can be anything. One is free to control people, places, and things. One is, as Laing notes,

omnipotent, and that omnipotence may be indulged and over-
extended (Laing, 1965, p. 84).

Laing (1965) and Sartre (1948) suggest that the divided
self exists divided between two worlds, the real and the imaginary. Laing (1965, p. 84) states: "The illusion of omnipotence
and freedom can be sustained only within the magic circle of its
own shut-upness in fantasy. And in order that this attitude be
not dissipated by the slightest intrusion of reality, fantasy and
reality have to be kept apart." Sartre concurs with this statement (Sartre, 1948, pp. 165-166, quoted above).

However, it is not true. That is, the real and the imaginary, or the fantastic, are one and the same for the emotionally
divided self. If the world of emotion is believed in as an absolute reality, as argued in Chapter Two, and if the world of fantasy merges with that world, then there can be no place for a
separate reality. The world of fantasy *is* the world for the person, just as the world of emotion is the real world during emotionality. In short, if it is assumed that the subject is joined with
the world in and through the circuit of selfness, and if consciousness is in the world, just as the subject is in consciousness,
then it is never possible to see the subject out of or against a
real world. The subject is the world. Reality is the person, just
as the person is reality. There are only different ways of constituting reality. The emotionally divided self constitutes reality in
and through emotion, violence, fantasy, imagination, distortion,
and distance. The subject cannot keep a distance between reality and fantasy. To believe that he or she can rests on a faulty
ontological conception of the subject and the world.

The divisions in the self that are felt are not posited in
terms of a real and unreal existence. The divisions hinge, rather, on the gaps the subject feels between his feelings and his inner core as a person. He is unable to relate his feelings back to a
core, inner self. He is a "they-self" cut adrift from an inner,
meaningful self. Here is where the division, in part, lies. The
subject cannot get back to the "who" of the "Who am I?" His
feelings are no longer felt in terms of an inner moral self.

It is true, however, that the emotionally divided self withdraws from reality, for she withdraws from her self as a lived

presence in the world. She disengages, or uncouples, herself from the world-at-hand.

The splitting that occurs is within the emotions and the selves that are felt and is not a splitting of two worlds, one imaginary and one real. Although Laing (1965, p. 85) can remark, quoting Marianne Moore, that "real toads invade the imaginary gardens and ghosts walk in the real streets," it is necessary to take exception: "Real toads invade real gardens and real ghosts in fact walk in real streets."

Although Laing's description below of the false self-system of the emotionally divided self appears correct, a reservation regarding his conclusions is in order. "The false self-system . . . exists as the complement of an 'inner' self which is occupied in maintaining its identity and freedom by being transcendent, unembodied, and thus never to be grasped, pinpointed, trapped, possessed. Its aim is to be pure subject, without any objective existence. Thus, except in certain possible safe moments the individual seeks to regard the whole of his objective existence as the expression of a false self. Of course . . . if a man is not two-dimensional, having a two-dimensional identity established by a conjunction of identity-for-others and identity-for oneself, if he does not exist objectively as well as subjectively, he has only a subjective identity, an identity-for-himself, he cannot be *real*" (Laing, 1965, p. 94-95). It is precisely because he is real, and knows it, that Laing's patient seeks treatment. The emotionally divided self is trapped in a reality, in a mode of inauthentic being that is intolerable. It is reality for him. The inner and outer worlds of experience that are his collide. He is trapped within an existence that will not allow him to be free. Reality crushes in from all sides. He wants to change himself and his reality. That is why he comes for treatment.

For analytic purposes the self-system of the emotionally divided subject may initially be divided into three categories— the good me, the bad me, and the not-me (Sullivan, 1953a, pp. 161-162). The "good me" refers to those self-personifications "which organize an experience in which satisfactions have been enhanced by rewarding increments of tenderness. . . . Good me, as it ultimately develops, is the ordinary topic of discussion

about "I" (Sullivan, 1953a, pp. 161–162). The good me encompasses those things about the self that the subject takes pride in,
cherishes, and values highly. The "bad me" is the "beginning
personification which organizes experiences in which increasing
degrees of anxiety are associated with behavior involving the
mothering one . . . bad me is based on this increasing gradient of
anxiety" (Sullivan, 1953a, p. 162). The bad me describes those
features of the self that cause the subject guilt and anxiety. The
mothering one may be replaced by any emotional associate of
the subject in later life. *Violence may be a part of the bad me.*
The "not-me" refers to those personifications characterized by
the "uncanny emotions" of awe, dread, loathing, and horror
(Sullivan, 1953a, p. 72). The not-me elements of the self may
include sexual acts that are taboo in the subject's culture (see
Lindesmith, Strauss, and Denzin, 1978, p. 473). These emotions
of the not-me persist throughout life, often erupting in night-
mares in adulthood. The not-me elements of the self refer to a
"private mode of living" (Sullivan, 1953a, p. 164).

Three features of the self-system are particularly significant. First, the self-system is based on interpersonal processes
(Sullivan, 1953a). The self is an interpersonal process. The emotions of the self are interpersonal phenomena. They are lodged,
in part, in the interactions and relationships that bind individuals to one another. The good me, bad me, and not-me are embedded in the social relationships that make up the subject's
world. Each is attached to certain recurring emotional themes,
whether these are the uncanny emotions (the not-me), the anxi-
ety-producing, negative emotions (the bad me), or the pleasura-
ble, positive emotions (the good me). These thematic structures
of the self are dynamically interrelated, for they are often
grounded in the same complex of interpersonal relationships
that makes up the core of the subject's social world. They may,
however, be separated or disassociated from one another. The
good-me themes of the self may be placed within the inner, true
self-feelings of the subject, and the not-me and bad-me themes
may make up the false, or public, self. Conversely, the not-me
and bad-me structures may, in the subject's eyes, be the real,
inner, true self. The good me is the false self, the public façade

the individual presents to others. The subject may seek out different interactional relationships for each of these selves, engaging in audience- or self-segregation processes (see Goffman, 1959). Or there may be a different set of selves for each relationship the person has (James, 1890/1950; Merton, 1957).

Second, there is a different language for each thematic structure of the self. The good me may be experienced within a language that is laden with consensually validated meanings. The bad me and not-me are linguistically conceptualized with terms and phrases that stutter with ambiguity, confusion, and high anxiety. As linguistic phenomena, the three thematic structures of the self may be experienced unreflectively in terms of Peirce's (1931, vol. 1, vol. 2, pp. 148-159) level of firstness, or within what Sullivan calls the "prototaxic mode." At the level of self-reflection, secondness without comparison to the level of thirdness may obtain. That is, the experience is not completely conceptualized reflectively. It remains within what Sullivan terms the "parataxic mode." Reflective thirdness may draw all the themes of the self together into a total system, "syntaxically" (Sullivan, 1953a, pp. 28-29). The subject's subjective awareness of selfness and of the divisions in self must be regarded, in part at least, as a linguistic process (Lacan, 1968; Mead, 1982a; Sullivan, 1953a, 1953b, 1956). A totalization of self, in which all the elements of the subject's self-system are brought together in a unified whole, does not occur for the divided self.

Third, the self-system is lodged in the interpersonal relationship the person has with his or her body (see Plessner, 1970, p. 38). The self and self-system of the subject are embodied and disembodied phenomena. The three levels of the human body discussed in Chapter Four—the physical body, the lived body for the person, and the lived body for others—are intimately rooted in the self-system of the person.

The good me, bad me, and not-me are, in Sullivan's words, "tangled up with the growing acquaintance of 'my body'" (1953a, p. 163). My body is an organization of experience. It is distinguished from other things in my world by its self-sentient character (Sullivan, 1953a, p. 161). My body feels, and I feel it feeling. Through those feelings I feel myself. The self that I feel in and through my body, whether it is a sexual self, a self in pain, a working self, a serious self, or a playful self, is "myself" feeling (Hegel, 1910, p. 259). The embodied feelings that I feel radiate into my inner selfness, disclosing me as a good me, a bad me, or a not-me.

Intersubjectively the subject may be in or out of touch with the feelings of his lived body. He may misunderstand his embodied feelings and have a spurious conception of the inner workings of his body. He may reflectively grasp his embodied feelings and embrace them fully. Or he may place a distance between himself and his embodied feelings, in which case he experiences his body at a distance, in a disembodied fashion. He may lose all ability to meaningfully enter into his embodied feelings. He is at a symbolic and physical distance from himself and his body. He lacks any sense of unity. He is split into a mind and a body, neither of which is his. He may disclaim ownership of his body and identify only with that part of himself that is not connected to his body (Laing, 1965, p. 65). He may place the not-me and the bad me in the dissociated parts of his body. All that is left of the self and its body is the good me, the "I," or the true inner self. The body shrinks in size as the subject disavows ownership over all or most of its parts.

The fully embodied self does not exist for the emotionally divided self. She has divorced herself from her body. The body becomes an object without subjectivity. It is no longer connected to the core, inner feelings of the person. It lies at the center of the false self of the person, which rests on the bad me and the not-me. The person has a disembodied self-system.

The disembodied self is split, or divided, into two categories: the true, inner self, and the false, outer self. The inner self diminishes in size as the outer, false self assumes horrible, terrifying dimensions. The inner self increasingly comes to rest on doubt as its principal emotional orientation to the world. The subject loses all sense of self-justification and meaning in the emotions he feels. The good feelings that he feels are regarded as illegitimate, stolen, and fraudulent. Guilt surrounds these feelings. The self that is revealed through emotion can no longer be trusted. He comes to doubt the very meaning of his being as a moral person. The surface and deep understandings of himself, which he had previously taken for granted, are no longer clear-cut. There is no firm center to the divided self.

The disembodied inner self feels threatened by its external relations in the world. The false self that is presented to the world is hated. It brings no satisfaction or security to the inner self. The false self-system becomes more and more autonomous and disconnected from the inner self (Laing, 1965, p. 144). It begins to spread inward, into the inner self, pushing out the person's last vestiges of sanity (Hegel, 1910). As it moves inward, the subject becomes more and more lifeless, until he may literally feel dead inside. (See the excerpt from William James near the beginning of this chapter.) Catatonia may represent a stance the subject takes toward self and the world (Laing, 1965, p. 163). As the self is increasingly divorced from its body, the inner self loses its own identity and integrity. It loses its realness. There is no longer any safe place that it can retreat into. Its body can no longer be trusted (Laing, 1965, p. 161). The inner self is full of doubt. Emotions no longer reveal an inner, feeling self. Nothingness engulfs the subject inside and out. He is an empty container filled with fear, terror, dread, doubt, and repulsion. Yet there is no place for these uncanny emotions to attach. Free-floating fear and terror overwhelm the person. He no longer has a direct relation with the world. He and the world are dead and lifeless.

The original splitting that occurred between self and body has now multiplied to the point at which the structure collapses inward, on itself. The true and false self can no longer be separated. The distinction between real and fantasy, or real and imaginary, can no longer be sustained. The line between inner and outer also slips away.

The disembodied, emotionally divided self feels objectless, or unmotived, emotions (James, 1890/1950, vol. 2, p. 459), which include dread, anger, apathy, and morbid fear. They may dominate the life of the emotionally divided self for long periods.

Situations. The emotional situations of the divided self have a threatening transparency that makes action within them nearly impossible. The subject can see through the situation to its other side. The situation acts back on him. It drives him out. He is pushed or forced into a corner. From that vantage point he may or may not gaze out and around himself, into the situation that he is afraid to enter. He may even turn his back on the situation, thereby turning his back on himself. Situations move toward him with a compelling force that cannot be stopped. The subject is literally unable to enter the situation. Yet, he is the situation. It is this fact that overwhelms him. He is trapped in the situation. He can neither enter nor leave.

William James (1890/1950, vol. 2, p. 285) offers an example, quoting from T. S. Clouston, *Clinical Lectures on Mental Diseases* (1883, p. 43): "Let me instance the other morning I went to walk. The day was biting cold, but I was unable to proceed except by jerks. Once I got arrested, my feet in a muddy pool. One foot was lifted to go, knowing that it was not good to be standing in water, but there I was fast, the cause of detention being the discussing with myself the reasons why I should not stand in that pool." The reflective self-awareness of the emotionally divided self makes action in the situation problematic, if not impossible. However, inaction is action, for not to act is to act. The divided self knows this. By not acting in the situation, the subject is acting in the situation. Consider the following account (James, 1885, pp. 55-56):

> In the spring of 1884 I was living with my family in the neighborhood of Windsor, England. . . . One day . . . towards the close of May, having eaten a comfortable dinner, I remained sitting at the table after the family had dispersed, idly gazing at the embers in the grate, thinking of nothing and feeling only the exhilaration incident to a good digestion, when suddenly—in a lightning-flash as it were—"fear came upon me, and trembling, which made all my bones to shake." To all appearance it was a perfectly insane and abject terror, without ostensible cause, and only to be accounted for, to my perplexed imagination, by some dammed shape squatting invisible to me within the precincts of the room, and raying out from his fetid personal-

ity, influences fatal to life. The thing had not
lasted ten seconds before I felt myself a wreck,
that is, reduced from a state of firm, vigorous, joyful manhood to one of almost helpless infancy.
The only self-control I was capable of exerting was
to keep my seat . . . this ghastly condition of mind
continued with me, with gradually lengthening intervals of relief for two years, and even longer.

Here William James's father is locked into the situation. All he
can do is keep his seat. By remaining immobile, one holds the
threat in the situation at a distance. More important, the only
fixed point the person has in the situation is himself. By remaining stationary, he strikes a balance with what appears to be
crushing in on him.

The senior James's account of his experience in the above
situation points to an additional feature of the emotional situation. It lies in front of the person, and it is occupied by threatening forces that are real (see Sartre, 1948, pp. 213-231, for a
contrary view). The person who hallucinates sees real Indians in
the cornfield next to her garden. She hears real voices singing
the national anthem. Squirrels are in her throat. She sees her
dead mother in front of her. These objects, which appear to be
imaginary, are real forces to the person. They are in the situation. Accordingly, part of the terror in the emotional situation
lies in the fact that is is occupied by "real-unreal" people and
things. The subject is not alone. But whom is she not alone with?

If the situation is occupied by "real" people, its threat increases. "Real" people draw the person out of her inner world
and require that interaction be attempted. In such situated moments the subject feels required to put on a "normal" self and
make the appearance of being in control. If appearing normal is
not possible, she may be placed in a situation where she is left
alone to be with herself. In any case she is unable to escape the
situated presence of her own presence.

The situations of the emotionally divided self are alien.
They appear to be filled with projects that need to be undertaken, but the subject is unable to move either forward or backward. Divided selves attempt, then, to distance themselves from

the situations that surround them. They are locked into an un-yielding present, for any movement through the situation would be a movement through time and space. Unable to accomplish such an action, they are forced to remain still, thereby stopping both time and space.

Temporality. Heidegger (1927/1962, p. 391) states that *"except on the basis of temporality,* moods *are not possible."* His thesis of the temporality of moods assumes that "moods temporalize themselves—that is, their specific ecstasis belongs to a future and a present in such a way, indeed, that these equiprimordial ecstases are modified by having been" (p. 390). Heidegger (p. 395) applies the thesis of the temporality of moods to the analysis of anxiety and fear, which I shall draw on shortly.

The thesis suggests that individuals may experience time in three reflective modes, or three "ecstases." The future is what moves towards them. The present is what they are alongside. The past is what has just been accomplished. If, as argued in Chapter Three, emotions are temporal phenomena, then it is possible to see how the emotions of the emotionally divided self are, in part, temporally static phenomena. That is, the subject can move neither forward nor backward in the situation that confronts him. If he attempts to stop the passage of time by remaining immobile, then his emotions are dead and lifeless. His emotions are stripped of all the liveliness that comes from the infusion of time into feeling and thinking.

Heidegger further argues that the person experiences time within two modes: the authentic and the inauthentic. Emotionally divided selves experience time both authentically and inauthentically. Authentic temporality is self-reflective and processual. Authentically the subject stands outside time as a static phenomenon. She is processually in time and in the world, confronting time and the meaning of her being within the three ecstases of the future, present, and past. Inauthentic temporality is chronological time, cut into bits and pieces. The past, the present, and the future are regarded as discretely different temporal sphers. Inauthentic time locates emotions in the subject's past, in the far-off threatening future, or in the hostile present.

Emotionally divided selves are caught reflectively between the edges of authentic and inauthentic time. Authentically they are able to view and grasp time processually. The past, the future, and the present come against them, as overpowering forces. Inauthentically, they feel trapped in the past and in the present. The future seems unapproachable. They hold to a double vision of time. On the one hand, time is reflectively understood as a process. On the other hand, they are rooted in an unreflective, inauthentic view of the past, the present, and the future as discrete temporal entities. To the extent that they are overwhelmed by the situations that confront them, they are driven deeper into an inauthentic view of themselves, their emotions, and temporality. They are the reflective victims of their own inauthentic temporality, trapped in the past and in the present. They cannot move forward. Every step backward is a step further into the past. The inability to enter the situation that lies in the present, in front of them, drives them further back into the past. By being driven into the past, emotionally divided selves find that their emotions are in the past. They live and feel in the past. Their emotional attachments, the selves they attach onto, and the others and the experiences they dwell on are in the past. Any liveliness they find in their world comes from and out of the past. They battle the past. They symbolically kill significant emotional others. They may even try to kill themselves. By killing themselves, they kill the other who has killed them. Since they make the decision to try to kill themselves and the other, they are the victors, for they have killed first. Such is the inner temporal logic of emotionally divided selves.

The Emotionality of the Divided Self

The emotionally divided self lives in a world dominated by backward-looking negative emotion. Fear, anger, depression, anxiety, feelings of worthlessness, despair, hostility, defiance, rejection, arrogance, smugness, self-pity, evasiveness, inadequacy, ressentiment, shame, and guilt are common. These are the negative personal and interpersonal emotions. They bear a close affinity to the uncanny emotions of awe, dread, loathing, and horror which Sullivan associates with the not-me personifications of the self. The emotionality of these emotions may be clarified by examining (1) their temporality, (2) their interpersonal structures, and (3) the self-feelings that are attached to them.

Temporality of the Negative Emotions. Anger, fear, and ressentiment are dominant negative emotions. They are accompanied by feelings of self-pity, inferiority in the eyes of others, hostility toward others, defiance, extreme criticism of the other, and continuing depression. These emotions are rooted in the past. Emotionally divided selves experience their past over and over again. They dwell in the past. Their dominant emotions are in the past. They are frozen in the present. They hold onto past accomplishments in the present. They are constantly resurrecting the past and holding it in front of them. They offer their past to others, as a measure of who they have been. Because they are unable to move into the future, the past is the only resource they have. The past and the present become entangled in their mind. They cannot separate yesterday from today. Time becomes a commodity that has slipped through their fingers. It has been lost, used up, wasted. The moods, feelings, and emotions they cling to are attached to the actions others have taken toward them in the past. Other people control their emotionality and their temporality.

Fear is an inauthentic state of mind. The meaning of fear lies in the past, as the past comes forward to threaten the subject in the present. Fear is fearing in the face of a threatening force that draws near (Heidegger, 1927/1962, pp. 179-182). The waiting for what is fearful is part of what the subject fears. Fear fears fear. The fear that fear fears cuts to the heart of the subject and leaves him open, empty, and without defense. He backs away from fear fearfully, as if backing into an abyss that is empty and dark. Fear is pushing him into fear. Fear turns back on itself, frightening him in the present and leaving him unable to act. He retreats into the past, but fear draws back with him. It comes around him from behind and engulfs him. He is surrounded by fear. Every way he turns, fear stands. The future is closed off to him.

A self-forgetting occurs. The subject forgets how he dealt with fear in the past. He feels empty-handed and defenseless in the face of fear. He seems unable to transform that which is fearful into something nonthreatening (Heidegger, 1927/1962, p. 392). Death may be considered the only possible resolution to fear's onslaught. The subject trembles in the face of fear. Feeling drains from him. The fear of destruction is imminent. Fear becomes a dominating state of mind.

The fear of divided selves comes from within, as well as from the world that surrounds. Inwardly they fear their own emotions, which terrify them and seem out of control. Caught in the swirl of inner emotionality, they seem unable to control the directions their feelings take. They even feel fear inside the other emotions that overcome them. They fear facing other people, for fear of exposing their inner self. They fear the ability of their false self to keep others at a distance. They fear actions they have taken in the past. Fear drives them deeper into themselves. But the deeper they go inside themselves, the more fearful it becomes. They are, in Joseph Conrad's words, plunging into a heart of darkness.

Fear's fearfulness comes from its threat of self-annihilation. The emotionally divided self has no inner defense against fear. Fear destroys and leaves only the nothingless of fear, the remains of which linger in the present. Hence the divided self is trapped within a circle of fear.

Anger exists alongside fear in the divided self. Like fear, anger is based in the past. It arises out of recent events in the subject's world. An other criticizes the self or overlooks the person. Someone speaks behind her back, makes a commitment for her in the future, or damages a valued object. These actions, which have occurred in the past, are carried into the present and made objects of emotionality. The anger-provoking act is brought toward the subject out of a future that is filled with anger. She angrily seeks retaliation. She strikes back, punishing the other for an action taken in the past. She attempts to get even.

She hurts or physically attacks the other. She will use actions taken in the past as a justification for striking out in the present. Anger is a cherished emotion, for it justifies action. Without anger the self might lack any foundations for acting in the world. Accordingly, the subject carefully constructs the grounds for justifiable anger. Divided selves rationalize their anger, thereby rationalizing themselves.

Anger may stem from an inward insecurity, ambiguity, or feeling of guilt the subject holds toward herself. By acting angrily, she overcomes that doubt and inner feeling. Anger becomes a way of overcoming the ontological insecurity the subject feels about herself in the world (Laing, 1965, p. 39). Anger becomes a way of emotionally joining the disjointed, separated, fragmented pieces of the self. Anger radiates through the false outer self into the "true" inner self. In anger the subject "feels as if" she were acting authentically, honestly, and openly. Anger becomes a mode of action that seizes the moment of the present. Anger cripples, though, for it is directed into the past. The floundering self-system of the subject is built on the past and on emotions that are lodged in the past. It is as if the person had nowhere to turn except into her past. This she does angrily. Anger approaches anger, much as fear approaches fear. The angry divided self is caught within the emotion of anger as its most "authentic" feeling. But anger is not authentic, in Heidegger's sense, for it reveals a person caught in the snare of her own temporality, unreflectively.

In anger the subject feels fear. Anger aroused by the other may stem from an inward feeling of threat, which is associated with fear. As anger intensifies, it overcomes fear, yet fear exists alongside anger. Anger exposes the self. The divided self fears self-exposure. Anger hurts. Embodied anger (as in violence) opens the subject to confrontation and attack by the other. The divided self fears confrontation. Confrontation exposes the weaknesses of the self and exaggerates feelings of inferiority, inadequateness, shame, guilt, and self-pity. Still, the divided self is an angry self, although the anger may be hidden beneath layers of deception, evasiveness, and bad faith.

Anger may turn into hatred, deep-seated hostility, and

ressentiment. *Ressentiment* (Scheler, 1912/1961) is a backward-looking emotionality that attaches to the emotional associates in the subject's world. Ressentiment is a form of self-hatred that is embedded in the real and imagined actions another has taken toward the subject. It is self-poisoning. It produces a mental attitude that turns the subject against close emotional associates, often the mothering or fathering figure (Scheler, 1912/1961; Lacan, 1968; Sartre, 1981, pp. 386-409). Ressentiment arises from the systematic repression or suppression of certain emotions, which may be normal components of human nature. Anger, envy, intense self-pride (and false pride), the desire for revenge, and self-conquest are all parts of ressentiment (Scheler, 1912/1961). Scheler's discussion of this complete emotion is instructive:

> We do not use the word *ressentiment* because of a special predilection for the French language, but because we did not succeed in translating it into German. Moreover, Nietzsche has made it a *terminus technicus*. In the natural meaning of the French word I detect two elements. First of all, *ressentiment* is the repeated experiencing and reliving of a particular emotional response reaction against someone else. The continual reliving of the emotion sinks it more deeply into the center of the personality but concomitantly removes it from the person's zone of action and expression. It is not a mere intellectual recollection of the emotion and of the events to which it "responded"—it is a re-experiencing of the emotion itself, a renewal of the original feeling. Secondly, the word implies that the quality of the emotion is negative, that is, that it contains a movement of hostility. Perhaps the German word *Groll* (rancor) comes closest to the essential meaning of the term. "Rancor" is just such a suppressed wrath, independent of the ego's activity, which moves obscurely through the mind. It finally takes shape through the repeated reliving of intentionalities of hatred or other hostile emotions. In itself it does not contain a specific hostile intention, but it nourishes any number of such intentions [1912/1961, pp. 39-40).

The English word *resentment*, which implies indignation or ill will felt as a result of a real or imagined offense, is too specific for Scheler's purposes. The emotions included in Scheler's formulations of ressentiment are revenge, hatred, malice, envy, impulse to detract, spite, rancor, wrath, vindictiveness, vengefulness, and joy at another's misfortune (Scheler, 1912/1961, pp. 45-46, 176). The subject resents another for actions he has taken toward her, for qualities he possesses that she lacks, and because the other often stands in an authority position over her. Each of these features of ressentiment is located in the past yet realized in the present.

Because the other stands over her (as a mothering or fathering figure, an employer, or the like), the subject cannot direct her emotion outward toward him. Ressentiment is turned inward as hatred, the repressed desire for revenge, the desire to get even, or a wish to destroy. As ressentiment spreads through the subject's divided self-system, the other becomes a part of all the negative emotions that are felt. Everywhere she turns, she is dominated by this other—in her imagination, in the world, and in her dealings with others. Forced submission to this other finds meaning in her ressentiment. The other deprives her of her sovereignty. Alienation and ressentiment are thereby produced, for she has been denied her right to choose who she will be (Sartre, 1981, p. 387). The subject feels inferior in the eyes of the resented other. Out of this feeling stems anger, then fear, then reinforced ressentiment. Anger becomes the vehicle for expressing ressentiment. Violence is the most active form of ressentiment. The subject strikes out in the present, as a means of getting back at this other who has harmed her. The other is slowly transformed into an object that does not feel. He becomes a thing, an obstacle, an unfeeling force to be dealt with.

Failure to act on the emotions that are contained within ressentiment leads to a constant tendency to indulge in certain kinds of value delusions and moral judgments regarding oneself and the other. The man or woman of ressentiment, Scheler (1912/1961, p. 76) remarks, cannot even justify his or her own existence in terms of positive values. Weakness, fear, and anxiety regarding self and a denial of the other's moral worth combine to produce a completely negative world view. The subject trapped in ressentiment has a false world view. "In reality he remains a captive of [the] past" (Scheler, 1912/1961, p. 67). The stages in life no longer have value or meaning. Things, including self, cease to have permanent value. A "they-self" mode of self-comparison dominates the subject.

The desire to strike out, to seek revenge, is blocked because of feelings of impotence. As impotence increases, inner insecurity amplifies. The subject loses control over her inner feelings. She seethes with inner rage and envy. She is dominated by a hatred of the other and of herself. She finds self-injury everywhere she looks. It is as if the entire world were against her. Her life is built on negation and negativity. She lives a false outer existence. Inwardly she has lost touch with an enduring, "true" self. She is so filled with hatred that she even hates herself.

Ressentiment is continually reexperienced by the subject. Every transaction with the world is an occasion for the feelings that accompany and are buried within this form of emotionality. Such a self is divided against itself. The inner emotions that are revealed through the transactions with the world reveal an empty, angry inner person.

Scheler suggests that certain social structures systematically produce the emotion of ressentiment. Social democracies that espouse equality of rights for all but permit wide gaps between expectations and what is in fact received engender ressentiment on the part of the young, the elderly, women, the handicapped, the stigmatized, and members of racial or ethnic minorities. Certain occupational groups also experience greater degrees of ressentiment, including the military, civil servants, certain clergy groups, members of the educational establishment, professional athletes, the unemployed, and those on welfare. Ressentiment is greatest when self- or group injury is experienced as destiny and as beyond one's control. When powerlessness is great, ressentiment increases. In such circumstances the other is transformed into an object deserving of revenge and perhaps violence.

Social structures that minimize the comparisons individuals make between themselves and others perhaps have less ressentiment than those that maximize invidious comparisons with others (Scheler, 1912/1961; Veblen, 1923). Structures without fixed places and stations for individuals and groups have large amounts of ressentiment. The structures of society produce emotions and forms of emotionality that turn back on the very structures that produced them (Scheler, 1912/1961; Marx, 1852/1983c; Sartre, 1976; Weber, 1946).

Joyce Carol Oates (1982) has commented on the self-feelings of women, particularly as women feel themselves when in the public's eye: "A woman often feels 'invisible' in a public sense precisely because her physical being—her 'visibility'—figures so prominently in her identity. She is judged as a body, she is 'attractive' or 'unattractive,' while knowing that her deepest self is inward, and secret: knowing, *hoping* that her spiritual essence is a great deal more complex than the casual eye of the observer will allow. It might be argued that the poet, inhabiting a consciousness and a voice, is 'invisible' as well; it might be argued that all persons defined to themselves rather more as what they think and dream, than what they do, are 'invisible' " (quoted by Donoghue, 1982, p. 12). The essence of being a woman is felt to be discontinuous with the public existence that is assigned to and felt by women (Donoghue, p. 12). Oates seems also to be suggesting that all people, if they dream, are invisible and essentially more complex than they appear to be in the "they-eye" of the public. The person of ressentiment feels invisible. The result may be " 'self-hatred,' 'self-torment,' and 'revenge against oneself' " (Scheler, 1912/1961, p. 72).

The words the person of ressentiment uses to describe his feelings are like shells, they are empty. They do not describe the feelings that are hidden inside him (Donoghue, 1982, p. 14). While it may be enough for some persons to have their words shelter their feelings, persons of ressentiment feel a rebellion against language. They feel trapped by the very words that are meant to express the feelings they feel. They feel frustration, desperation, anxiety, and futility in the face of this linguistic gap. They cannot put their feelings into words. The words do not feel for them.

The body of the person of ressentiment becomes the container for his feelings. Scheler remarks (1912/1961, p. 71) that the repression of feeling that accompanies ressentiment affects the emotion itself. Further: "Detached from their original objects, the affects melt together into a venomous mass. . . . All these sensations are unpleasant or even painful. . . . The man in question no longer feels at ease in his body, it is as though he moves away from it and views it as an unpleasant object. . . . It would be wrong to follow a well-known theory (William James) which believes that the affects are entirely composed of such visceral sensations. But they do make up a substantial component of hatred, wrath, envy, revenge, etc. Yet they determine neither the particular intentionality or quality of an impulse nor the moment of its greatest intensity . . . only its passive and static aspect, which varies for the different affects" (pp. 71–72).

The body of the person of ressentiment becomes a source of pain. That pain builds on itself and on the feelings of self-hatred and self-torment that rack the subject's consciousness. The divided self hates itself, the world, and its body. Its invisibility to itself and to the world that views it increases its inner self-hatred. Deprived of an inner base for its feelings, the emotionally divided self feels only negativity.

Anxiety and depression are correlates of fear, anger, and ressentiment. They too are produced by structural and interpersonal relationships, but less so. Anxiety, in contrast to fear, arises from within the subject. There is nothing immediately threatening him except his own anxiety. The world has sunk into insignificance (Heidegger, 1927/1962, p. 303). The person can find no meaning. He turns inward, into himself. He becomes preoccupied with his current presence in the world. He is locked into the present and can move neither forward nor backward. He cannot give himself to a future and move into a line of action that would overcome his anxiety. Anxiety moves into his inner core, leaving him weakened and without purpose, except to be in a state of anxiety.

In high anxiety the subject's visceral sensations preoccupy her attention. She feels ill at ease with herself and with her body. She cannot get comfortable. She cannot stand to be irritated. Yet she is self-irritated. This amplifies her anxiety. Time rushes in on her. She is trapped by her past. She feels undone by all her actions. Overwhelmed by her anxiety, she is driven into a corner. She attempts to escape from herself and from the situations that surround her.

Anxiety accompanies depression, which settles in the present. Depression appears as an inability to confront the on-slaught of the future. It may arise out of feelings that others have let the subject down. They have not given him the inner se-curity, the prestige, the economic rewards, or the self-confi-dence that is sought. The physical weakness and pain that ac-companies the self-hatred of ressentiment may also turn against the subject, leaving him unable to confront and act on the world. Major and minor setbacks in the world may also contrib-ute to the development of depression.

As a mood, depression focuses on the present and on the residues of the past that are most accessible to the subject. De-pression dwells in the unmoving present. The subject is afraid to move forward. He is depressed over his past. He is the in-authentic victim of his own temporality. Every attempt to move forward turns back on him. He is constantly thrown back into the past and the present.

Depression is circular in its effects. It is self-fulfilling and self-defeating. It may produce nausea and feelings of nothing-ness. Unable to strike a stance toward the future, the subject finds himself locked in the dead timelessness of the past. The pres-ent, too, is devoid of liveliness. He is morbidly drawn back to the past. His reflective ressentiment draws him to the past. Feel-ings of death, dying, denial, decay, waste, and unworthiness be-come permanent parts of the person's inner, feeling self. In this negation of his being the subject in his passivity becomes a blind spot to himself. Sartre (1981, p. 398) states, "I would willingly call his ego the blind spot of his reflexive vision." He cannot see or grasp his own ressentiment or the divisions that exist in his divided self. His reflexive insight into himself is indirect and dis-torted.

Interpersonal Structure of the Negative Emotions. The temporality of anger, fear, ressentiment, anxiety, and depres-sion is attached to the past. The emotionally divided self lives in the past. The interpersonal structure of the negative emotions reveals a similar attachment to the past. Consider the following description of Peter, one of R. D. Laing's patients. "The patient described his life in the following way: His own feeling about his birth was that neither his father nor his mother had wanted him and, indeed, that they had never forgiven him for being born. His mother, he felt, resented his presence in the world because he had messed up her figure and damaged and hurt her in being born. He maintained that she had cast this up to him frequently during his childhood. His father, he felt, resented him simply for existing at all, 'He never gave me any place in the world . . . .' He thought too that his father probably hated him because the damage and pain he had caused his mother by his birth had put her against having sexual intercourse. He entered life, he felt, as a thief and criminal" (Laing, 1965, p. 122). Peter felt ressentiment toward his parents, as well as anger and fear. He confronted the world with anxiety and insecurity. He split his self into an inner self and an outer, false self. He lived a lie. He was unable to interact with others. He interacted *at* others, through deception, veiled anger, ressentiment, and self-disgust.

The emotionally divided self does not have interpersonal relationships with others, except in the negative sense. That is, the negative emotions are lodged in the subject's relations with others. Peter dwelled on his birth and early childhood. His relationships with his parents were grounded in the past. He was unable to move forward into the present or the future. His emotions rested on deceptions, lying, and criticism and destructive appraisal of the other. There was no sharing of experience with the other, no sense of loyalty or attachment (except negatively). He felt trapped by the other in a past that would not let him move into the future where he could be himself.

The emotionally divided self hates the others who make up her world (see Dostoevsky, 1864/1960, p. 233). She is unable to have sharing relationships with them. She fears the others and resents them for what they have done to her. She feels victimized by the others. Furthermore, she feels that the others have unfairly judged her. Accordingly, no positive emotions can be felt toward them.

The interpersonal focus of the negative emotions is on feelings that detract from the other while building up the (false) self of the subject. The authoritarian other is a constant emotional associate of the subject. Such persons are negative, significant emotional others. By (symbolically) destroying the other and by surrounding her with negative emotionality, the subject accomplishes two things. First, he ensures that the other will have negative experiences with him, thereby increasing her discomfort. Second, he elevates his own self-esteem, for he draws pleasure from inflicting pain on the other. This pleasure comes from the feeling that the other has harmed him in the past. The production of negative emotionality places the emotionally divided self in a position of control over the other. It is this control that is sought. It must be seen, however, that this emotionality dwells in the past.

The emotionally divided self keeps the other in the past, for this is safe country. She may not be able to act in the future, and she may find the present threatening and anxiety-provoking, but the past is hers. Hence she continually draws the other into the past, finding refuge and control in events that may have happened days, months, or even years ago.

This is why criticism is so important to the divided self. By attacking the other who threatens her, she keeps him at a safe distance. Criticism, joined with deception, dishonesty, malicious gossip, invective, hatred, slander, profanity, temper tantrums, and guilt-invoking actions, keeps the other at a distance and under control. Pain is inflicted through these actions. By causing pain to others, the divided self, full of ressentiment, derives self-pleasure and support. An empty inner self that is incapable of generating its own positive emotionality must rely on others. The negative emotions have a symbiotic quality that allows them to live off the past actions of the negative other who has controlled and destroyed the world of the divided self.

The control that is purchased through generation of negative emotionality is tenuous and unstable. Because the divided self must rely on the other as the source of whatever inner stability he possesses, a high risk is taken when the other is confronted with negative experiences. The other may terminate interactions with the divided self. Furthermore, the other may reply in kind, thereby increasing the likelihood that the outer shell of the subject will be penetrated, if not shattered. An interpersonal relationship built on negativity contains the seeds of its own destruction.

A paradox is experienced at this level of interpersonal life. The emotional barrier that is built between the divided self and the other is founded on emotional infection and spurious emotionality (see Chapter Five). The grounds for true emotional understanding, characteristic of emotional embracement and shared emotionality, are missing in this relationship. The other's intersubjective understanding of the emotionality of the divided self is minimal. The emotions that draw the divided self near to the other are the very emotions that keep the two apart. The others who surround the divided self can neither tolerate nor understand the field of emotionality that places them in the company of this person. The negative emotions produce a jointly felt "alienation" from place. Neither party can long stand the presence of the other.

Self-Feelings and the Negative Emotions. If the interpersonal relations of the divided self are threaded through with negative, hostile emotionality, the subject's self-feelings have the same foundation. The emotions of fear, anger, ressentiment, and self-loathing govern the divided self. From these forms of emotionality come selfishness, self-pity, and feelings of uselessness. The divided self constructs a façade of false-pride that serves both to keep others at a distance and to hold up a faltering inner self. The inner emotions of guilt and shame underpin the entire self-system of the divided self. These are deep, master emotions (Sullivan, 1953b; Lynd, 1958; Freud, 1933; Lacan, 1968; Lewis, 1971; Piers and Singer, 1971). The subject feels responsible and remorseful over his past actions toward the other. He takes blame for these past actions and holds himself inwardly responsible for the self-destructive emotional cycle he finds himself in. The shame that accompanies this guilt is painful and contributes to the sense of unworthiness and disgrace the self feels. The divided self feels dishonored and blames itself for this shameful state it has constructed. The subject's inward moral self-awareness turns against him. He feels morally irresponsible and morally disrespectful in the face of himself. He is ashamed and guilty to be in the presence of himself. He may routinely obliterate his consciousness of himself. The subject requires the recurrent use of false pride, anger, hostility, and criticism of the other to keep from seeing himself. Outwardly he attempts to place guilt, remorse, and responsibility for his state of mind on the other. The shame and disgrace the other feels take responsibility away from the divided self. By placing blame on the other, the subject absolves himself of responsibility for the negative emotionality he is experiencing. He locates his loss of dignity and grace in the actions the other has taken toward him. His false pride and false self-system foster this belief. He is in bad faith.

In contrast, the morally respectful subject (Heidegger, 1975/1982, p. 133) feels respect for herself in the face of something greater than herself. This something greater is a moral law or moral code that she willingly and freely submits to. Her feelings of self-respect are revealed through this act of submission. The feeling self appears in the act of submission to the moral code.

> In subjecting myself to the law, I subject myself to myself as pure reason; but that is to say that in this subjection to myself I raise myself to myself as the free, self-determining being. This submissive self-elevation of myself to myself reveals, discloses as such, me to myself in my *dignity*. . . . The moral feeling, as respect for the law, is nothing but self's being responsible to itself for itself. This moral feeling is a distinctive way in which the ego understands itself as ego directly, purely, and free of all sensuous determination.
>
> This self-consciousness in the sense of respect constitutes the personalitas moralis. . . . In respect, as a feeling, there is present . . . self-subjection. This self-subjection, in conformity with the content of that to which I subject myself and *for which* I have a feeling in my respect, is at the same time a self-elevation as a becoming self-evident in my ownmost dignity [Heidegger, 1975/1982, pp. 135-136].

The emotionally divided self does not feel self-respect. He has not subjected himself, freely and rationally, to himself in the face of something outside himself. He has submitted, instead, to his own out-of-control emotionality. He feels and reveals himself only through false, spurious, negative emotionality. He has no apparent self-control over his emotionality. He is locked inside himself and unable to see out, except through negativity. Self-pity dominates him. The feelings he continually feels only contribute to this self of self-pity and self-loathing. He is the unreflective victim of his own emotionality. He is in a vicious circle of self-destruction.

The dignity and self-respect that the subject clings to are fragile and false. She has nothing to stem the onslaught of fear that sweeps across her. There is no inner core of respect, dignity, finality, or certainty that she can turn to, in surrender or submission (see James, 1904/1961, pp. 148-161). She is suffering from inauthentic guilt (Heidegger, 1927/1962, p. 353). She and her emotionality have fallen through that thin wall that separates her and her feelings from the feelings she thinks others want her to have (Heidegger, 1927/1962, p. 323). She is guilty (in her eyes) in the eyes of the other. She feels that she deserves self-punishment. Being inauthentically guilty in the eyes of the other is a mode of self-feeling that diverts the subject from feeling her own inner feelings. Inauthentic guilt, together with anger and ressentiment, sustains the false self of the subject (see Rebeta-Burditt, 1977).

Authentic guilt, which arises from the breach of a moral agreement the subject has with herself, is not felt by the divided self. Inauthentic guilt over not submitting oneself to a moral code, to one's *inner* moral conscience, plagues the emotionally divided self. The subject has lost touch with her inner moral conscience. She has violated her own inner morality. She experiences a denial of self-respect, which only she can give herself.

Self-pity is the feeling that traps the divided self. The subject is caught within a mode of temporality that freezes him in the dividing line between the past and the present. His world is filled with guilt, shame, and disgrace. His final act of false pride proclaims his self-pity and his hatred. King Lear pleads:

You heavens, give me that patience, patience I need!
You see me here, you gods, a poor old man,
As full of grief as age; wretched in both!
If it be you that stir these daughters' hearts
Against their father, fool me not so much
To bear it tamely; touch me with noble anger,
And let not women's weapons, water drops,
Stain my man's cheeks!—No, you unnatural hags,
I will have such revenges on you both
That all the world shall,—I will do such things,—
What they are yet I know not; but they shall be
The terrors of the earth. You think I'll weep;
No, I'll not weep:—
I have full cause of weeping; but this heart
Shall break into a hundred thousand flaws
Or ere I'll weep.—O fool, I shall go mad!
[*King Lear*, act 2, scene 4]

Collapse and Repair

The emotionally divided self is described by James (1904/
1961, pp. 145-146): "There are persons whose existence is little more than a series of zigzags, as now one tendency and now
another gets the upper hand. Their spirit wars with their flesh,
they wish for incompatibles, wayward impulses interrupt their
most deliberate plans, and their lives are one long drama of re-
pentance and of effort to repair misdemeanors and mistakes.
. . . In the haunting and insistent ideas, in the irrational impulses, the morbid scruples, dreads, and inhibitions which beset
the psychopathic temperament when it is thoroughly pro-
nounced, we have exquisite examples of heterogeneous personality." Not only are such persons left with an emotionally divided self, which is torn and left in shreds, but more important,
they lose the capacity to feel. They can feel only objectless
emotionality, as discussed earlier in this chapter. The sharpness
of feeling that comes from anger, wrath, joy, envy, or the thirst
for revenge is gone. The emotions have become dulled, dead-
ened, lifeless experiences. The subject fears to feel, for feeling
would bring him or her back into time and the world. It is safe
to not feel. Thus temporality disappears from the world of the
divided self.

Still, the divided self may draw back together and find a sense of unity of its parts that was heretofore missing. James remarks that "the process of unification, when it occurs . . . may come gradually, or it may occur abruptly; it may come through altered feelings, or through altered powers of actions; or it may come through new intellectual insights, or through experiences which we shall later have to designate as 'mystical.' However it comes, it brings a characteristic sort of relief" (1904/1961, p. 150). Religion, madness, therapy, geographical moves, and changes in occupation or in interactional associates all may combine to unify the torn, divided self. Repair, however, if it comes, moves the self out of itself.

In order for the self to change itself, it must get outside itself. A communicative and meaning system that stands in a metarelationship to the self-system of the subject must be entered into (Bateson, 1972, pp. 177–193). If such communication is not possible, the self remains trapped within itself. It is faced by the following dilemma: "Perhaps the only answer, I thought then, was that by the time we understand the pattern we are in, the definition we are making for ourselves, it is too late to break out of the box. We can only live in terms of the definition, like the prisoner in the cage in which he cannot lie or stand or sit, hung up in justice to be viewed by the populace. Yet the definition we make of ourselves is ourselves. To break out of it, we must make a new self. But how can the self make a new self when the selfness which it is, is the only substance from which the new self can be made? At least that was the way I argued the case back then" (Warren, 1946, p. 351).

Repair and rebuilding necessarily require an opening up of the divided self to the world of interactional associates. The negative emotions and negative interpersonal relations that tie the subject to the past must be broken. A new mode of temporality and being-in-the-world must be entered into. New interactional experiences that draw the self together yet outside itself must be generated. The subject must relinquish her inauthentic views of time and being. In such transformations, the future, the present, and the past take on new meanings to the person. Heidegger (1927/1962) suggests the conceptualization shown in Table 1.

Table 1. Authenticity and Temporality.

Mode of Being-in-the World	Temporality of Emotions		
	Past	Present	Future
Authentic	acceptance	anticipation	caring
Inauthentic	rejection ressentiment	fear, anxiety, anger	avoidance, depression

The lines that divide and split the self are implicitly drawn in Table 1. Repair and unification involve an entire temporal restructuring of the world of divided selves, their emotionality, and their relations with others. Only by getting outside time and outside themselves can they regain a new view of themselves. From such a view will come the positive interpersonal and personal emotions of friendship, love, "we-ness," caring, sharing, solidarity, warmth, calm, and inner honesty. The surface and deep levels of the subject will be drawn back together. The emotionality that Scheler (1916/1973, p. 343) describes as "bliss," serenity, and inner peace may be given through a transformation of the person. Scheler (1916/1973, p. 344) states: "Since these feelings are *not conditioned* by value-complexes exterior to the person and his possible acts, it is clear that they take root in the value-nature of the person *himself* and his being and value-being, which stand above all acts. Therefore these feelings are the only ones which cannot be conceived as feelings that could be produced, or even *merited,* by our comportment. Both possibilities contradict the *essence* of these feelings."

The divided self must be resocialized through a drawing out of new abilities and "facilities that are in him" (Scheler, 1916/1973, p. 236). A rediscovery of old forms of emotionality and old forms of feeling must be accomplished. At the same time, new forms of self-feeling will be learned. A sense of self-responsibility for one's actions must be produced. The self-pity of bad faith will disappear as honest self-appraisal enters the subject's world. Through emotionality the subject will discover new views of self. That emotionality will reveal a new, inner essence to the self that was previously lost. The divided self will come home to itself, finding a new person inside the skin of an old body that was hated and despised.

Conclusions

Detailed examination of the inner life of the emotionally divided self has served to develop my major thesis that self-feelings lie at the core of emotionality. An expanded view of emotions and emotionality has emerged from the discussion. In particular, the following points deserve highlighting:

1. The body is central to the feelings of the self.
2. The other figures centrally in all self-feelings of the person.
3. The thematic structures of the self divide and work against one another.
4. Temporality is basic to emotionality.
5. Negative emotionality destroys positive emotionality.
6. Repair of the self is an interpersonal process involving metacommunication and the location of the self outside itself.

The violent self, the topic of the previous chapter, can now be seen to be a divided self. Violence is one mode of striking out at the "false" world that surrounds the subject. Through violence the self attempts to regain support for its faltering inner self-system. Yet the divided self, like the violent self, is an interpersonal process, subject to the same schismogenic forces that destroy families of violence.

The processes that produce persons, families, selves, self-feeling, and emotionality are interactional and are governed by their own inner logic and force. A part of the very process that they produced, individuals often find that they are trapped by their own creations. Not wishing to take responsibility for these creations, they retreat into a divided self; one part of the self wants credit for what it has created, the other part wants to destroy it. Such is the fate of the violent self and the emotionally divided self.

Conclusion:
Reflections
on Emotion

The continual examination of the basic question that has guided this investigation, how emotionality as a form of consciousness is lived, experienced, articulated, and felt, has served a double purpose. On the one side, the structures and essence of emotionality have been revealed. On the other, investigation of the substantive dimensions of emotionality (lived emotion, intersubjectivity, violence, the divided self) has revealed the central place that emotionality must occupy in a theory of interpretation and understanding. In this conclusion I offer preliminary observations and reflections on emotionality, interpretation, and understanding. If interpretive sociology is to gain a stronger footing within the human disciplines, then basic elements of the emotional theory of interpretive understanding warrant presentation.

The following topics will be examined: emotionality, in-

terpretation and understanding, hermeneutics, the subject matter of interpretation, understanding, the criteria of interpretation, meaning, and situating emotionality within the lives of
ordinary people.

Emotionality

On reading Charles Dickens's *Christmas Books,* Robert
Louis Stevenson was moved to write the following lines: "I
wonder if you have ever read Dickens's *Christmas Books?* ...
they are too much perhaps. I have only read two yet, but I have
cried my eyes out, and had a terrible fight not to sob, But, oh,
dear God, they are good ... and I feel so good after them—I
shall do good and lose no time—I want to go out and comfort
someone—I *shall* give money. Oh, what a jolly thing it is for a
man to have written books like these and just filled people's
hearts with pity" (Stevenson, 1920/1971, p. 200).

Emotion moves the subject. That movement has a double
structure. In this text Stevenson is moved first by Dickens's
Christmas Books. He is moved emotionally to "have cried my
eyes out" and "to go out and comfort someone." "I *shall* give
money," he states. This decision to give money reflects the second element of emotion's ability to move the subject. That is,
emotionality is connected to an object, whether that is a Christmas book, a painting, a musical score, the vision of another suffering or in joy, or the person feeling a feeling. In that relationship to the object the subject's emotionality leads him to act.
These actions are based on the subject's sympathetic, moral,
and emotional identification with the object(s) of his feelings
and emotional attention (see Smith, 1911, pp. 480–481). Hence,
the double structure of emotion's movement: a feeling toward
the object, in which a feeling self is revealed to the self, and the
movement into a course of action which enacts that emotionality and feeling.

On the basis of emotionality, the person is moved to act
morally, on behalf of himself and of others. The moral person is
revealed through emotionality. That moral person has a sense of
duty, dignity, and self-respect. These qualities are produced by

submission to a moral code, or moral law. In yielding to moral respect, the individual gains that respect for himself. He reveals himself to himself respectfully. This sense of self-respect permeates the subject's inner essence as a moral person (see Chapter Three).

If the subject is moved by emotionality both to feel and to act, then a theory of emotionality and moral sympathy can be seen as offering one answer to the question "How is society possible?" (Simmel, 1950). In contrast to the utilitarians, who argue for a rational, cost/benefit, economic model of the human being and social conduct, the argument presented here is aligned with that of Georg Simmel, Adam Smith, and the Scottish moralists David Hume, Adam Ferguson, Thomas Reid, Francis Hutcheson, Dugald Stewart, Lord Kames, and Lord Monboddo (see Schneider, 1967; Bryson, 1945).

The basic elements of this view are as follows. Through their feelings and emotionality individuals are connected to others. Through emotionality they come to know others. Cognitions, thoughts, and meanings are lodged in the horizons of emotionality. Understanding and interpretation are interrelated processes that rest on the feelings individuals feel when they grasp the meaning of another's actions (see Dilthey, 1900/1976, pp. 226–228). Emotionality is interwoven through the acts that connect a subject to others and to herself. It is in and against emotionality that the subject comes to know, interpret, and understand herself and others. Emotionality is thus a basic underlying feature of human consciousness and human interaction. On this Adam Smith (1911) observes: "But whatever may be the cause of sympathy or however it may be excited, nothing pleases us more than to observe in other men a fellow-feeling with all the emotions of our own breast; nor are we ever so much shocked as by the appearance of the contrary. . . . In the same manner, we either approve or disapprove of our own conduct, according as we feel that, when we place ourselves in the situation of another man, and view it, as it were, with his eyes from his station, we either can or cannot entirely enter into and sympathize with the sentiments and motives which influenced it" (pp. 10, 161). The other person is the looking glass before which "we examine our persons limb by limb [endeavoring] as much as possible to view ourselves . . . with the eyes of other people" (Smith, 1911, p. 163). The impressions we are met with from the other are then judged cognitively and emotionally with approval or disapproval as well as some sort of self-feeling, or emotion (Cooley, 1902/1956, p. 184). The feelings that are directed to the other arise from their having first been felt by ourselves.

Smith, the other Scottish moralists, and the Romantic poets Blake, Wordsworth, Coleridge, Byron, Shelley, and Keats (see Heath, 1973; Engell, 1981; Abrams, 1953) assumed that humans had the ability to enter one another's fields of experience, to take the other's attitude (Mead, 1934, 1982a), and to act on that experience sympathetically, through imagination, empathy, and emotionality. They assumed, too, that this process produced a shared feeling that drew persons to become "in some measure the same person" with the other (Smith, 1911, p. 4).

The "emotional imagination" heightens the person's awareness of another's feelings "until we feel them just as intensely as he does—perhaps more so" (Engell, 1981, p. 150). This awareness of the other's situation, and the emotional imagination of his feelings, awakens feelings in oneself. But they now become one's own feelings.

This appropriation of the other's feelings is based both on the emotional imagination of the subject and on her willingness to suspend doubt or disbelief regarding the other's feelings and state of mind. Emotionality overrides cognitive doubt. It produces sufficiently plausible reasons for adopting the other's feelings and believing in them. Emotionality constructs its own compelling and complete structure of plausible belief, thereby removing or momentarily neutralizing the perceiver's nagging doubts of implausibility, illogicality, or irrationality. Emotionality moves the perceiver to accept the grounds for the other's acts, feelings, and thoughts (see Canby, 1983, pp. 1, 13).

In these respects emotionality and the emotional imagination lead the subject, as the poet urges, to accept on faith the feelings of the other. On this Coleridge (1817/1973, p. 516) reports an agreement made with William Wordsworth concerning the directions their poetry would take: "In this idea originated the plan for the 'Lyrical Ballads': in which it was agreed that my endeavors should be directed to persons and characters supernatural, or at least romantic; yet so as to transfer from our inward nature a human interest and a semblance of truth sufficient to procure for these shadows of imagination *that willing suspension of disbelief for the moment* which constitutes poetic faith" (italics added). Emotionality shapes a willingness to believe and transfers "a semblance of truth" to the "shadows of imagination" felt and thought by the person. Emotionality depends on the willing suspension of disbelief for its existence, while furnishing the very grounds for that belief. Emotionality produces a "bracketing of the natural attitude of doubt." It lends a sense of authenticity and a structure of plausibility to actions and feelings that would ordinarily be cast aside, doubted, not believed. The emotional imagination presumes a willingness to believe in the emotionality of the other.

This willingness to believe in the emotionality of the other, to feel her pain or her joy, rests on the ability to feel and imagine her feelings. It thus overrides the subject's own selfish impulses and inclinations. It gives pleasure and support to others by leading the subject not only to feel for their feelings but to be moved to come to their assistance (Engell, 1981, p. 150; Smith, 1911). Such actions also release pleasures for the individual. But these actions are influenced by duty, custom, tradition, belief, obligation, the presence or absence of others, the novelty of the situation, the fear of sanction, the person's current state of mind and emotionality, and other factors (see Latané, 1970; Baron and Byrne, 1981, pp. 271-310; Smith, 1911, pp. 30-50).

Society is possible, in part, because of the moral foundations of emotionality and sympathy. These processes, through the operation of the emotional imagination, produce concern for and interest in the feelings and situations of others. We are led to "act for the sake of others" (Engell, 1981, p. 151). The emotional imagination, coupled with the principle of emotional sociality, becomes the vehicle for the exercise of our basic sociality and moral conscience.

This argument replaces or challenges a theory of society based on pure self-interest and economic exchange. It is essentially the "theory of moral sympathy" of Adam Smith and Charles Horton Cooley. It may now be given more explicitly in terms of the following points.

First, the primary objects of the subject's moral and emotional judgments are the actions of other people from whom the meanings of emotion are learned. Second, the subject's moral and emotional judgments regarding his own actions are judgments and feelings that were first formed and felt in terms of the conduct of others (Stewart, 1911, p. xxi). Third, the understanding the subject gains of his *own* moral and emotional conduct is derived through the processes of emotional intersubjectivity. Fourth, the understanding a subject has of *another's* conduct is gained from the same processes. That is, the subject enters into the experiences of another by placing himself in the circumstances of the other and generating for himself the feelings of the other. These feelings then become his. Fifth, through the processes of emotional intersubjectivity (feelings in common, fellow-feeling, emotional infection, emotional identification, shared emotionality, spurious emotionality) a sense of *joining with* the other is produced. In this interaction the other and the subject join their respective forms of emotionality into a field of common experience. The self that is revealed to the subject through these feelings then passes judgment on those feelings, finding them appropriate or inappropriate, morally right or morally wrong, despicable or attractive. Sixth, the motives and emotional accounts that appear to underlie the other's actions and emotionality are judged as fitting and appropriate or as inappropriate. Seventh, on the basis of this judgment, actions of a positive or negative nature are taken toward the other. The subject may come to her assistance, turn away from her in disgust, seek her out for interaction, or be moved by her feelings (Smith, 1911; Latané, 1970; Latané and Darley, 1968). As just noted, it is on the basis of emotionality and interpretive understanding that persons act on one another's behalf. The self of the other enters the interaction through the process of emotional sociality (see Chapter Five). However, G. H. Mead's principle of sociality, which was modified in Chapter Five into the principle of emotional sociality, now requires one additional change. Selves enter the interaction process through the process of moral, not just emotional and cognitive, understanding. The self is a moral object. The principle of moral sociality underlies the emotional-interpretive view of society and person set forth in this investigation. This principle connects this work to that of the Scottish moralists, to James, Freud, Heidegger, Scheler, Cooley, Durkheim, Mead, and Goffman.

Eighth, the moral foundations of sympathy and emotional understanding rest on this ability of one person to imagine the feelings, motives, and meanings that another brings to her conduct in a concrete social situation. Because the emotional understanding one person has of another is always incomplete and partial, subject to the ambiguities of interaction and inter-subjectivity, the social understandings that underlie everyday life are ambiguous and often contradictory (Lefebvre, 1971; Manning, 1977, pp. 81-82; L. Lofland, 1973; J. Lofland, 1976, 1981, pp. 414-415). As a consequence, interpretation is always incomplete and is contingent on the interpretations that individuals bring to their situations of interaction.

The implications of the perspective on emotionality and interpretation set forth in Chapter Five can now be drawn out in fuller detail. Stated succinctly, the argument suggests the following five conclusions. First, emotionality is at the basis of interpretation and understanding in everyday and scientific life. Second, emotionality underlies the social and moral foundations of society. This bold statement requires specification. Material scarcity in all the senses stressed by Sartre (1976) and Marx sets the raw skeletal realities against which moral sympathy, emotionality, interpretation, and understanding are lived and experienced. This problem will be addressed in my next work. It is through emotionality, imagination, sympathy, fellow-feeling, and revealed self-feelings that persons come to know themselves and one another. Third, on the basis of those emotional understandings, actions toward others are taken. Fourth, those actions affirm and reaffirm the subject's own sense of moral worth. Fifth, the moral worth of the other is determined by this same process.

The theory of moral sympathy and emotional understanding locates emotionality in the center of the transactions of self and society. It is to be contrasted to utilitarian models of the human being and society that strip emotionality, tradition, custom, and ritual from everyday life and locate meaning in economic cost/benefit exchanges. Such views are devoid of an interpretive theory of understanding, as well as a theory of the moral, feeling person. The topic of interpretation must now be taken up in greater detail.

Interpretation and Understanding

Figure 2 depicts the hermeneutic circle of interpretation and understanding. It assumes the presence of the interactional and phenomenological streams of experience discussed in Chapter 2 and Figure 1. The person stands in the center of this circle, attached to the world through the circuit of selfness. The circle begins with the hermeneutic situation (Heidegger, 1927/1962, p. 232; Dilthey, 1900/1976, pp. 10, 203, 259, 262). A situation is never approached free of prior interpretations. As Gadamer (1976, p. 9) states, "It is our prejudices that constitute our being." An impulse to action presents itself to the subject, located in the world. This impulse, which may come from self-indications from others, alters the line of action the person is currently pursuing. It involves the mobilization and direction of action, perception, and interpretation toward an object or project that is "spatiotemporally away from" the person (Mead, 1938, p. 141). Through action and perception the subject draws herself near to the object, perhaps engaging it with her hands as well as visually. In this, the manipulatory phase of interpretation, the subject engages in reflective and unreflective (habitual) interpretive conduct (Dewey, 1922). As she moves into the manipulatory phases of action and interpretation, she anticipates the conclusions of her actions. She brings the conclusion of her act in front of her, as she undertakes movements toward that conclusion. As action and interpretation unfold, problematics are confronted. Action may be interrupted because of prior commitments. The object on which the person acts may resist her actions. Prior interpretations may not fit the specifics

Figure 2. The Hermeneutic Circle of Interpretation and Understanding.

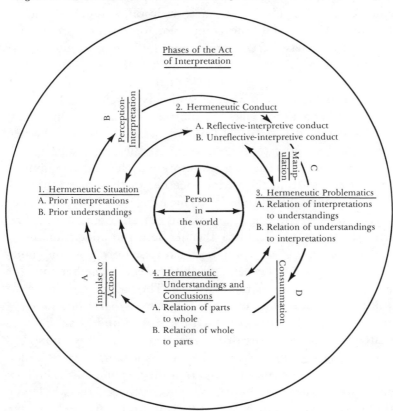

of the project once she finds herself in the midst of action. Fatigue, emergent emotionality, loss of interest, or simple recalcitrance on the part of the object may lead to the complete abandonment of the interpretive project she has undertaken. Or, in the face of problematics, she may redefine the conclusions of her act and come to an early consensual conclusion, perhaps producing a half-finished job of the proposed project.

In the manipulatory phase of interpretive conduct, the subject assesses the relation between his prior and emerging interpretations of the project and the interactional (pragmatic) utility of those interpretations for the project undertaken. In turn, his understandings of the completed project are reassessed in light of the prior and emergent interpretations. Should a fit emerge among manipulation, interpretation, and understanding, the subject moves to the completion of the interpretive act. Here, in the phase of consummation, he brings his interpretive conduct to conclusion. This consummatory conclusion is now evaluated and interpreted in light of the relation of the preceding interpretive steps to what was initially sought out.

This conclusion gives the subject a concrete picture of the total completed act. In light of this totality, which is the hermeneutically understood conclusion of the act, the parts that went into the whole act are reinterpreted. The understanding of the act comes from the fitting together of these parts into the whole. Conversely, the whole has meaning only in relation to its parts. Similarly, the meaning of this (or any) sentence as a reflective statement regarding the hermeneutic understanding of understanding and interpretation can arise only from the simultaneous fitting of the parts of the sentence together into the whole that constitutes this sentence. The meaning of the whole sentence cannot be given only through its parts but must be given as a totality of assembled parts. The understanding of a sentence consists in this fitting together of parts to whole. Understanding, as Dilthey remarks, gives meaning: "Here understanding of the sentence results from the meaning of the individual words. But there is an interaction between the whole and the parts through which ambiguities of meanings are eliminated and the meaning of individual words determined" (1900/1976, p. 237).

Understanding works back through interpretation, just as interpretation begins with prior understandings. As the parts that fit together into the whole are unraveled, the whole takes on new meanings. There is a critical interaction between interpretation and understanding. They do not stand apart as unrelated activities. Mead's (1938, 1982a) model of the act, Peirce's (1931) theory of firstness, secondness, and thirdness, Dilthey's (1900/1976) elaborations of understanding, Saussure's (1959) theory of the sign, Heidegger's (1927/1962) views on the hermeneutics of interpretation, and Sartre's (1963) progressive-regressive method of analysis are all statements about this interactive relation between interpretation and understanding.

The essence of understanding involves the grasping of what will come after interpretation, before interpretation actually begins. Understanding leaps in front of itself to its own anticipated conclusions. It involves a grasping of the whole before the parts that constitute the whole have been fitted together, as when one glimpses a striking painting, finds one's interest held, and then returns to study the painting.

Interpretation does the footwork of understanding, in three senses. First, interpretation lays out the ground rules under which the parts of the understood whole will be pieced together. For sentences, this would be the rules of syntax; for music, the rules of composition; for the exegesis of a text, the rules of hermeneutic interpretation; for cockfighting, the rules of a cockfight; and so on. Second, interpretation is a part of understanding, for each interpretation in a sequence yields a partial understanding of what has thus far been interpreted. Interpretation releases itself from understanding. As Dilthey observes, "the gesture and the terror are not two separate things but a unity" (1900/1976, p. 221). Third, interpretation provides partial grounds for judging understanding. That is, if the parts that go into an understood totality are not themselves understood and interpreted in relation to one another, the finished understanding is incomplete and thereby weakened or made tentative.

The late classical Canadian pianist Glenn Gould conceived of interpretation in a manner consistent with Dilthey's. On Mr. Gould's views of recording, Rothstein (1982, p. 19) observes:

> Mr. Gould's approach to recording . . . has been different from that of most musicians. The record, traditionally, is supposed to be an imitation of a concert, a sort of "testimony" to the way music is "actually" made. In Mr. Gould's view, the recording is nothing of the kind. It is constructed, pieced together, controlled. The continuous result is an illusion, just as a filmmaker creates an illusion with his splices. This is how a writer works . . . or, for that matter, how a composer composes . . . discarding drafts, fitting in pieces, rearranging, expanding and contracting . . . Mr. Gould has a formidable technique. . . . But once the dialect is

> learned, the interpretations can be formidable. . . .
> Hence the autumnal eloquence of Mr. Gould's ear-
> ly Brahms, the refined and provocative perfor-
> mance of the Beethoven 'Emperor' Concerto. . . .
> Paradoxically, this intense spareness finally speaks
> to the listening body. It can be difficult to sit still
> for this playing. Its compression and tensile strength
> can make much of it seem like an ecstatic dance.

These comments on Mr. Gould's recordings of Brahms and Beethoven suggest that interpretation has a meaning that makes it more than a prelude to understanding. An interpretation of a musical text, painting, or poem can itself produce a new text of interpretation, just as a new reading or new interpretation of a classical sociological theorist can produce a new interpretive text (see Barthes, 1975; Becker, 1982). Interpretations, then, are layered on one another, for there is only interpretation. Fur-thermore, interpretations are produced as interpretive produc-tions in their own right. Mr. Gould's manner of interpretation, like that of a writer, involves a fitting together of bits and pieces, drafts and redrafts, arranged and rearranged in different formats.

Interpretation requires the interpreter to rethink the text being interpreted. This involves a rethinking of the activity of interpreting. To interpret suggests an understanding of the text that will be interpreted, for one reaches forth and grasps the meaning of the totality of the text before one works one's way back through the text, moving forward piece by piece to the conclusions one perhaps reached before one began.

The results of such a view of interpretation make inter-pretation a new act of understanding. But more is involved, for new interpretations are meant to challenge the reader, listener, or spectator. She is drawn into an interpretive act that chal-lenges her preconceived understandings. She is startled, alarmed, tantalized, seduced, put at ease, forced to rethink her own rela-tionship to herself and to that which she is asked to interpret (Barthes, 1975).

Such a view of interpretation makes it more than a cogni-tive task that follows well-developed lines of thought and discourse. The end of interpretation, as Wordsworth argued with respect to poetry, is to "produce excitement in coexistence with an overbalance of pleasure; but by the supposition, excitement is an unusual and irregular state of mind; ideas and feelings do not, in that state, succeed each other in accustomed order. . . . Poetry is the spontaneous overflow of powerful feelings: it takes its origin from emotion recollected in tranquility: the emotion is contemplated till, by the species of re-action, the tranquility gradually disappears, and an emotion, kindred to that which was before the subject of contemplation, is gradually produced, and does itself actually exist in the mind. In this mood successful composition generally begins, and in a mood similar to this it is carried on" (1800/1973, pp. 405–406).

A goal of interpretation is to produce in the interpreting subject an emotional relationship with the text that is being interpreted. From such an identification comes a lodging of the feeling self in the text. The self that secures the text for its own can hope to better understand that text. This seems to be the point of Mr. Gould's and Mr. Wordsworth's arguments concerning interpretation, understanding, and emotionality.

The act of interpretation (see Davis, 1978) re-creates through feelings and thoughts an original relationship to the text of experience that is before the interpreter. This new relationship requires and produces a new interpretation. From that new interpretation comes a new and different form of understanding. The interpreter stands midway between text and understanding. In interpretation the interpreter must use a language that speaks at once to the text and to the reader, listener, or viewer of the work. The "real language" of the world must be the language used, not a peculiar language that speaks only to other interpreters (Wordsworth, 1800/1973, p. 405).

Interpretation and understanding stand in a dynamic, dialectical, interactional relationship with each other. Each reflects on the other. Each needs the other for its existence. Each, to a certain extent, negates the other. There are, of course, uninterpreted understandings. Freud's and Lacan's patients, for example, felt their bewilderment and psychological discomfort but were unable to interpret that self-understanding. Similarly, there are interpretations that do not yield understanding. One can interpret each word in a sentence and still be unable to grasp the structural totality of the sentence. Spurious emotionality, discussed in Chapter Five, is an instance of an interpretation that is not understood. Interpreted understandings move all the way through the hermeneutic circle of interpretation and understanding. Uninterpreted understandings are blocked by hermeneutic problematics. The subject wrestles with an unresolved, uninterpreted understanding. In interpreted understandings the totality of what is problematic is grasped, as an understanding. Interpretation both unravels what is understood and produces understanding. Understanding, in turn, rewrites interpretation.

A theory of interpretive understanding must be a theory of the interpretive subject as a feeling self. Emotionality, as argued in Chapters Three and Five, is at the basis of understanding. All emotionality refers back to the feeling self, even if it initiates in the other. The interpretive subject is the feeling subject and the subject of its own interpretations. This subject enters into and directs its own intersubjective interpretations of the world. As an interpretive subject, the person stands inside a network of interpretive understandings and practices that render the world "feelable," meaningful, interpretable, and understandable. These interpretive practices (Chapter Three) repeatedly move the person through the hermeneutic circle of interpretation and emotionality.

Persons can never be free of interpretation or prejudgment toward understanding, nor can they be free of emotionality, of temporality, or of themselves. As a consequence, all interpretations work outward from the feeling, thinking, intuiting, interpreting, prejudiced, understanding subject.

This subject is well known in the phenomenological, interactionist, and structural literature (see, for example, Cicourel, 1974; Knorr-Cetina and Cicourel, 1981; Foucault, 1980, 1982; Dreyfus and Rabinow, 1982; Finkelstein, 1982; Secord, 1982; Sharron, 1981, 1982; Rabinow and Sullivan, 1979; Sartre, 1943/ 1978; Blumer, 1969; Gadamer, 1976; Manning, 1973; Giddens,

1982; Geertz, 1983). Its characteristics need not be repeated or debated here. All that must be noted is that this subject, both reflectively and unreflectively, is attached to the world and draws its interpretive schemes from transactions with that world. This subject engages and makes the world into a dwelling place for itself, its emotionality, its projects, and its meanings. How the world is to be made into a dwelling place is the problem that continually confronts the feeling, thinking, interpretive subject.

Hermeneutics

Hermeneutics is the work of interpretation and understanding. The methodology of interpretation is hermeneutics (Dilthey, 1900/1976, p. 261). All interpretations are mediated by the interpreter's own intersubjectivity (Grossberg, 1979, 1982). Interpretations are conditioned by prior understandings, which are open-ended and are based on previous interpretations and understandings. Interpretation proceeds through the hermeneutic circle with the projection of meanings and the anticipation of understanding. In interpretation there is a "dialogical-dialectical mediation of subject and object" (Bleicher, 1980, p. 3). A task of hermeneutics is the avoidance of misunderstanding (Bleicher, 1980, p. 2). Misunderstanding is an overwhelming of the text with the interpreter's own prior understandings and prejudices. Misunderstandings arise when interpreters force their interpretations on that which is to be understood. Hermeneutics describes the interaction that occurs between subject and object, interpretation and understanding. The hermeneutical process is a conversation of voices—silent and loud, active and passive, reluctant and open, distorting and opaque, transparent and visible. It is a conversation that produces a new form of discourse, transforming what was previously invisible into the visible, the felt, and the held (Merleau-Ponty, 1968; Mead, 1938). Hermeneutics brings into reach what was previously at a distance. Meaning arises in this process of reaching toward the object that is at a distance.

The Subject Matter of Interpretation

The subject matter of hermeneutic interpretation is inter-actional experience. This experience is rooted in the conduct of individuals. The starting point of hermeneutic inquiry, then, is the individual located in the world, interacting with others. Reversing Goffman's dictum (1967, p. 3), the interpreter examines "persons and their moments," not "moments and their men." The moments of persons, ordinary and routine, problematic and turning-point, solitary and joint, collective and large-scale, join individual lines of action into moving fields of experience that are symbolic, temporal, relational, situational, structural, historical, and meaningful. Interactional experience connects the lifetimes of persons with history, structure, and society. The processes that weave persons into and through one another's lives are made visible in the moments of interactional experience.

The grounding of interpretation in the lives of interacting individuals ensures a continual and firm foundation in the world of lived experience. If the goal of interpretive inquiry is the examination of how persons give meaning to their lives, then the joining of lives with interactional experiences seems mandatory. To sever persons from their moments, and moments from their persons, produces a formal sociology of forms that can find meaning only in structures that are posited as standing outside the realms of directly lived experience (Jameson, 1972; Hall, 1980; Denzin, in press-c). Such a sociology violates the basic principle of interpretive interactionism that phenomena be examined and interpreted from within.

The Study of Interactional Emotional Experience. Interactional emotional experiences, as projects connected to the lifetimes of interacting individuals, may be studied in terms of what Heidegger (1927/1962, p. 232) terms the hermeneutical situation. The hermeneutical understanding of a lived emotional experience involves six steps:

1. Uncovering the emotional understandings that persons hold prior to the production of the experience; this includes

revealing their motives, feelings, intentions, images, accounts, and relational bonds.

2. Actually presenting the emotional experience, through thick description and experience-near concepts, as a temporal, practical accomplishment.

3. Uncovering the embodied practices involved in the accomplishment and production of the experience.

4. Revealing the foreinterpretations that justify, compel, and perhaps neutralize the self (and life) of the person in relation to the acts that make up the experience and the project.

5. Displaying the afterinterpretations of the act and the experience after it has been accomplished. The meanings of the experience to all parties involved must be fitted into an articulated structural totality.

6. Laying bare the raw skeletal features of social structures, including class structures, power relations, material scarcity, and systems of law, exchange, kinship, education, and language, as these obdurate realities intrude into, shape, and modify the emotionality of interactional experience (see Denzin, 1982b, p. 123).

Strategically and interpretively, the study of interactional, emotional experiences requires a view from the interior side of the experience. Interpretation lies in grasping this inner perspective, for it is from that view that individuals organize and give meaning to their unfolding action. Interpretation cannot be given from the outside. The inner side of the act as seen and lived by the person is essential to interpretive understanding.

Inner interpretation is circular. What begins as a foreinterpretation of an act becomes a part of the act that is now subjected to new interpretation in light of what has just been interpreted. In the inner arc of interpretation, the future draws out the meanings of previous interpretations, while past meanings slide alongside acts that are undergoing new interpretation. The line between interpretation and action dissolves in the experiential field. Embodied emotional conduct, like language, is process in motion producing its meaning as it moves along and through the past, the future, and the present.

This interplay among interpretation, action, and embodied conduct, so well discussed and portrayed in the works of Blumer and Mead, is lifted to a new level of meaning in Heidegger's hermeneutic analysis of interpretation in *Being and Time* (1927/1962). Interpretive interactionism thus proposes a move to a perhaps deeper view of interpretation as a practice that operates at both the everyday and scientific levels of discourse.

The Process of Hermeneutic Interpretation. There are, as the foregoing discussion suggests, two basic steps in the process of hermeneutic interpretation. The first is linguistic and involves a stepwise progression from part to whole. That is, a grammatical, linguistic interpretation "proceeds from link to link to the highest combinations of the whole of the work [in question] " (Dilthey, 1900/1976, p. 259). The separate acts, utterances, and sequential speech acts that make up an interactional experience are pieced together, offering a text of the interaction (see Goffman, 1981b, pp. 5-25). That text consists of linguistic units, separate acts, gestures, and movements, and what Stanislavski (1936, pp. 105-119) calls "units" and "objectives," which are constituent elements of scenes.

The second step in hermeneutic interpretation is, to alter Dilthey slightly, social psychological. It starts by "penetrating the inner creative process and proceeds to the outer and inner form of the work [text] and from there to a further grasp of the unity of all his works in the mentality and development of their author" (Dilthey, 1900/1976, p. 259). The investigator endeavors to uncover the inner meanings of the act in question. These meanings, which unfold during the act, are displayed in the act's outer forms, including the author's gestures, utterances, actions, and interactions with others. Interpretation follows the interpretations of the author of the action. The act and its meanings are seen from within, as interactive productions, having the characteristics of impulse, interpretation, manipulation, and termination. The acts studied are temporal productions that reach forward for meaning as they move forward. "The advance of (interpretive) time leaves more and more of the past behind and moves into the future" (Dilthey, 1900/ 1976, p. 234). The temporality of action must be contextualized in interpretation. That is, time must be seen from the author's point of view.

"The final goal of the hermeneutic procedure is to understand the author better than he understood himself; a statement which is the necessary conclusion of the doctrine of unconscious creation" (Dilthey, 1900/1976, pp. 259-260). Without excepting Dilthey's (and Schleiermacher's) conclusion regarding the doctrine of unconscious creation, it can be seen that hermeneutic interpretation wishes to give to an individual's actions an interpretation that perhaps even he would not give to it. This is so because the totality of the individual's actions are not visible to him as he acts. Nor is the full range of factors that play on his actions apparent to him. The interpreter has access to a picture of the author's text that the author often lacks, because the interpreter has a "method" of interpretation that the subject may not possess. *Method,* in the Greek, implies, as Coleridge (1817/1973, p. 523) notes, a "progressive transition, literally a way or path of transit." The method of the interpreter moves through preconception to an understanding that is continuous, revealing, and disclosing. The "method" of the subject may be neither continuous nor a way to understanding. Instead, it is a way of securing meaning in the here and now. It is an unproblematic interpretive structure that does not need to dwell on hidden meaning, inner self-deceptions, the foreclosure of habit, or the narrowness of self-interest. The interpretive method of the natural attitude is pragmatic and workable. It works, insofar as it works, because it gives meaning to the subject. Little more need be asked of it.

The interpreter who seeks to understand the subject better than she understood herself seeks a level of understanding that is interpreted at the ontological level (discussed later). Surface interpretations and understandings, which are often workable for the subject, are framed against deeper-level interpretations. These may be foreign to the subject or seldom given by her. Thus the interpretive understandings that are rendered for a sequence of action may well have meanings that are initially "uninterpretable" and "irrelevant" for the subject. At some point, however, the interpretations must be understood by or made understandable to the person(s) to whom they apply. If they do not meet this criterion, they are unacceptable. The producers of the texts of interaction are the ultimate interpretive authority on their own work, for it is they who give it its initial and final (to them) meaning. Once it leaves their hands, however, they lose control over the meanings that are brought to it.

Only in these senses can Dilthey's statements, now perhaps brought full circle, be understood and rendered acceptable. The interpreter must express his or her interpretation "as other men express themselves" (Wordsworth, 1800/1973, p. 404). Not to do so is to lift interpretation to a level that is out of touch with the world of directly lived emotionality and experience (see Garfinkel, 1967; Garfinkel and Sacks, 1970; Garfinkel, Lynch, and Livingston, 1981; Wordsworth, 1800/1973, pp. 403-405; Coleridge, 1817/1973, pp. 519-521).

The essential point of interpretation is to start with a problem (Sartre, 1981, p. x). The problem must be set by the subject. Furthermore, it must always be the uncovering of the project, event, act, or feeling that gives primary meaning to the subject's life. That project, act, event, or feeling will be woven through the life of the subject. It will be the object that he seeks in order to understand himself, seeks to attain, to possess, or to be free of. It will be the act or event that gives primary, deep ontological meaning to his life and to his work. The interpreter must discover that event and unveil its multiple meanings and forms in the subject's life. It will be from the elusive vantage point of this event or object that the subject seeks to bring cognitive and emotional meaning into his life.

The uncovering of the meanings that surround this event or object may well place investigators in a position where, in the end, they know more about the subject's life than the subject does. Such was Sartre's last project in his study of Gustave Flaubert. He remarks, beginning with a quotation from Flaubert: " 'It is by the sheer force of work that I am able to silence my innate melancholy. But the old nature often reappears, the old nature that no one knows, the deep, always hidden wound.'

What is the meaning of this? Can a wound be innate? In any event, Flaubert refers us to his prehistory. What we must try to understand is the origin of the wound that is 'always hidden' and dates back to his earliest childhood. That will not, I think, be a bad start" (Sartre, 1981, p. x). Clearly one must know a great deal about the subject before the relevant question can be phrased. That would appear to be the first requirement of interpretive studies.

The second phase of hermeneutic interpretation involves the sympathetic identification of the interpreter with the author of the text being interpreted (see Weber, 1977; Znaniecki, 1934; MacIver, 1931; Cooley, 1902/1956; Dilthey, 1900/1976). This involves more than using the author's language and more than grasping her meanings. It requires bringing the author's experience into the interpreter's field of experience, so that it becomes the interpreter's. Just as emotional understanding involves an appropriation of another's emotionality, so does interpretation. A failure to see the other's experience from her standpoint results in the worst kind of scientific objectivism, wherein observers substitute their perspective for that of the person they are studying (see Blumer, 1969; Denzin, 1978). Hermeneutics attempts to avoid this objectivist fallacy by requiring entry into the other's world as the first prerequisite for interpretation (see B. Stone, 1981, 1982, 1984).

The interpreter must live his way *through* the life of the other so that he can come back on her experiences from the double vantage point of having been where she has been while being able to see her experiences through her eyes and her voice. He then speaks through her, and she through him. (See Krieger, 1983, for an outstanding display of this commitment.)

The temporal work of hermeneutics involves the following steps:

1. Securing the total text to be interpreted, through observations, field notes, recordings, film, printed texts, autobiographies, life-story narratives, and so on.
2. Subdividing that text into experiential units, or discrete fields of experience.

3. Situational, relational, and interactional specification of each subtext regarding the who, what, when, where, and how of the specific interactions (McCall and Simmons, 1981).
4. Serial display of the text as an interactional unit, from beginning to end.
5. Internal analysis of the text, linguistically, unit by unit, phrase by phrase, act by act.
6. Serial unfolding and display of the inner meanings of the text to its author, grasping the shifting temporal meaning as the act(s) and the experiential field unfold.
7. Development of "working hypotheses" (Flaherty, 1982, 1983; Mead, 1982a) and "working interpretations" for each subtext as the overall text unfolds.
8. Checking these working interpretations against the text that has unfolded and in light of the text that follows.
9. Grasping the text as a totality, fitting the subtextual interpretations into an overall interpretive scheme that now gives total meaning, recognizing that multiple interpretations of the text will be produced and necessarily laid side by side.
10. Displaying these multiple interpretations, compared with the interpreter's own interpretations and understandings.

Understanding

If hermeneutics does the work of interpretation and understanding, then understanding must be understood as an unfolding process that turns on itself. Two phases to understanding can be distinguished. The first concerns the prior understandings that individuals bring to a situation. The second concerns the interpreted understandings that have been produced once interpretation has been accomplished. Interpreted understandings modify prior understandings, just as prior understandings initially shape and determine interpreted understandings.

Against these two phases of understanding are the two levels of understanding. The first level is methodological and epistemological; the second is ontological. By and large, the extensive literature on interpretation and understanding in the social sciences has focused on the first level to the neglect of the second (see Rabinow and Sullivan, 1979; Heidegger, 1927/1962; Geertz, 1973; Dilthey, 1900/1976; Foucault, 1982; Krieger, 1983; Weber, 1977). A passage from Dilthey (1900/1976, p. 261) exemplifies this imbalance: "It follows from the fundamental role of understanding in the human studies that *the epistemological, logical and methodological analysis of understanding is one of the main tasks involved in establishing the foundations of the human studies.* The significance of the task emerges when one considers what difficulties the nature of understanding raises for the practice of valid scholarship."

The epistemology of understanding, which Dilthey, Weber, and others have raised to the position of paramount importance, requires a consideration of such topics as validity, verifiability, reliability, the empirical and logical adequacy of conceptual categories, first-order and second-order concepts, ideal types, the scientific status of one's theory, its empirical presuppositions, its theoretical logic and generalizability, its objectivity, its falsification, and its paradigmatic status. These topics set problems that impede understanding and interpretation (B. Stone, 1981; but see Alexander, 1982). They represent topics turned into questions that reflect a "normal science" point of view. How they become problems that guide inquiry is a topic of inquiry in its own right (Garfinkel, 1967). These topics will not be treated here (see Denzin, 1978, 1982a, 1982c, 1983a).

Insight into the interpretation and understanding of human emotionality must always begin with ontological, not epistemological, questions. As interpretive sociologists, we must ask and answer the question of what "kind of being" it is we are studying. Ontological questions force a movement beyond method and logic to the underlying question of meaning in human affairs. It must be seen that our investigations and interpretations can be conducted only from within the lifetimes and the lives of those we study. Our interpretations, like the lives we study, will always be unfinished projects.

Concern, then, should not be with methods of logic but with interpretation. The subject matter of interpretation is interpretation. The topic of inquiry is how people bring meaning to their lives, their projects, and their moments. The ordinary people we study are "singular instances of the universality of human history" (Sartre, 1981, p. ix). If meaning is the topic, and if meaning is made apparent through emotionality (as discussed later), then the ontology of understanding, not the epistemology of understanding, requires our most serious concern.

The ontological level of understanding requires a deep, reflective concern for the multiple levels of human being and meaning. Surface expressions of meaning must be contrasted to the meanings that individuals give to themselves at the deep ontological level. A concern for the epistemology of understanding is not likely to reveal how individuals reveal themselves to themselves at the deep levels of their moral being. Accordingly, interpretive phenomenology, with symbolic interactionism, sets questions of method momentarily aside in favor of a preoccupation with the problems of meaning, interpretation, and understanding. Ontology precedes epistemology.

The Criteria of Interpretation

In the Introduction nine criteria of interpretation were set forth. These included the ability of an interpretation to illuminate, disclose, and reveal the phenomenon in question, as well as the extent to which the interpretation was thickly contextualized, historical, relational, and interactive. The other criteria were the ability of the interpretation to incorporate prior understandings, to cohere, to produce understanding, to coalesce into a meaningful whole, and to remain fundamentally unfinished, to be taken up anew in another investigation.

These criteria can be reduced to a single question: "Does the interpretation produce and reveal meaning?" If it does not reveal how the phenomenon in question—in the present study, emotion—is given meaning in the lives of interacting individuals, then it has fallen short of this stated goal. Furthermore, if the investigation does not contribute to our ability to better understand ourselves, and if it does not become, rather than merely a record of humans, one "of the props, the pillars to help them endure and prevail" (Faulkner, 1967, p. 724), then it has failed. This directive appears consistent with the commitment expressed above to ontology over epistemology. It is to the topic of meaning that I now turn.

Meaning

The pragmatic theory of meaning, as elaborated by Blumer, drawing on the works of James, Peirce, Dewey, and Mead, rests on three assumptions: (1) Humans act toward things "on the basis of the meanings that the things have for them" (Blumer, 1969, p. 2). Such things may be physical objects, other humans, institutions, ideas, or the activities of others. (2) Meaning is "derived from, or arises out of, the social interaction that one has with one's fellows." (3) Meanings "are handled in, and modified through, an interpretive process used by the person in dealing with the things he encounters" (Blumer, 1969, p. 2).

This formulation of meaning draws on Mead's triadic view of meaning. It suggests that the meaning of a gesture one person makes to another signifies "what the person to whom it is directed is to do, what the person who is making the gesture is planning to do, . . . the joint action that is to arise by the articulation of the acts of both" (Blumer, 1969, p. 9). Meaning lies in interaction, in proposed action, and in joint action. Meaning is *pragmatically* established by working back from the anticipated consequences of an action to its antecedents. Meaning is a temporal projection that moves forward and backward in time, while the action and interpretation that alter meaning arise in the present. Thus temporality is central to meaning simply because the interpretive subject is temporal in its very being (Heidegger, 1927/1962; Couch, 1984).

The temporality of meaning and interpretation is located in the future, as the future moves toward the person and the person moves toward it. Meaning is located in the past, for actions taken in the present and the future are assessed against what has just been accomplished. Meaning is in the present, as the present slides alongside the person as action that is now being taken.

The interpretive process that underlies meaning arises out of the interactions the subject has with herself and with others. That process is circular, temporally grounded, and self-referential. Meaning is always meaning with respect to the subject and the action she is undertaking and interpreting. Meaning's interpretations work outward from the self to a social object and then back to the self.

With slight variation, the pragmatic theory of meaning can be altered to read as the pragmatic-emotional theory of meaning. Since the self or the interpretive subject is at the center of the process that confers meaning on social objects, and since that subject is a feeling subject, self-feelings lie at the core of the meanings conferred on objects. Meaning has a dual location: in the interaction process and in the feelings and thoughts of the interpretive subject. The meanings that are referred back to the self are felt, are emotional in tone, are believed in, not doubted, and are taken as real. Meaning is rooted in emotionality. The meaning of meaning is verified through self-feelings. Self-feelings are interactional, emergent, temporal, relational, and intersubjectively established. They are historical phenomena as well. Meaning is historical, for the self is historical.

The pragmatic-emotional theory of meaning assumes that the meaning a person confers on an object or on herself expresses something in her stream of consciousness—that is, a feeling or a thought. This meaning contains emotional elements, or expressive meaning. Of course, meaning also contains cognitive elements, which may or may not be intertwined with emotionality.

The meanings expressed in and through emotionality are less subject to the power of fleeting interests, the demands of practicality, the contingencies of logic, or the struggles of practical concern than are primarily cognitive and taken-for-granted meanings (Dilthey, 1900/1976, p. 220). Emotional expressions of meaning are related to the person in a way that other expressive actions are not. These expressions reveal the inner meaning of actions to the person as they are felt and interpreted at the deep, ontological level. These expressions break through the natural attitudes that constrain the expression of deep emotionality and meaning. They are, however, conventionalized and subject to the pressures of daily etiquette, good manners, and proper conduct. Interpretive, phenomenological investigation must cut through these conventionalized expressions of meaning. Inquiry must display the underlying emotional meanings that are hidden, perhaps disembodied, masked, and even distorted by the constraints of convention and the contingencies of practical concern. The laying bare of these inner meanings will reveal not just the pragmatic but also the emotional meanings held by the person. It is these meanings that interpretive inquiry seeks to reveal, illuminate, interpret, and understand.

The expression of meaning is given through the person's actions, gestures, facial expressions, choice of words, word inflection, posture, spatial distance from others, intensity of speech—in short, through what David Sudnow (1979) calls "talk's body" and what I have termed "emotion's body."

Through talk—emotional, commonplace, ordinary, violent, and out of control—subjects convey emotional and cognitive definitions of self. Through emotional talk, which is talk that makes self-feelings the topic of discourse, the subject allows others to enter into his emotionality, if only briefly. Emotional talk reveals the interior self-feelings of the subject. Such talk reveals the subject as an emotional being. It thus provides the avenue for the emotionality of others to emerge and appear in the interaction process. In emotional talk the inner meanings of action to the subject, including his own meanings to himself, are revealed.

In emotional talk the subject establishes an emotional footing in the situation. (On "footing" see Goffman, 1981b, pp. 124-157.) Such footing, or anchoring, aligns the subject with a sequence of embodied emotional utterances and actions. In emotional footing the subject's "projected self is somehow at issue" (Goffman, 1981b, p. 128). The projection of self is done through emotional talk that extends across a line of action that is presented to others. A transition from ritual, cognitively expressive talk to emotional talk is accomplished in and through emotional footing. Through changes in stance, shifts in voice tone, use of the personal pronoun *I,* and use of words that refer to internal emotional states, the subject establishes her emotional footing in the situation (Goffman, 1981b, p. 128). A code signaling a switch into an emotional vocabulary is usually evident, as are explicit references to the speaker's biography. Sound markers indicating emotionality—"pitch of voice, volume, rhythm, stress, and tonal quality"—are involved as well (Goffman, 1981b, p. 128). Interpretively, the subject establishing emotional footing asks that others give her the speaker's floor for emotional talk. This may involve a bracketing of previous talk—a setting aside of previous utterances, so to speak. Now, that talk over, the person can get down to emotional business (see Labov and Fanshel, 1977).

Footing established, the speaker can now talk personally about her self-feelings and emotions. She will often begin her remarks with "I," as in "I feel" or "I felt." The personal pronoun "I" draws talk into the speaker and indicates that the reference of the talk is to the speaker's self-feelings. The "I" of emotional talk is the platform from which the speaker's emotionality is expressed. From that platform past emotions may be presented, the fear of the future may be brought forward, and emotional ambiguities of the present may be disclosed. On this platform the feelings of others may be discussed, and the person's feelings in relation to those feelings may be argued, debated, and put forth. The footing for emotional talk may be fleeting, for a person may lose her station in an emotional conversation and be unable to regain it, or it may involve routinized turn-taking (see Jenkins, 1982).

The forms of emotionality that are discussed in emotional talk may range from the deeply personal and potentially discrediting to the surface level of light expressive discourse. The talk may be purely rhetorical, discursive, emotional self-propaganda. It may be indirect talk about emotionality, relying on metaphor, metonymy, and symbolism. Or it may be ritual emotional talk, in which the meaning of emotionality is hidden inside the ritual words the person speaks. Such talk may be metacommunicative; here the subject talks about the meaning of the meaning of emotional words. Consider the following conversation excerpted from tapes from the popular *Mary Tyler Moore* television show (see Denzin and Keller, 1981, pp. 57–58). The conversationalists are Mary Tyler Moore and Dan, her boyfriend and recently ex-fiancé. They are seated outside Mary's apartment on the stairway to Rhoda's room. Dan begins the conversation.

Dan: Let's talk.
Mary: OK. I thought you'd start.
Dan: No, you start.
Mary: OK. Dan, I don't want to get married.
Dan: (Smiles, chuckles, laughs to himself)
Mary: What are you laughing about?
Dan: I'm laughing because we know you don't mean no.
Mary: Dan, how do we know that?
Dan: We know that because we know you don't mean no. We know you really want to get married.
Mary: No, we don't know that. It's not that I don't want to get married. It's not that I don't love you. It's just that I don't want to get married now.
Dan: Oh.

Here the meaning of the word *no* must be established before meaningful talk can continue. Does *no* mean "no" or "know"? And how do the two speakers know the difference between the two forms of the word? Before the meaning of love and marriage could be established, the two meanings of *no* had to be clarified. Metaemotional talk shifts the emotional footing of the two speakers back and forth. Each speaker attempts to anchor the other in a particular line of action that would secure the desired emotional bond that might obtain between them.

Emotional talk turns on the use of three kinds of words: emotional words themselves (for example, *anger, fear, love, hate*); ordinary words that surround emotional words and phrases, embedding them with interpretation, ambience, and subtlety; and the personal pronouns, especially *I, me, mine, you, your, yours, ours, we, they, them,* and *theirs.* Ordinary words locate emotional talk interactionally, by time, place, others, and the intentions of the speaker (see Chappell, 1964).

These words express a connection between the speaker and others or between the speaker and an emotional social object, event, or experience. These three categories of words lodge emotionality in the interaction process. They simultaneously direct emotionality outward from the speaker toward others while maintaining a constant self-reference toward the speaker.

The words of emotionality are always available to the subject, for the ordinary language is filled with them. Indeed, any word can be turned to emotional purposes. All that is required is that the subject emotionally locate herself within the words she uses. Through her embodied presence in the situation, she makes herself and her words emotional. The following transaction, which occurs in the lobby of a bank, displays this feature of emotional talk. The speakers are a customer and a bank teller. They speak through the glass that divides them across the counter. Customer (male, age fifty-five, dressed in a suit) speaks:

Customer: You've taken down the Christmas tree.
Teller: (Approximate age twenty-eight, dressed in sweater and skirt) Yes, we took it down yesterday. (Smiling as she speaks, blushes slightly; looks over to where the tree stood) We have so much more room now. It's so nice. (Smiles again) Have a good day. Look, it's gone. I didn't really like it. The lights weren't right. We tried, though! Oh, well!
Customer: Thank you.

Here the teller attaches herself and her talk to the Christmas tree that has been taken down. Spreading her arms, she indicates where it stood. Disclaiming the decorations, she indicates how the employees tried to make it look nice. The statement "You've taken down the Christmas tree" brings forth an embodied line of action that calls out a series of emotional expressions on her face. The words she uses catch her emergent emotionality. In this brief transaction two speakers engage each other in an emotional interaction that barely touches the surface of either person's underlying, deep self. This surface display of emotionality is to be contrasted to the episode (below) in which a speaker deeply discredits herself through an emotional performance. Whether emotionality (and its displays) is surface or deep, however, its presence in the interactional stream depends on the use of ordinary words and the ordinary practical accomplishments of speakers.

The problematic of such talk involves the securing of personal emotional meaning for these three categories of words. The words themselves must be endowed with emotionality, as they express the emotional self-feelings of the speaker and draw others into the speaker's talk. Here sound markers and the other features of emotional footing are critical. Without the proper emotionality infused into the words that are intended as emotional expressions of self, a dull, lifeless, cold, unfeeling self is communicated to others. A self that cannot feel its own emotionality cannot express its emotionality, except lifelessly, to others. Such a self is also unable to reveal itself to itself through emotion. It is thereby cut off from itself.

The self that is projected through emotional talk and emotional footing is a line of embodied action. That self is the person presented to others through emotional talk. It is a biographical presence that establishes its own dramatic presence. That is, the subject dramatically enacts and reenacts himself before himself and others, claiming through the use of emotional words and actions an emotional definition of self. He becomes a part of his own emotionality and in that action perhaps finds that he has extended himself too far. Consider the following sequence of actions, also taken from the *Mary Tyler Moore* show. In this situation Mary has been harrassed for weeks by a man named Warren who has fallen in love with her. He hung a banner outside the newsroom proclaiming his love for her. He chained the two of them together to a parking meter. He drove around her house with a loudspeaker atop his car telling everyone he loved her.

As the scene opens, Mary is in a restaurant with a "normal" date. She is about to tell the story of Warren when he appears behind her, introducing himself to her date and calling a group of gypsy musicians to her table.

Mary: Warren! Oh! No! You did this! Well, Warren, let me
             tell you something. You're not going to do this to
             me again. Oh, no, not again! Well, Warren. What will
             it be now?

As Mary is speaking these lines, a woman in her midthirties
moves behind Warren and listens to Mary. A waiter approaches
and hands Warren a large frosted cake with "Will you marry
me?" written on it. As the cake is handed to Warren, Mary
speaks:

Mary: So this is it. Will I marry you? Well, let me answer
             you, Warren. No! I will not marry you. Let me spell
             it out.

As this last line is spoken, Mary puts her finger in the frosting
on the cake and begins writing the words "No, I will not" on
Warren's face.

Mary: Let me spell it out for you, Warren. "No, *N-O,* no,
             I will not!" Is that clear? No, I will not marry you!
Warren: (Turning to the woman standing behind Mary) Mary,
             let me introduce you to the woman who I was going
             to give this cake to. Mary, I would like you to meet
             my fiancée.
Fiancée: (To Mary) You're terrible! (To Warren) Warren,
             let's get out of here.
Warren: Come on, gypsies, follow me.
Mary: Oh, no! (A look of defeat and embarrassment comes
             over her face)

The scene closes, showing Mary apologetically confronting the
other diners in the restaurant, saying, "I'm sorry."
    In this interaction Mary is caught up in her own emotion-
ality. She interacts at, not with, Warren. He is a vehicle for the
display of her pent-up emotions. The self Mary presents is an
emotional self. The line of action she projects builds on itself
and attains an inner authenticity that is not doubted. She is in

the world of emotion. Its reality totally absorbs her. She experiences a sequence of emotions, moving from shock to alarm, self-assertion, self-indignation, embarrassment, self-defeat, degradation, and humiliation.

It is not a single self that Mary presents, but a sequence of selves that are revealed and disclosed through the shifting forms of emotionality she expresses and experiences. As emotionality unfolds, it assumes new forms, new meanings, and new interpretations. With these new forms and meanings come new displays and interpretations of self. Hence, a single slice of the self is never presented in an interaction episode. Rather, multiple slices or instances of the person are revealed in and through interaction and emotionality. These instances of the self constitute a continuous thread that is woven round the embodied presence of the person (see Strauss, 1959; G. P. Stone, 1962, 1977, 1981). Each presence is a part of the continuous talk and action of the person. The self is not discontinuous, for the being that is the person is constantly present to itself.

The emotional footing that Mary establishes gives her a platform from which multiple versions of herself are presented. She becomes different persons to herself, to Warren, to the gypsies, to her date, and to the other diners as she moves through her talk. She is her talk and her gestures, yet she is more than this, for she is all that Mary is and has been before she came into this situation. All of Mary is before her as she acts. Yet because she acts in a sequence, through a series of interrelated statements, assertions, and actions, she reveals herself slowly and then quickly to herself. She is not, in this sense, fully and totally aware of herself all at once.

Only after she has completed her speech to Warren, and then after he speaks to her, does she become aware of who she has become in the situation. In this sense action must be completed before it can be situated, interpreted, and understood. As acts unfold, they have meaning only in relation to what has been and what will be. Once a sequence has been completed, it can then be assessed as a structural totality—as a unified instance of the-person-in-a-situation. It is that unified instance that is then interpreted. But the interpretations themselves must be laid side by side in order for a total interpretation to be produced.

The circularity of interpretation can now be seen, for it is only after Warren acts and leaves the situation that Mary can understand who she has become. That is, his actions have to be interpretively turned back on the sequence of utterances she produced. By reading her actions in terms of his, she can see that she acted inappropriately. She could not know this until he acted.

There is a double interpretive structure to emotional interaction. There are, first, the feelings and self-interpretations the person feels during, before, or just after an action. These may be glossed feelings, as in Mary's apparent feelings of shock that carried over into her self-assertive attack on Warren. Second, and following on these interactionally contextualized feelings and interpretations, are the interpretations produced after the completion of a sequence of action. These retrospective feelings and interpretations build on the previously felt meanings. They need these previous interpretations and could not be built without them. The feelings that are felt after action has been completed are layered on the previous feelings. A new feeling structure is thereby produced. It may contradict the previous meanings that were given to the interaction. The meanings that the subject gives to herself as interaction unfolds, runs to a conclusion, and then turns back on itself, shift and change as new feelings are felt, and new interpretations are formed while old ones are smashed. The consequence is that multiple instances and images of the person may be produced from the same sequence of interaction and emotionality.

The selves that are revealed to the subject during emotionality express a depth of attachment that is altogether different from the self that remains coldly aloof from others. It is a self attached to a sequence of action that appears to come from the inner depths of the person. The self attached to emotionality, as Mary's is in the above account, is one that cannot be doubted, shrugged off, or ignored. It is a self attached to a person who has made a fool of herself in a social situation.

But it is not necessary to turn to embarrassment and social scenes to find selves attached to persons through emotionality. The previous discussions of the violent and the emotionally divided self (Chapters Six and Seven) revealed this point. Persons are, in many significant ways, the emotions they feel. Emotionality reveals persons to themselves in ways that pure reflection and thinking cannot.

The subject, then, must learn his emotions if he is to learn who he is and who he can be. He must learn how to feel inside his emotions. He must learn how to place words in front of, alongside, and behind his emotionality. He must learn, too, how to weave his emotions into himself and into his thoughts about himself. He must learn how to dwell within his own emotionality, both reflectively and unreflectively. By reflecting on his emotions, he reflects on himself, and in such reflections he finds new as well as old and familiar answers to the question "Who am I?"

Emotionality, then, reveals the self to itself in a way that no other line of action can. Emotionality awakens inner feelings and thoughts. It enlivens the person's own presence before himself. It announces itself with a certainty and a conviction that are not doubted.

Situating Emotionality Within the Lives of Ordinary People

The kind of human being that interpretive sociology studies is an ordinary man, woman, or child. Like Faulkner's characters, such people are seldom verbally articulate about themselves, their emotionality, their projects, or their plans (see Denzin, in press-b; Faulkner, 1961, 1964, 1965). They keep their thoughts and their feelings to themselves. Many are self-taught. Others are poor, living off someone else's land, job, or reputation—or living out someone else's life for him. Ordinary people speak through their actions, their small habits, their routines, their daily hard work, their commitments to others. They live on dreams and promises and defer gratification. They often take a deep, inquisitive interest in the doings of one another, especially neighbors, coworkers, kin, employers, and persons in positions of high power. They participate in a deep, sprawling oral tradition that ties them to a common past yet separates each of them within his or her own unique world of experience. They live lives tied to the rhythms of the seasons, the economy, and the political and moral order, and they take agendas from society at large. Their lives are tied to one another in fragmented ways, yet they are bonded to others through kin, moral, ideological, friendship, legal, and economic ties. They have power over their own lives, if by *power* is meant control of one's own fate and life. They may be powerless over their own or others' lives, but the power to make that admission is theirs. They gain power by admitting to their powerlessness.

Ordinary people live within a small social world, often defined by a few square miles. They know of and about everyone who makes up that world, often having dealings that extend through several generations. These people often are born, live, marry, have children, divorce, steal, murder, go insane, find inner peace, and die within a few miles of where their parents lived and died. They always return home, where blood, social, and friendship bonds remain, as if timelessly. They live out lives fated for them by others, and they wrestle with sexual and biological desires, reproducing themselves in men and women they barely understand. They have few degrees of freedom in their lives, but they act, make choices, tell stories about themselves, engage in recreational activities, drink, read the classics, work for others, and search for eternal meaning, truth, and justice in their everyday dealings with one another. They leave their stamp on the world. Long after they pass on, they are felt in the lives of those they touched.

The truths and meanings which they seek, and by which they judge one another, cover such matters as honor, honesty, pride, pity, justice, compassion, courage, and love. The human emotions that reveal the deep meanings individuals hold about themselves and others are the stuff ordinary people are made of. Such people endure in the face of moral and social decay. They persist in spite of defeat. They live inside empty dreams and deep poverty. They may know few or many material possessions. They seek meaning from such things and travel great distances to find themselves, often finding that the person they find there is not to their liking. Disappointed, they return home, to pick up the routines and daily habits that give unproblematic meaning to them.

For many their name is what they value most, as that name is attached to the deep meanings they pursue in their everyday, ordinary lives. These people are the cement of society. They are society as it is lived, felt, and experienced (see Broyard, 1981). They are the proper subject matter of interpretive phenomenology and sociology. They and their lives and meanings must be brought back into the human disciplines as living, breathing, feeling people.

Ordinary people come and go from one another's presence. They touch one another in ways that they do not understand. They savor their own uniqueness. They are bewildered by one another, become outraged over tiny actions, feel deep remorse about actions taken long ago. They carry ressentiments toward one another, harbor grudges, try to get even. They dwell in the past and in the far-off future. They take small pleasures in daily accomplishments of others and set high goals for themselves. They laugh and smile inwardly as they catch the glimpse of a stunning sunset. They talk behind one another's backs and brag about their own accomplishments.

They express their emotionality conventionally and seldom let themselves get too far out of hand. They keep their emotions in check, keeping their flights of feeling confined to dreams and fantasies. The daily world and its commitments command their unrelenting attention. Work, the demands of existence, the need to pay the bills and eat, these matters cut through their daily lives like a knife, leaving them suspended between dreams and hard realities. They have little time of their own, and what time they have, they lose in their wandering streams of consciousness. Yet they return to themselves constantly, checking their appearance in mirrors and in store windows. Pleased or displeased by what they see, they move quickly ahead to a late appointment or an unfinished project, which may involve bringing the day to a close. They reflectively move through the lives they organize for themselves or find have been given them by others. This project, which is theirs and which is who they are, at times scarcely seems under control. It simply is, as they simply are.

Emotionality suddenly appears before them, or to them. They trip and stumble over a curb and make a cry of apology to whoever is there to see and hear (Goffman, 1981b, pp. 88-89). They chastise themselves for having stumbled. They get mad at themselves and experience a self-feeling that was not there before. They have violent interior thoughts, dreaming, like Thurber's Walter Mitty, of killing their wives, or of engaging life in a dance, as Jules Feiffer's dancer does. They stop on the way home and have a drink, a beer, a cup of coffee, and relax, letting the day they have just had feel its way into them. In these feelings that they allow to seep in, they feel themselves in ways that they have not permitted all day.

They come close and next to themselves, and here, in these feelings, become, if only for a moment, the person they dream about or have put off being. Now a smile creeps across their faces. They joke, banter, tell a story about their day to anyone who will listen. They engage the evening news and have an argument with their favorite newscaster. They invidiously compare their lives with the tragedies and bad weather of others, whether they are located in Denver, Minneapolis, San Francisco, London, Beirut, Moscow, Chicago, or New Orleans. They bring emotionality into their lives by viewing and hearing of the lives of others, and later in the day they will move into the world of the theater, opera, sports, or evening television. Here, in this world, they may permit their minds to wander, tendering emotional thoughts and dreams and feelings they would not otherwise or elsewhere feel.

In these moments they dream and dream meaning into their lives. They imagine themselves feeling new or put-off feelings. In these feelings they find and feel, more deeply than usual, answers to who they are and who they want to be. Built-up images of self, plans for the future, and reworked dialogues with the past occur during these times of the person. Finding that time is slipping away, checking the clock, they put these thoughts aside and turn to the completion of the mundane, familiar assignments they have set for themselves.

Emotionality, or feeling, is threaded through the person's day. It does not just appear at appointed times, in preselected places; nor is it far off. It is with the person all the time, contextualized and interwoven through their thoughts and actions. This world of emotion and the reality it invites is always there, waiting to be entered and embraced.

There are two ways to enter this world (Sartre, 1939/1962). It may force itself on a person, as when a terrifying face appears at the window or a favorite song appears on the radio. Or a person may move into emotionality, by building up and locating emotional lines of action and interpretation within herself and the world. That is, people may bring their own emotionality into the world. They may greet others cheerily or reluctantly. They may pull themselves along into a line of action or embrace a task with relish and fervor. They may criticize others who make small talk with them, turn away when conversation is offered, or simply refuse to talk. In these ways and others people choose how they will engage the world emotionally. By giving and withholding emotionality, they give or withhold themselves from others, thereby altering the emotional meanings of self that others receive from them. The person's emotionality, then, is never strictly and solely hers and hers alone. The person's self enters and is given to the world of interaction through the processes of moral and emotional sociality. Hence, to be present before others is to always be potentially present as an emotional social object.

The subject's world holds emotion for him. Emotionality is there to be grasped and engaged, if the subject is so inclined. Emotionality, in all its forms, is a choice he makes. To be or not to be emotional, to lend a bit of self-feeling to one's actions or to withhold feeling, to be overcome by emotion or to hold it in check, these are choices the person has and makes in everyday life.

In these choices and others like them, individuals shape and determine how they will see themselves and how they will be seen by others. Emotionality transforms them in a way that no other line of action they might take toward themselves or toward others can. By engaging themselves and others in and through emotionality, they enter into a social contract with the social order that surrounds them. Through emotionality, sympathy, violence, fellow-feeling, shared emotionality, emotional footings, and emotional presentations of self they draw others into their world. The shared world of emotionality is one where understanding, interpretation, and meaning are located. It is that world that individuals seek because their sociality demands it. This contract, that draws individuals into the presence of others so that they may be more than they can be alone, need not be sociologically tragic, as Simmel (1950) and others have often implied. This is so because through emotionality the person can become more than he ever imagined. The tragedy arises when the person fulfills only part of the contract—that is, when he withholds his emotionality from others.

Herein lies the cardinal significance of emotionality and its study. It lifts ordinary people into and out of themselves in ways that they cannot ordinarily achieve. People, then, must engage themselves and their emotionality if they are to more meaningfully enter the affairs of others. They must, in a certain sense, work at and take this emotionality seriously. Yet they are free to engage their emotionality. They may do so playfully and freely, finding in the play of emotionality a playfulness about the world that is not ordinarily there (see Hans, 1981; Denzin, 1977, 1981; Denzin and Keller, 1981).

In this final respect, without the presence of emotionality and its paradoxes, "life would be . . . an endless interchange of stylized messages, a game with rigid rules, unrelieved by change or humor" (Bateson, 1972, p. 193; see also Flaherty, 1982, 1983; Lynch, 1980, 1982). Emotionality and its reflections give the everyday world and the ordinary people who live in that world a sense of joy, bewilderment, pain, confusion, satisfaction, and pleasure that no other form of conduct can. For this reason emotionality and its investigation must lie at the heart of the human disciplines; for to understand and reflect on *how* this being called human *is*, and how it *becomes what it is*, it is necessary to understand how emotionality as a form of consciousness is lived, experienced, articulated, and felt by persons. In the dwelling places of emotion people will be found. And there, in those places, will be found self-feelings, meaning, and understanding. This inquiry, which has reflected on the dwelling places of emotionality, unfinished as it is, has, I hope, revealed new dimensions of this process and the places it occupies.

Glossary

Circuit of selfness. The moving field of experience that connects the person to the world.

Cognitive understanding. The bracketing out of emotionality from the interpretive process so as to proceed through interpretation step by step in a rational, orderly fashion.

Emotion. Self-feeling.

Emotional abstract. The knowledge of an emotion such as fear, but not the actual experiencing of the emotion in an interactional episode.

Emotional account. Justification of a self-feeling.

Emotional associate. A person who is implicated in the subject's emotional world of experience.

Emotional consciousness. The flow of conscious experience that has inner phenomenological and outer interactional dimensions, which are united in the stream of emotional experience.

It is directed toward itself and the person as its own objects of consciousness. It is both reflective and unreflective.

Emotional intersubjectivity. The interactional appropriation of another's emotionality such that one feels one's way into the feelings and intentional feeling states of another.

Emotionality. The process of being emotional.

Emotionally divided self. A self turned against itself, disembodied, characterized by self-loathing and ressentiment.

Emotional practice. An embedded practice that produces anticipated and unanticipated alterations in the person's inner and outer streams of emotional experience.

Emotional understanding. Knowing and comprehending through emotional means, including sympathy and imagination, the intentions, feelings, and thoughts expressed by another.

Enacted emotionality. The interactional articulation of an emotional definition of self and other in a situation.

Feelings. Sensations of the lived body.

Field of experience. The temporal structure of meanings, definitions, and feelings that surround and situate the person in the world.

Hermeneutics. The work of interpretation.

Intentional value feelings. Intentional objects of feeling, independent of actual, subjective emotional states, such as the feeling of sorrow before, during, and after a funeral.

Interactional stream. The copresent, actually observable flow of interaction between two or more parties.

Interiority. The inner structure of experience as interpreted and felt by the person.

Interpretation. The clarification of meaning.

Interpretive sociology. The sociology that takes as its focus the study of meaning as meaning is grounded in the lives of ordinary people. Also termed *interpretive interactionism*.

Intersubjectivity. The shared knowledge that exists between two persons regarding one another's conscious mental (emotional) states. Intersubjectivity produces an intersection, or intertwining, of two fields of experience into a single synthesis of shared experience. In contrast, *subjectivity* refers to a subject's knowledge of her own mental states.

Lived feelings. Feelings, such as nausea, that express a particular value content or meaning found in the world.

Mood. An emotional state of mind that transcends particular situational experiences.

Person. That temporal being already present in the world, ahead of itself, aware of itself, and capable of expressing and acting on that awareness, being, and presence.

Phenomenological stream. The inner side of interaction, in which the subject symbolically interacts with self and other in a social situation.

Phenomenological thesis. The principle that there is an interconnection between the essence of an object and the essence of intentional experience.

Principle of emotional sociality. The principle that the self as a social object enters the field of experience on the same basis of emotionality as does the self of the other person.

Psychic body. The interior field of experience against which one's feelings and sensations are felt.

Ressentiment. The repeated experiencing and reliving of a particular emotional reaction against another. The emotion is negative, hostile, and includes a cluster of interrelated feelings—anger, wrath, envy, intense self-pride, and desire for revenge.

Self. That process that unifies the stream of thoughts and experiences the person has about himself around a single pole or point of reference; not a thing, but a process. It is consciousness conscious of itself, referring always to the sameness and steadiness of something always present to the person in his thoughts, as in "I am here, now, in the world, present before and to myself." Involves moral feelings for self, including all the subject

calls his at a particular moment in time, such as material possessions, self-feelings, and relations to others. Also includes the
meaning the person gives to himself as a distinct object and subject at any given moment, involving the meaning of the person
to himself as he turns back on himself in reflection. The self is
not in consciousness, but in the world of social interaction. It
haunts the subject.

Self-feelings. Sequences of lived emotionality having self-referents, including a feeling for self, a feeling of this feeling, and a
revealing of the moral self to the person through this feeling.

Sensible feelings. Feelings given in particular parts of the lived
body as sensations or feeling states—for example, pain—felt
against and within the psychic body.

Social phenomenological method. That mode of inquiry that returns to the things of experience and studies them from within.
Involves five phases: deconstruction of previous theories of the
phenomenon, capture, reduction, construction, and contextualization.

Understanding. The process of interpreting, knowing, and comprehending the meaning intended, felt, and expressed by another.

Violence. The attempt to regain, through the use of emotional
and physical force, something that has been lost or taken away
from the self.

References

Abbott, J. H. *In the Belly of the Beast: Letters from Prison.* New York: Random House, 1981.

Abrams, M. H. *The Mirror and the Lamp: Romantic Theory and the Critical Tradition.* New York: Norton, 1953.

Albee, E. *Who's Afraid of Virginia Woolf?* New York: Atheneum, 1962.

Alexander, J. C. *Theoretical Logic in Sociology.* Vol. 1. Berkeley: University of California Press, 1982.

Allport, G. W. *Becoming: A Basic Consideration for a Psychology of Personality.* New Haven, Conn.: Yale University Press, 1955.

Althusser, L. *For Marx.* (B. Brewster, trans.) Harmondsworth, England: Penguin, 1969.

Althusser, L., and Balibar, E. *Reading Capital.* (B. Brewster, trans.) New York: Pantheon, 1970.

Althusser, L., and Balibar, E. *"Lenin and Philosophy" and Other Essays.* (B. Brewster, trans.) New York: Monthly Review Press, 1971.

Arnold, M. B. *Emotion and Personality.* Vol. 1: *Psychological Aspects.* New York: Columbia University Press, 1960a.

Arnold, M. B. *Emotion and Personality.* Vol. 2: *Neurological and Physiological Aspects.* New York: Columbia University Press, 1960b.

Arnold, M. B. (Ed.). *Feelings and Emotions.* New York: Academic Press, 1970.

Athens, L. H. *Violent Criminal Acts and Actors: A Symbolic Interactionist Study.* Boston: Routledge & Kegan Paul, 1980.

Averill, J. R. "Emotion and Anxiety: Sociocultural, Biological, and Psychological Determinants." In A. Rorty (Ed.), *Explaining Emotions.* Berkeley: University of California Press, 1980.

Averill, J. R., Opton, E. M., Jr., and Lazarus, R. S. "Cross-Cultural Studies of Psychophysiological Responses During Stress and Emotion." *International Journal of Psychology,* 1969, *4,* 83-102.

Bain, A. *The Emotions and the Will.* London: John W. Parker, 1859.

Baldwin, J. M. "The Origins of Emotional Expression." *Psychological Review,* 1894, *1,* 610-623.

Baron, R. A., and Byrne, D. *Social Psychology.* (3rd ed.) Boston: Allyn & Bacon, 1981.

Barthes, R. *The Pleasure of the Text.* New York: Hill & Wang, 1975.

Bateson, G. *Steps to an Ecology of the Mind.* San Francisco: Chandler, 1972.

Bateson, G. *Mind and Nature.* New York: Dutton, 1979.

Bauman, Z. *Hermeneutics and Social Science.* New York: Columbia University Press, 1976.

Becker, H. S. *Art Worlds.* Berkeley: University of California Press, 1982.

Bedford, E. "Emotions." In V. C. Chappell (Ed.), *The Philosophy of Mind.* New York: Dover, 1981.

Berger, P., and Luckmann, T. *The Social Construction of Reality.* New York: Doubleday, 1967.

Bergson, H. L. *Matter and Memory.* New York: Humanities Press, 1970. (Originally published 1896.)

Bergson, H. L. *Time and Free Will: An Essay on the Immediate Data of Consciousness.* New York: Humanities Press, 1971. (Originally published 1908.)

Bertaux, D. (Ed.). *Biography and Society: The Life History Approach in the Social Sciences.* Beverly Hills, Calif.: Sage, 1981.

Binswanger, L. *Being-in-the-World: Selected Papers of Ludwig Binswanger.* (J. Needleman, trans.) New York: Basic Books, 1963.

Bleicher, J. *Contemporary Hermeneutics: Hermeneutics as Method, Philosophy, and Critique.* London: Routledge & Kegan Paul, 1980.

Blumer, H. *Symbolic Interactionism: Perspective and Method.* Englewood Cliffs, N.J.: Prentice-Hall, 1969.

Blumer, H. "The Social Situation." Address given to the annual meetings of the Pacific Sociological Society, 1972.

Blumer, H. "Social Unrest and Collective Protest." In N. K. Denzin (Ed.), *Studies in Symbolic Interaction.* Vol. 1. Greenwich, Conn.: JAI Press, 1978.

Blumer, H. "Preface." In L. Athens, *Violent Criminal Acts and Actors.* Boston: Routledge & Kegan Paul, 1980.

Boyle, R. P. "The Structures of Mystical Teachings: Implications for Social Theory." In N. K. Denzin (Ed.), *Studies in Symbolic Interaction.* Vol. 6. Greenwich, Conn.: JAI Press, 1984.

Brentano, F. *Psychology from an Empirical Standpoint.* New York: Humanities Press, 1973. (Originally published 1924.)

Broyard, A. "Ordinary People." *New York Times Book Review,* December 13, 1981, p. 43.

Bryson, G. *Man and Society: The Scottish Inquiry of the Eighteenth Century.* Princeton, N.J.: Princeton University Press, 1945.

Burke, K. *A Grammar of Motives.* Englewood Cliffs, N.J.: Prentice-Hall, 1945.

Burke, K. *A Rhetoric of Motives.* Englewood Cliffs, N.J.: Prentice-Hall, 1950.

Butler, S. *The Way of All Flesh.* London: Grant Richards, 1903.

Canby, V. "When a Movie Doesn't Pass the Plausibility Test."

New York Times, January 2, 1983, Arts and Leisure section, pp. 1, 13.

Candland, D. K. "The Persistent Problems of Emotion." In D. K. Candland and others, *Emotion.* Monterey, Calif.: Brooks/Cole, 1977.

Cannon, W. B. *Bodily Changes in Pain, Hunger, Fear, and Rage: An Account of Recent Researches into the Function of Emotional Excitement.* (2nd ed.) New York: D. Appleton, 1929.

Capote, T. *In Cold Blood: A True Account of a Multiple Murder and Its Consequences.* New York: Random House, 1965.

Chappell, V. C. (Ed.). *Ordinary Language: Essays in Philosophical Method.* Englewood Cliffs, N.J.: Prentice-Hall, 1964.

Charmaz, K. C. "The Social Construction of Self-Pity in the Chronically Ill." In N. K. Denzin (Ed.), *Studies in Symbolic Interaction.* Vol. 3. Greenwich, Conn.: JAI Press, 1980.

Cicourel, A. V. *Cognitive Sociology.* New York: Free Press, 1974.

Cicourel, A. V. "The Role of Cognitive-Linguistic Concepts in Understanding Everyday Social Interactions." In R. H. Turner and J. F. Short, Jr. (Eds.), *Annual Review of Sociology.* Vol. 7. Palo Alto, Calif.: Annual Review of Sociology, 1981.

Clough, P. T. "The Interactional Work of Women: Conceptualizing the Ideological Component." Paper presented at annual meeting of the American Sociological Association, San Francisco, September 1982.

Cockerham, W. *Sociology of Mental Disorders.* Englewood Cliffs, N.J.: Prentice-Hall, 1981.

Coleridge, S. T. *Biographia Literaria.* In W. Heath (Ed.), *Major British Poets of the Romantic Period.* New York: Macmillan, 1973. (Originally published 1817.)

Collins, R. *Conflict Sociology: Toward an Explanatory Science.* New York: Academic Press, 1975.

Collins, R. *Sociology Since Midcentury: Essays in Theory Cumulation.* New York: Academic Press, 1981.

Cooley, C. H. *The Two Major Works of Charles H. Cooley, Social Organization and Human Nature and the Social Order.* New York: Free Press, 1956. (Originally published 1902.)

Couch, C. J. *Constructing Civilizations.* Greenwich, Conn.: JAI Press, 1984.

Coward, R., and Ellis, J. *Language and Materialism: Developments in Semiology and the Theory of the Subject.* London: Routledge & Kegan Paul, 1977.

Cowley, M. (Ed.). *The Portable Faulkner Reader.* (rev. ed.) New York: Viking Press, 1967.

Darwin, C. *On the Origin of Species by Means of Natural Selection.* New York: D. Appleton, 1859.

Darwin, C. *The Expression of the Emotions in Man and Animals.* New York: Philosophical Library, 1955. (Originally published 1872.)

Davis, F. *Yearning for Yesterday: A Sociology of Nostalgia.* New York: Free Press, 1979.

Davis, W. A. *The Act of Interpretation: A Critique of Literary Reason.* Chicago: University of Chicago Press, 1978.

Deleuze, G., and Guattari, F. *Anti-Oedipus: Capitalism and Schizophrenia.* New York: Viking Press, 1977.

Denzin, N. K. "The Significant Others of a College Population." *Sociological Quarterly,* 1966, *7,* 298-310.

Denzin, N. K. "Symbolic Interactionism and Ethnomethodology: A Proposed Synthesis." *American Sociological Review,* 1969, *34,* 922-934.

Denzin, N. K. *Childhood Socialization: Studies in the Development of Language, Social Behavior, and Identity.* San Francisco: Jossey-Bass, 1977.

Denzin, N. K. *The Research Act.* (2nd ed.) New York: McGraw-Hill, 1978.

Denzin, N. K. "A Phenomenology of Emotion and Deviance." *Zeitschrift Für Soziologie,* 1980, *9*(3), 251-261.

Denzin, N. K. "The Paradoxes of Play." In J. Loy (Ed.), *The Paradoxes of Play.* West Point, N.Y.: Leisure Press, 1981.

Denzin, N. K. "Contributions of Anthropology and Sociology to Qualitative Research Methods." In E. Kuhns and S. V. Martorana (Eds.), *New Directions for Institutional Research: Qualitative Methods for Institutional Research,* no. 34. San Francisco: Jossey-Bass, 1982a.

Denzin, N. K. "Notes on Criminology and Criminality." In H. E. Pepinsky (Ed.), *Rethinking Criminology.* Beverly Hills, Calif.: Sage, 1982b.

Denzin, N. K. "On Time and Mind." In N. K. Denzin (Ed.),

Studies in Symbolic Interaction. Vol. 4. Greenwich, Conn.: JAI Press, 1982c.

Denzin, N. K. "The Significant Others of Young Children: Notes Toward a Phenomenology of Childhood." In K. M. Borman (Ed.), *The Social Life of Children in a Changing Society.* Norwood, N.J.: Ablex, 1982d.

Denzin, N. K. "Interpretive Interactionism." In G. Morgan (Ed.), *Beyond Method.* Beverly Hills, Calif.: Sage, 1983a.

Denzin, N. K. "A Note on Emotionality, Self, and Interaction." *American Journal of Sociology,* 1983b, *89,* 402-409.

Denzin, N. K. "On Interpreting an Interpretation." *American Journal of Sociology,* in press-a.

Denzin, N. K. "Interpreting the Lives of Ordinary People: Heidegger, Sartre, and Faulkner." [In Portuguese.] *Dados, Revista de Ciencias Socias,* in press-b. English translation in *Oral History,* 1984, *9.*

Denzin, N. K. "Towards an Interpretation of Semiotics and History." *Semiotica,* in press-c.

Denzin, N. K., and Keller, C. M. "Frame Analysis Reconsidered." *Contemporary Sociology,* 1981, *10,* 52-59.

Derrida, J. *Speech and Phenomena.* Evanston, Ill.: Northwestern University Press, 1973.

Dewey, J. "The Theory of Emotion: I. Emotional Attitudes." *Psychological Review,* 1894, *1,* 553-569.

Dewey, J. "The Theory of Emotion: II. The Significance of Emotions." *Psychological Review,* 1895, *2,* 13-32.

Dewey, J. *Human Nature and Conduct: An Introduction to Social Psychology.* New York: Holt, 1922.

Dey, J. "91-Year-Old Tells Jury of Attack." *Champaign-Urbana News Gazette,* October 6, 1982, pp. 1-2.

Dickens, C. *The Christmas Books.* Vol. 1. (M. Slater, Ed.) Harmondsworth, England: Penguin Books, 1971. (Originally published 1843.)

Dilthey, W. L. *Selected Writings.* (H. P. Rickman, ed. and trans.) Cambridge: Cambridge University Press, 1976. (Originally published 1900.)

Dobash, R. E., and Dobash, R. P. *Violence Against Wives.* New York: Free Press, 1979.

Dobash, R. E., and Dobash, R. P. "The Antecedents and Nature of Violent Episodes." Paper presented at annual meeting of the American Sociological Association, San Francisco, September 1982.

Donoghue, D. "Wonder Women: A Review of Joyce Carol Oates, *A Bloodmoor Romance.*" *New York Review of Books,* July 1982, pp. 12-16.

Dostoevsky, F. *Crime and Punishment.* New York: Vintage Books, 1950. (Originally published 1866.)

Dostoevsky, F. *Notes from the Underground.* In A. Yarmolinsky (Ed.), *Three Short Novels of Dostoevsky.* (C. Garnett, trans.) New York: Doubleday, 1960. (Originally published 1864.)

Dreyfus, H. L., and Rabinow, P. *Michel Foucault: Beyond Structuralism and Hermeneutics.* Chicago: University of Chicago Press, 1982.

Dubus, A. *The Times Are Never So Bad.* Boston: Godine, 1983.

Durkheim, É. *The Elementary Forms of the Religious Life.* London: Allen and Unwin, 1912.

Durkheim, É. *The Rules of Sociological Method.* New York: Free Press, 1964. (Originally published 1895.)

Durkheim, É. "Elementary Forms of the Religious Life." In R. Bellah (Ed.), *Émile Durkheim on Morality and Society.* Chicago: University of Chicago Press, 1973. (Originally published 1912.)

Ekman, P. (Ed.). *Darwin and Facial Expression: A Century of Research in Review.* New York: Academic Press, 1973.

Ekman, P. "Biological and Cultural Contributions to Body and Facial Movement in the Expression of Emotions." In A. Rorty (Ed.), *Explaining Emotions.* Berkeley: University of California Press, 1980.

Engell, J. *The Creative Imagination: Enlightenment to Romanticism.* Cambridge, Mass.: Harvard University Press, 1981.

Erchak, G. M. "Escalation and Maintenance of Child Abuse: A Cybernetic Model." *Child Abuse and Neglect,* 1981, *5,* 153-157.

Fagerhaugh, S. Y., and Strauss, A. *Politics of Pain Management: Staff-Patient Interaction.* Menlo Park, Calif.: Addison-Wesley, 1977.

Faulkner, W. *The Town.* New York: Vintage Books, 1961.

Faulkner, W. *The Hamlet.* New York: Vintage Books, 1964.

Faulkner, W. *The Mansion.* New York: Vintage Books, 1965.

Faulkner, W. "Address upon Receiving the Nobel Prize for Literature." Stockholm, December 10, 1950. In M. Cowley (Ed.), *The Portable Faulkner Reader: Revised and Expanded Edition.* New York: Viking Press, 1967.

Faulkner, W. *The Uncollected Stories of William Faulkner.* (J. Blotner, Ed.) New York: Random House, 1981.

Felson, R. B. "Aggression and Violence Among Siblings." Paper presented at annual meeting of the American Sociological Association, San Francisco, September 1982.

Ferraro, K. J., and Johnson, J. M. "How Women Experience Battering: The Process of Victimization." *Social Problems,* 1983, *30,* 325–339.

Finkelstein, J. "Considerations for a Sociology of the Emotions." In N. K. Denzin (Ed.), *Studies in Symbolic Interaction.* Vol. 3. Greenwich, Conn.: JAI Press, 1980.

Finkelstein, J. "Self and Civility: The Politics of Social Psychology." In N. K. Denzin (Ed.), *Studies in Symbolic Interaction.* Vol. 4. Greenwich, Conn.: JAI Press, 1982.

Finkelstein, J. "Dining Out: A Sociology of Modern Manners." In N. K. Denzin (Ed.), *Studies in Symbolic Interactions.* Vol. 6. Greenwich, Conn.: JAI Press, 1984.

Flaherty, M. "Reality Play: A Sociological Analysis of Amusement." Unpublished doctoral dissertation, University of Illinois at Urbana–Champaign, 1982.

Flaherty, M. "A Formal Approach to the Study of Amusement in Social Interaction." In N. K. Denzin (Ed.), *Studies in Symbolic Interaction.* Vol. 5. Greenwich, Conn.: JAI Press, 1983.

Foucault, M. *The Order of Things: An Archaeology of the Human Sciences.* New York: Random House, 1970.

Foucault, M. *Discipline and Punishment.* New York: Pantheon Books, 1977.

Foucault, M. *Power/Knowledge: Selected Interviews and Other Writings 1972-1977.* New York: Pantheon Books, 1980.

Foucault, M. "Afterword: The Subject and Power." In H. L. Dreyfus and P. Rabinow, *Michel Foucault: Beyond Structuralism and Hermeneutics.* Chicago: University of Chicago Press, 1982.

Franks, D. D. "Social Power, Role-Taking, and the Structure of Imperceptiveness: Toward a Redefinition of False Consciousness." *Annals of Phenomenological Sociology,* 1976, *1,* 93–111.

Freud, S. "On the Internalization of the Sex Role: The Feminine Case." In S. Freud, *New Introductory Lectures.* New York: Norton, 1933.

Freud, S. *The Basic Writings of Sigmund Freud.* New York: Random House, 1938.

Freud, S. *The Standard Edition.* London: Hogarth, 1954.

Freud, S. *The Interpretation of Dreams.* New York: Avon Books, 1965. (Originally published 1900.)

Freud, S., and Breuer, J. *Studies in Hysteria.* New York: Avon Books, 1966. (Originally published 1895.)

Frisch, M. *I'm Not Stiller!* New York: Knopf, 1958.

Frye, N. *The Great Code: The Bible and Literature.* New York: Harcourt Brace Jovanovich, 1982.

Funkenstein, D. "The Physiology of Fear and Anger." *Scientific American,* 1955, *192,* 74–80.

Gadamer, H. G. *Truth and Method.* London: Sheed and Ward, 1975.

Gadamer, H. G. *Philosophical Hermeneutics.* (D. E. Linge, ed. and trans.) Berkeley: University of California Press, 1976.

Garfinkel, H. *Studies in Ethnomethodology.* Englewood Cliffs, N.J.: Prentice-Hall, 1967.

Garfinkel, H., Lynch, M., and Livingston, E. "The Work of a Discovering Science Construed with Material from the Optically Discovered Pulsar." *Philosophy of the Social Sciences,* 1981, *11,* 131–158.

Garfinkel, H., and Sacks, H. "On Formal Structures of Practical Actions." In J. C. McKinney and E. A. Tiryakian (Eds.), *Theoretical Sociology: Perspectives and Developments.* New York: Appleton-Century-Crofts, 1970.

Geertz, C. *The Interpretation of Cultures.* New York: Basic Books, 1973.

Geertz, C. *Negara: The Theater State in Nineteenth Century Bali.* Princeton, N.J.: Princeton University Press, 1980.

Geertz, C. *Local Knowledge: Further Essays in Interpretive Anthropology.* New York: Basic Books, 1983.

Gelles, R. J. *The Violent Home: A Study of Physical Aggression Between Husbands and Wives.* Beverly Hills, Calif.: Sage, 1972.

Gelles, R. J. *Family Violence.* Beverly Hills, Calif.: Sage, 1979.

Gelles, R. J., and Cornell, C. P. "International Perspectives on Family Violence." Paper presented at annual meeting of the American Sociological Association, San Francisco, September 1982.

Gelles, R. J., and Straus, M. A. "Determinants of Violence in the Family: Toward a Theoretical Integration." In W. R. Burr and others (Eds.), *Contemporary Theories About the Family.* New York: Free Press, 1979.

Gerth, H. H., and Mills, C. W. "Introduction: The Man and His Work." In *From Max Weber: Essays in Sociology.* (H. H. Gerth and C. W. Mills, ed. and trans.) New York: Oxford University Press, 1946.

Giddens, A. *Central Problems in Social Theory: Action, Structure, and Contradiction in Social Analysis.* Berkeley: University of California Press, 1979.

Giddens, A. *A Contemporary Critique of Historical Materialism.* Vol. 1: *Power, Property, and the State.* Los Angeles: University of California Press, 1981.

Giddens, A. "On the Relation of Sociology to Philosophy." In P. Secord (Ed.), *Explaining Human Behavior: Consciousness, Human Action, and Social Structure.* Beverly Hills, Calif.: Sage, 1982.

Gilbert, S. M., and Gubar, S. "Alphabet Soup: Women, Language, and Sexuality." University Miller Lecture, University of Illinois, April 13, 1982.

Giorgi, A. *Psychology as a Human Science: A Phenomenologically Based Approach.* New York: Harper & Row, 1970.

Glaser, B., and Strauss, A. "Awareness Contexts and Social Interaction." *American Sociological Review,* 1967, *29,* 669-679.

Goffman, E. "Embarrassment and Social Organization." *American Journal of Sociology,* 1956, *62,* 264-271.

Goffman, E. *The Presentation of Self in Everyday Life.* New York: Doubleday, 1959.

Goffman, E. *Asylums*. New York: Doubleday, 1961a.

Goffman, E. *Encounters*. Indianapolis: Bobbs-Merrill, 1961b.

Goffman, E. *Behavior in Public Places*. New York: Free Press, 1963.

Goffman, E. *Interaction Ritual*. New York: Doubleday, 1967.

Goffman, E. *Relations in Public*. New York: Basic Books, 1971.

Goffman, E. *Frame Analysis*. New York: Harper, 1974.

Goffman, E. "A Reply to Denzin and Keller." *Contemporary Sociology*, 1981a, *10*, 60-68.

Goffman, E. *Forms of Talk*. Philadelphia: University of Pennsylvania Press, 1981b.

Goffman, E. "The Interaction Order." *American Sociological Review*, 1983, *48*, 1-17.

Goode, W. J. "Force and Violence in the Family." *Journal of Marriage and the Family*, 1971, *33*, 624-636.

Gordon, S. L. "The Sociology of Sentiments and Emotions." In M. Rosenberg and R. H. Turner (Eds.), *Social Psychology: Sociological Perspectives*. New York: Basic Books, 1981.

Gross, E., and Stone, G. P. "Embarrassment and the Analysis of Role Requirements." *American Journal of Sociology*, 1964, *70*, 1-15.

Grossberg, L. "Language and Theorizing in the Human Sciences." In N. K. Denzin (Ed.), *Studies in Symbolic Interaction*. Vol. 2. Greenwich, Conn.: JAI Press, 1979.

Grossberg, L. "Intersubjectivity and the Concept of Communication." *Human Studies*, 1982, *5*(3), 213-235.

Hall, S. "Cultural Studies and the Centre: Some Problematics and Problems." In S. Hall, D. Hobson, A. Lowe, and P. Willis (Eds.), *Culture, Media, and Language: Working Papers in Cultural Studies, 1972-1979*. London: Hutchinson, 1980.

Hammond, M. "The Sociology of Emotions and the History of Social Differentiation." In R. Collins (Ed.), *Sociological Theory 1983*. San Francisco: Jossey-Bass, 1983.

Hans, J. S. *The Play of the World*. Amherst: University of Massachusetts Press, 1981.

Harré, R., and Secord, P. F. *The Explanation of Social Behavior*. Totowa, N.J.: Littlefield, Adams, 1973.

Hartmann, H. "The Unhappy Marriage of Marxism and Feminism: Towards a More Progressive Union." *Women and Revolution*, 1982, *1*, 1-41.

Heath, W. (Ed.). *Major British Poets of the Romantic Period*. New York: Macmillan, 1973.

Hegel, G. W. F. *The Phenomenology of Mind*. (J. B. Baillie, trans.) London: Allen & Unwin, 1910.

Heidegger, M. *Being and Time*. New York: Harper & Row, 1962. (Originally published 1927.)

Heidegger, M. *Basic Writings from* Being and Time *(1927) to* The Task of Thinking *(1964)*. (D. F. Krell, ed.) New York: Harper & Row, 1977.

Heidegger, M. *The Basic Problems of Phenomenology*. Bloomington: Indiana University Press, 1982. (Originally published 1975.)

Heise, D. *Understanding Events: Affects and the Construction of Social Action*. New York: Cambridge University Press, 1981.

Hewitt, J. P., and Stokes, R. "Disclaimers." *American Sociological Review*, 1975, *40*, 1-11.

Hochschild, A. R. *The Unexpected Community*. Englewood Cliffs, N.J.: Prentice-Hall, 1973.

Hochschild, A. R. "The Sociology of Feeling and Emotion: Selected Possibilities." In M. Millman and R. M. Kanter (Eds.), *Another Voice: Feminist Perspectives on Social Life and Social Science*. New York: Anchor, 1975.

Hochschild, A. R. "Comments on Thomas J. Scheff's 'The Distancing of Emotion in Ritual.' " *Current Anthropology*, 1977, *18*(3), 494-495.

Hochschild, A. R. "Emotion Work, Feeling Rules, and Social Structure." *American Journal of Sociology*, 1979, *85*(3), 551-575.

Hochschild, A. R. *The Managed Heart: Commercialization of Human Feeling*. Berkeley: University of California Press, 1983.

Howe, R. H. "Weber's Kant." Unpublished doctoral dissertation, Department of Sociology, University of Illinois, 1982.

Husserl, E. *Ideas: General Introduction to Pure Phenomenology*. New York: Collier Books, 1962. (Originally published 1913.)

Icheiser, G. *Appearances and Realities: Misunderstanding in Human Relations*. San Francisco: Jossey-Bass, 1970.

"Inmate Links Drinking, Murder." *Champaign-Urbana News Gazette,* October 6, 1982, p. C9.

Irigaray, L. "When Our Lips Speak Together." In E. Marks and I. de Courtivron (Eds.), *New French Feminisms*. Amherst: University of Massachusetts Press, 1980.

Irons, D. "Professor James' Theory of Emotions." *Mind,* 1894, *3,* 78.

Irons, D. "Recent Developments in the Theory of Emotion." *Psychological Review,* 1895, *2,* 179-184.

Izard, C. E. *The Face of Emotion*. New York: Appleton-Century-Crofts, 1971.

Izard, C. E. *Patterns of Emotions: A New Analysis of Anxiety and Depression*. New York: Academic Press, 1972.

Izard, C. E. *Human Emotions*. New York: Plenum Press, 1977.

James, W. *The Literary Remains of the Late Henry James*. Boston: Houghton Mifflin, 1885.

James, W. "The Physical Basis of Emotion." *Psychological Review,* 1894, *1,* 516-529.

James, W. *The Principles of Psychology*. New York: Dover, 1950. (Originally published 1890.)

James, W. *Pragmatism and Four Essays from The Meaning of Truth*. New York: Humanities Press, 1955.

James, W. *The Varieties of Religious Experience: A Study in Human Nature*. New York: Collier Books, 1961. (Originally published 1904.)

Jameson, F. *The Prison-House of Language: A Critical Account of Structuralism and Russian Formalism*. Princeton, N.J.: Princeton University Press, 1972.

Jenkins, M. M. "Stories Women Tell: An Ethnographic Study of the Life Stories in a Women's Rap Group." Unpublished doctoral dissertation, Department of Speech Communications, University of Illinois at Urbana-Champaign, 1982.

Joyce, J. *The Portable James Joyce*. New York: Penguin Books, 1976.

Keen, E. "Emotion in Personality Theory." In D. K. Candland and others, *Emotion*. Monterey, Calif.: Brooks/Cole, 1977.

Kelly, G. A. *The Psychology of Personal Constructs.* Vol. 1. New York: Norton, 1955.

Kempe, C., and others. "The Battered-Child Syndrome." *Journal of the American Medical Association,* 1962, *181*(July 7), 17-24.

Kemper, T. D. "Toward a Sociological Theory of Emotions: Some Problems and Some Solutions." *American Sociologist,* 1978a, *13,* 30-41.

Kemper, T. D. *A Social Interactional Theory of Emotions.* New York: Wiley, 1978b.

Kemper, T. D. "Sociology, Physiology, and Emotions: Comment on Shott." *American Journal of Sociology,* 1980, *85,* 1418-1423.

Kemper, T. D. "Social Constructionist and Positivist Approaches to the Sociology of Emotions." *American Journal of Sociology,* 1981, *87,* 336-361.

Knorr-Cetina, K., and Cicourel, A. V. (Eds.). *Advances in Social Theory and Methodology: Toward an Integration of Micro- and Macro-Sociologies.* Boston: Routledge & Kegan Paul, 1981.

Krieger, S. *The Mirror Dance: Identity in a Women's Community.* Philadelphia: Temple University Press, 1983.

Krim, S. *Views of a Nearsighted Commoner.* New York: Dutton, 1961.

Kristeva, J. "Sexual Differences." *Signs,* 1981, *7,* 2-25.

Kuhn, M. "The Reference Group Reconsidered." *Sociological Quarterly,* 1964, *5,* 5-24.

Labov, W., and Fanshel, D. *Therapeutic Discourse: Psychotherapy as Conversation.* New York: Academic Press, 1977.

Lacan, J. A. *Écrits.* Paris: Edition du Seuil, 1966.

Lacan, J. A. *Speech and Language in Psychoanalysis.* (A. Wilden, trans.) Baltimore: Johns Hopkins University Press, 1968.

Lacan, J. A. *Écrits: A Selection.* (A. Sheridan, trans.) New York: Norton, 1977.

Lacan, J. A. *The Four Fundamental Concepts of Psycho-Analysis.* (J. A. Miller, ed.; A. Sheridan, trans.) New York: Norton, 1978.

Laing, R. D. *The Divided Self: An Existential Study in Sanity and Madness.* Harmondsworth, England: Penguin Books, 1965.

Latané, B. *The Unresponsive Bystander: Why Doesn't He Help?* New York: Appleton-Century-Crofts, 1970.

Latané, B., and Darley, J. M. "Group Inhibition of Bystander Intervention in Emergencies." *Journal of Personality and Social Psychology,* 1968, *10,* 215-221.

Lazarus, R. S., and Averill, J. R. "Emotion and Cognition: With Special Reference to Anxiety." In C. D. Spielberger (Ed.), *Anxiety: Contemporary Theory and Research.* New York: Academic Press, 1972.

Lazarus, R. S., Averill, J. R., and Opton, E. M., Jr. "Towards a Cognitive Theory of Emotion." In M. B. Arnold (Ed.), *Feelings and Emotions.* New York: Academic Press, 1970.

Lefebvre, H. *Everyday Life in the Modern World.* London: Allen Lane, 1971.

Lemert, E. M. "Paranoia and the Dynamics of Exclusion." *Sociometry,* 1962, *24,* 2-20.

Lewis, H. B. *Shame and Guilt in Neurosis.* New York: International Universities Press, 1971.

Lindbergh, A. M. *Hour of Gold, Hour of Lead: Diaries and Letters of Ann Morrow Lindbergh, 1929-1932.* New York: Harcourt Brace Jovanovich, 1973.

Lindesmith, A., Strauss, A., and Denzin, N. K. *Social Psychology.* (5th ed.) New York: Holt, Rinehart and Winston, 1978.

Lofland, J. *Doing Social Life: The Qualitative Study of Human Interaction in Natural Settings.* New York: Wiley-Interscience, 1976.

Lofland, J. "Collective Behavior: The Elementary Forms." In M. Rosenberg and R. H. Turner (Eds.), *Social Psychology: Sociological Perspectives.* New York: Basic Books, 1981.

Lofland, L. *A World of Strangers: Order and Action in Urban Public Space.* New York: Basic Books, 1973.

Luria, A. R. *The Selected Writings of A. R. Luria.* (M. Cole, ed.) White Plains, N.Y.: M. E. Sharpe, 1978.

Lynch, R. "Social Play: An Interactional Analysis of Play in

Face-to-Face Interaction." Unpublished doctoral dissertation, Department of Leisure Studies, University of Illinois at Urbana–Champaign, 1980.

Lynch, R. "Play, Creativity, and Emotion." In N. K. Denzin (Ed.), *Studies in Symbolic Interaction*. Vol. 4. Greenwich, Conn.: JAI Press, 1982.

Lynd, H. M. *On Shame and the Search for Identity*. New York: Harcourt Brace Jovanovich, 1958.

McCall, G. J., and Simmons, J. L. *Social Psychology*. New York: Free Press, 1981.

MacIver, R. M. "Is Sociology a Natural Science?" *American Journal of Sociology*, 1931, *25*, 25–35.

Mailer, N. *The Executioner's Song*. New York: Warner Books, 1979.

Maines, D. R. "Bodies and Selves: Fundamental Dilemmas in Demography." In N. K. Denzin (Ed.), *Studies in Symbolic Interaction*. Vol. 2. Greenwich, Conn.: JAI Press, 1978.

Maines, D. R. "Biography and Time in Diabetic Experience." *Mid-American Review of Sociology*, 1983, *8*, 103–117.

Manning, P. K. "Existential Sociology." *Sociological Quarterly*, 1973, *15*, 200–225.

Manning, P. K. *Police Work*. Cambridge, Mass.: M.I.T. Press, 1977.

Marcus, P. *Criminal Law, Part II*. Champaign: University of Illinois College of Law, 1982.

Marks, E., and de Courtivron, I. (Eds.). *New French Feminisms: An Anthology*. Amherst: University of Massachusetts Press, 1980.

Marx, K. "From the Economico-Philosophical Manuscripts of 1844." In *The Portable Karl Marx*. (E. Kamenka, ed.) New York: Penguin Books, 1983a. (Originally published 1844.)

Marx, K. "The German Ideology, Volume One." In *The Portable Karl Marx*. (E. Kamenka, ed.) New York: Penguin Books, 1983b. (Originally published 1845–1846.)

Marx, K. "From the Eighteenth Brumaire of Louis Bonaparte." In *The Portable Karl Marx*. (E. Kamenka, ed.) New York: Penguin Books, 1983c. (Originally published 1852.)

Marx, K. "Theses on Feuerbach." In *The Portable Karl Marx*.

(E. Kamenka, ed.) New York: Penguin Books, 1983d. (Originally published 1888.)

Matthiessen, F. O. *The James Family: Including Selections from the Writings of Henry James, Senior, William, Henry, and Alice James.* New York: Knopf, 1947.

May, R. "The Origins and Significance of the Existential Movement in Psychology." In R. May, E. Angel, and H. F. Ellenberger (Eds.), *Existence: A New Dimension in Psychiatry and Psychology.* New York: Basic Books, 1958.

Mayfield, C. W. Conversation. Urbana, Ill., March 17, 1982.

Mead, G. H. "A Theory of the Emotions from the Physiological Standpoint." *Psychological Review,* 1895, *2*(1), 162-164.

Mead, G. H. *Mind, Self, and Society.* Chicago: University of Chicago Press, 1934.

Mead, G. H. *The Philosophy of the Act.* Chicago: University of Chicago Press, 1936.

Mead, G. H. *The Philosophy of the Present.* Chicago: University of Chicago Press, 1938.

Mead, G. H. *George Herbert Mead on Social Psychology: Selected Papers.* (A. L. Strauss, ed.) Chicago: University of Chicago Press, 1956.

Mead, G. H. *Selected Writings: George Herbert Mead.* (A. J. Rock, ed.) Indianapolis: Bobbs-Merrill, 1964.

Mead, G. H. *The Individual and the Social Self: Unpublished Work of George Herbert Mead.* (D. L. Miller, ed.) Chicago: University of Chicago Press, 1982a.

Mead, G. H. "Unpublished Lecture Notes," Box X, Folder 1, pp. 9-13, at Regenstein Library of the University of Chicago. Transcribed by C. V. Smedley, Department of Sociology, University of Illinois, Urbana–Champaign. November 22, 1982b.

Meinong, A. *On Emotional Presentation.* Evanston, Ill.: Northwestern University Press, 1972.

Meisenhelder, T. "The Life-World." *Sociological Inquiry,* 1979, *49*(1), 65-68.

Merleau-Ponty, M. *Phenomenology of Perception.* (C. Smith, trans.) London: Routledge & Kegan Paul, 1962.

Merleau-Ponty, M. *The Structure of Behavior.* (A. L. Fisher, trans.) Boston: Beacon Press, 1963.

Merleau-Ponty, M. *The Primacy of Perception.* (J. M. Edie, ed.; W. Cobb and others, trans.) Evanston, Ill.: Northwestern University Press, 1964a.

Merleau-Ponty, M. *Sense and Non-Sense.* (H. L. Dreyfus and P. A. Dreyfus, trans.) Evanston, Ill.: Northwestern University Press, 1964b.

Merleau-Ponty, M. *Signs.* (R. C. McCleary, trans.) Evanston, Ill.: Northwestern University Press, 1964c.

Merleau-Ponty, M. *The Visible and the Invisible.* (C. Lefort, ed.; A. Lingis, trans.) Evanston, Ill.: Northwestern University Press, 1968.

Merleau-Ponty, M. *Humanism and Terror.* (J. O'Neill, trans.) Boston: Beacon Press, 1969.

Merleau-Ponty, M. *Adventures of the Dialectic.* (J. J. Bien, trans.) Evanston, Ill.: Northwestern University Press, 1973a.

Merleau-Ponty, M. *Consciousness and the Acquisition of Language.* (H. J. Silverman, trans.) Evanston, Ill.: Northwestern University Press, 1973b.

Merleau-Ponty, M. *The Prose of the World.* (C. Lefort, ed.: J. O'Neill, trans.) Evanston, Ill.: Northwestern University Press, 1973c.

Merleau-Ponty, M. *Phenomenology, Language, and Sociology: Selected Essays of Maurice Merleau-Ponty.* (J. O'Neill, ed.) London: Heinemann Educational Books, 1974.

Merton, R. K. *Social Theory and Social Structure.* (Rev. ed.) New York: Free Press, 1957.

Mills, C. W. "Situated Actions and Vocabularies of Motive." *American Sociological Review,* 1940, *5,* 904–913.

Monahan, J., and Klassen, D. "Situational Approaches to Understanding and Predicting Individual Violent Behavior." In M. E. Wolfgang and N. A. Weiner (Eds.), *Criminal Violence.* Beverly Hills, Calif.: Sage, 1982.

Mowrer, O. H. *Learning Theory and Behavior.* New York: Wiley, 1960.

Natanson, M. (Ed.). *Philosophy of the Social Sciences.* New York: Random House, 1963.

Natanson, M. *The Journeying Self: A Study in Philosophy and Social Role.* Reading, Mass.: Addison-Wesley, 1970.

Novak, A. *In the Night*. Los Angeles: ABM Books, 1967.

Oates, J. C. *Invisible Women*. Toronto: Ontario Review Press, 1982.

O'Neill, E. *Long Day's Journey into Night*. New Haven, Conn.: Yale University Press, 1955.

Osgood, C. E., Suci, G. J., and Tannenbaum, P. H. *The Measurement of Meaning*. Urbana: University of Illinois Press, 1957.

Palmer, R. E. *Hermeneutics: Interpretation Theory in Schleiermacher, Dilthey, Heidegger, and Gadamer*. Evanston, Ill.: Northwestern University Press, 1969.

Parsons, T. *Action Theory and the Human Condition*. New York: Free Press, 1978.

Peirce, C. S. *Collected Papers of Charles Sanders Peirce*. Vols. 1 and 2. (C. Hartshorne, ed.; P. Weiss, trans.) Cambridge, Mass.: Belknap Press of Harvard University Press, 1931.

Peirce, C. S. *Collected Papers of Charles Sanders Peirce*. Vols. 3 and 4. (C. Hartshorne, ed.; P. Weiss, trans.) Cambridge, Mass.: Belknap Press of Harvard University Press, 1933.

Peirce, C. S. *Collected Papers of Charles Sanders Peirce*. Vols. 5 and 6. (C. Hartshorne, ed.; P. Weiss, trans.) Cambridge, Mass.: Belknap Press of Harvard University Press, 1934.

Peirce, C. S. *Collected Papers of Charles Sanders Peirce*. Vols. 7 and 8. (C. Hartshorne, ed.; P. Weiss, trans.) Cambridge, Mass.: Belknap Press of Harvard University Press, 1958.

Perinbanayagam, R. S. *The Karmic Theater: Self, Society, and Astrology in Joffna*. Amherst: University of Massachusetts Press, 1982.

Piers, G., and Singer, M. B. *Shame and Guilt*. New York: Norton, 1971.

Plessner, H. *Laughing and Crying: A Study of the Limits of Human Behavior*. Evanston, Ill.: Northwestern University Press, 1970.

Plutchik, R. *The Emotions: Facts, Theories, and a New Model*. New York: Random House, 1962.

Plutchik, R. "Cognitions in the Service of Emotions: An Evolutionary Perspective." In D. K. Candland and others, *Emotion*. Monterey, Calif.: Brooks/Cole, 1977.

Power, M. B. "The Child's Emotionality: A Naturalistic Investigation." Doctoral dissertation in progress, Department of Sociology, University of Illinois at Urbana–Champaign, 1982.

Power, M. B. "The Language of Emotions in Early Childhood: The Ritualization of Emotional Conduct." In N. K. Denzin (Ed.), *Studies in Symbolic Interaction.* Vol. 6. Greenwich, Conn.: JAI Press, 1984.

Pribram, K. H. "Emotions." In S. B. Filskov and T. J. Boll (Eds.), *Handbook of Neuropsychology.* New York: Wiley, 1981.

Rabinow, P., and Sullivan, W. M. (Eds.). *Interpretive Social Science: A Reader.* Los Angeles: University of California Press, 1979.

Rebeta-Burditt, J. *The Cracker Factory.* New York: Macmillan, 1977.

Rickman, H. P. (Ed.). *Pattern and Meaning in History: Thoughts on History & Society, William Dilthey.* New York: Harper & Row, 1961.

Ricoeur, P. *Hermeneutics and the Human Sciences.* (J. B. Thompson, ed. and trans.) Cambridge: Cambridge University Press, 1981.

Riezler, K. *Man—Mutable and Immutable: The Fundamental Structure of Social Life.* Chicago: Regnery, 1950.

Rogers, C. R. *On Becoming a Person.* Boston: Houghton Mifflin, 1961.

Rorty, A. O. (Ed.). *Explaining the Emotions.* Los Angeles: University of California Press, 1980.

Rothstein, E. "Glenn Gould Revisits a Bach Masterwork." *New York Times,* September 16, 1982, Section 2, pp. 1, 19.

Sahlins, M. *Historical Metaphors and Mythical Realities: Structure in The Early History of the Sandwich Island Kingdom.* Association for Social Anthropology in Oceania, Special Publications No. 1. Ann Arbor: University of Michigan Press, 1981.

Sartre, J.-P. *The Psychology of Imagination.* New York: Philosophical Library, 1948.

Sartre, J.-P. *Nausea.* Norfolk, Conn.: New Directions, 1949.

Sartre, J.-P. *The Transcendence of the Ego.* New York: Noonday Press, 1957.

Sartre, J.-P. *Sketch for a Theory of the Emotions.* (P. Mariet, trans.) London: Methuen, 1962. (Originally published 1939.)

Sartre, J.-P. *Search for a Method.* New York: Knopf, 1963.

Sartre, J.-P. *Imagination: A Psychological Critique.* Ann Arbor: University of Michigan Press, 1972. (Originally published 1940.)

Sartre, J.-P. *Critique of Dialectical Reason.* London: NLP, 1976.

Sartre, J.-P. *Being and Nothingness.* New York: Simon & Schuster, 1978. (Originally published 1943.)

Sartre, J.-P. *The Family Idiot, Gustave Flaubert.* Vol. I: *1821-1857.* Chicago: University of Chicago Press, 1981.

Saussure, F. de. *The Course in General Linguistics.* New York: Philosophical Library, 1959.

Schachter, S. *Emotion, Obesity, and Crime.* New York: Academic Press, 1971.

Schachter, S., and Singer, D. "Cognitive, Social, and Physiological Determinants of Emotional States." *Psychological Review,* 1962, *68,* 379-399.

Scheff, T. J. "The Distancing of Emotion in Ritual." *Current Anthropology,* 1977, *18,* 500-505.

Scheff, T. J. *Catharsis in Healing, Ritual, and Drama.* Berkeley: University of California Press, 1979.

Scheff, T. J. "Toward Integration in the Social Psychology of Emotions." *Annual Review of Sociology,* 1983, *9,* 333-354.

Scheler, M. *Ressentiment.* (L. A. Coser, ed.; W. W. Holdeim, trans.) New York: Free Press, 1961. (Originally published 1912.)

Scheler, M. *The Nature of Sympathy.* (P. Heath, trans.) Hamden, Conn.: Archon Books, Shoe String Press, 1970. (Originally published 1913.)

Scheler, M. *Formalism in Ethics and Non-Formal Ethics of Values: A New Attempt Toward the Foundation of an Ethical Personalism.* (M. S. Frings and R. L. Funk, trans.) Evanston, Ill.: Northwestern University Press, 1973. (Originally published 1916.)

Schmalenbach, H. *On Society and Experience.* (G. Lueschen and G. P. Stone, ed. and trans.) Chicago: University of Chicago Press, 1977.

Schneider, L. (Ed.). *The Scottish Moralists on Human Nature and Society*. Chicago: University of Chicago Press, 1967.

Schutz, A. *Collected Papers*. Vol. 1: *The Problem of Social Reality*. (M. Natanson, ed.) The Hague: Martinus Nijhoff, 1962.

Schutz, A. *Collected Papers*. Vol. 2: *Studies in Social Theory*. (A. Brodersen, ed.) The Hague: Martinus Nijhoff, 1964.

Schutz, A. *The Phenomenology of the Social World*. Evanston, Ill.: Northwestern University Press, 1967.

Schutz, A. *Collected Papers*. Vol. 3: *Studies in Phenomenological Philosophy*. (I. Schutz, ed.) The Hague: Martinus Nijhoff, 1968.

Schutz, A., and Luckmann, T. *The Structures of the Life World*. Evanston, Ill.: Northwestern University Press, 1973.

Scott, M. B., and Lyman, S. M. "Accounts." *American Sociological Review*, 1968, *33*, 46–62.

Searle, J. *Speech Acts*. Cambridge: Cambridge University Press, 1970.

Secord, P. (Ed.). *Explaining Human Behavior, Consciousness, Human Action, and Social Structure*. Beverly Hills, Calif.: Sage, 1982.

Shakespeare, W. *The Complete Book of William Shakespeare*. (The Cambridge Text established by J. D. Wilson.) London: Octopus Books, 1981.

Sharron, A. "Time and the Mainstream of Consciousness." Unpublished doctoral dissertation, Department of Sociology, University of Illinois at Urbana–Champaign, 1981.

Sharron, A. "Dimensions of Time." In N. K. Denzin (Ed.), *Studies in Symbolic Interaction*. Vol. 4. Greenwich, Conn.: JAI Press, 1982.

Shibutani, T. *Social Psychology*. Englewood Cliffs, N.J.: Prentice-Hall, 1961.

Shils, E. *Center and Periphery: Essays in Macrosociology*. Chicago: University of Chicago Press, 1975.

Shott, S. "Emotion and Social Life: A Symbolic Interactionist Analysis." *American Journal of Sociology*, 1979, *84*, 1317–1334.

Simmel, G. "Sociology of the Senses: Visual Interaction." In

R. E. Park and E. Burgess (Eds.), *Introduction to the Science of Sociology*. Chicago: University of Chicago Press, 1924.

Simmel, G. *The Sociology of Georg Simmel*. (K. Wolf, ed. and trans.) New York: Free Press, 1950.

Singer, J. L. *The Child's World of Make-Believe: Experimental Studies in Imaginative Play*. New York: Academic Press, 1973.

Singer, J. L. *Imagery and Daydream Methods in Psychotherapy and Behavior Modification*. New York: Academic Press, 1974.

Smith, A. *The Theory of Moral Sentiments*. London and New York: G. Bell, 1892.

Smith, A. *A Theory of Moral Sentiments*. London: G. Bell, 1911.

Smith, M. B. *Humanizing Social Psychology*. San Francisco: Jossey-Bass, 1974.

Spitzer, S. P., and Denzin, N. K. (Eds.). *The Mental Patient: Studies in the Sociology of Deviance*. New York: McGraw-Hill, 1968.

Stanislavski, C. *An Actor Prepares*. New York: Theatre Arts Books, 1936.

Stanislavski, C. *Building a Character*. New York: Theatre Arts Books, 1949.

Stark, R., and McEvoy, J. "Middle Class Violence." *Psychology Today*, 1970, (November), pp. 52-65.

Steinmetz, S. K. *The Cycle of Violence: Assertive, Aggressive, and Abusive Family Interaction*. New York: Praeger, 1977.

Steinmetz, S. K., and Straus, M. A. *Violence in the Family*. New York: Harper & Row, 1974.

Stevenson, R. L. "To an Unidentified Correspondent." *Dickensian*, Vol. 16, 1920. As quoted in M. Slater, "General Critical Introduction." In *Charles Dickens, The Christmas Books*. Vol. 1. Harmondsworth, England: Penguin Books, 1971. (Originally published 1920.)

Stewart, D. "Account of the Life and Writings of Adam Smith, LL.D." In A. Smith, *The Theory of Moral Sentiments*. London: G. Bell, 1911.

Stone, B. "Toward a Hermeneutic of Meaningful Social Action."

Unpublished doctoral dissertation, Department of Sociology, University of Illinois at Urbana-Champaign, 1981.

Stone, B. "Saussure, Schutz, and Symbolic Interactionism on the Constitution and Interpretation of Signitive Behavior." In N. K. Denzin (Ed.), *Studies in Symbolic Interaction*. Vol. 4. Greenwich, Conn.: JAI Press, 1982.

Stone, B. "Interpretive Sociology and the New Hermeneutics." In N. K. Denzin (Ed.), *Studies in Symbolic Interaction*. Vol. 6. Greenwich, Conn.: JAI Press, 1984.

Stone, G. P. "Appearance and the Self." In A. M. Rose (Ed.), *Human Behavior and Social Process*. Boston: Houghton Mifflin, 1962.

Stone, G. P. "Personal Acts." *Symbolic Interaction*, 1977, *1*, 2-19.

Stone, G. P. "Appearance and the Self: A Slightly Revised Version." In G. P. Stone and H. A. Farberman (Eds.), *Social Psychology Through Interaction*. (2nd ed.) New York: Wiley, 1981.

Stone, G. P., and Farberman, H. A. (Eds.). *Social Psychology Through Symbolic Interaction*. (2nd ed.) New York: Wiley, 1981.

Strasser, S. *Phenomenology and the Human Sciences*. New York: Humanities Press, 1963.

Strasser, S. "Feeling as Basis of Knowing and Recognizing the Other as an Ego." In M. B. Arnold (Ed.), *Feelings and Emotions*. New York: Academic Press, 1970.

Stratton, G. M. "The Sensations Are Not the Emotions." *Psychological Review*, 1895, *2*, 173-174.

Straus, M. "Foreword." In R. J. Gelles, *The Violent Home*. Beverly Hills, Calif.: Sage, 1972.

Straus, M., Gelles, R. J., and Steinmetz, S. K. *Behind Closed Doors: Violence in the American Family*. New York: Doubleday, 1980.

Strauss, A. *Mirrors and Masks: The Search for Identity*. New York: Free Press, 1959.

Strauss, A. *Negotiations: Varieties, Contexts, Processes, and Social Order*. San Francisco: Jossey-Bass, 1978.

Sudnow, D. *Ways of the Hand*. New York: Knopf, 1978.

Sudnow, D. *Talk's Body*. New York: Knopf, 1979.

Sugrue, N. "Emotions as Property and Context for Negotiation." *Urban Life,* 1982, *11,* 280-292.

Sullivan, H. S. *The Interpersonal Theory of Psychiatry.* New York: Norton, 1953a.

Sullivan, H. S. *Conceptions of Modern Psychiatry.* New York: Norton, 1953b.

Sullivan, H. S. *Clinical Studies in Psychiatry.* New York: Norton, 1956.

Sykes, G. M., and Matza, D. "Techniques of Neutralization: A Theory of Delinquency." *American Sociological Review,* 1959, *22,* 664-670.

Thomas, W. I., and Znaniecki, F. *The Polish Peasant in Europe and America: Monograph of an Immigrant Group.* Vol. 5: *Organization and Disorganization in America.* Boston: Richard G. Badger, Gorham Press, 1920.

Toch, H. *Violent Men.* Chicago: Aldine, 1969.

Tomkins, S. S. *Affect, Imagery, Consciousness.* Vol. 1: *The Positive Affects.* New York: Springer, 1962.

Tomkins, S. S. *Affect, Imagery, Consciousness.* Vol. 2: *The Negative Affects.* New York: Springer, 1963.

Turner, R. *Family Interaction.* New York: Wiley, 1970.

Turner, R. "The Real Self: From Institution to Impulse." *American Journal of Sociology,* 1976, *81,* 989-1016.

Turner, V. *Dramas, Fields, and Metaphors.* Ithaca, N.Y.: Cornell University Press, 1974.

Turner, V. *From Ritual to Theatre: The Human Seriousness of Play.* New York: Performing Arts Journal Publication, 1982.

Veblen, T. *The Theory of the Leisure Class.* New York: Scribner's, 1923.

Vygotsky, L. S. *Mind in Society.* (M. Cole and others, eds.) Cambridge, Mass.: Harvard University Press, 1978.

Warren, R. P. *All the King's Men.* New York: Bantam Books, 1946.

Weber, M. *From Max Weber: Essays in Sociology.* (H. Gerth and C. W. Mills, eds.) New York: Oxford University Press, 1946.

Weber, M. *Critique of Stammler.* (G. Oakes, trans.) New York: Free Press, 1977.

Weber, M. *Max Weber: Selections in Translation.* (W. G. Runciman, ed.; E. Matthews, trans.) Cambridge: Cambridge University Press, 1978.

Wilden, A. "Lacan and the Discourse of the Other." In J. Lacan, *Speech and Language in Psychoanalysis*. (A. Wilden, trans.) Baltimore: Johns Hopkins University Press, 1968.

Wiley, N. "Notes on Self Genesis: From Me to We to I." In N. K. Denzin (Ed.), *Studies in Symbolic Interaction*. Vol. 2. Greenwich, Conn.: JAI Press, 1977.

Wiley, N. "Comments on Gregory Bateson's 'Double Bind.' " Unpublished manuscript, 1980.

Wittgenstein, L. *Remarks on the Philosophy of Psychology*. 2 vols. Chicago: University of Chicago Press, 1981.

Wolfe, T. *The Hills Beyond*. New York: New American Library, 1982.

Wolfgang, M. E., and Ferracuti, F. *The Subculture of Violence: Toward an Integrated Theory in Criminology*. Beverly Hills, Calif.: Sage, 1982.

Worcester, W. I. "Observations on Some Points in James's Psychology. II: Emotion." *Monist*, 1893, *3*, 285.

Wordsworth, W. Preface to the Second and Subsequent Editions of "Lyrical Ballads." In W. Heath (Ed.), *Major British Poets of the Romantic Period*. New York: Macmillan, 1973. (Originally published 1800.)

Wundt, W. "Zur Lehre von den Gemüthsbewegungen." ("Towards a Theory of Emotional Movements.") *Philosophische Studien*, 1891, *6*, 335-393.

Znaniecki, F. *The Method of Sociology*. New York: Farrar and Rinehart, 1934.

Index